THE OTHER PARENT

The Inside Story of the Media's Effect on Our Children

JAMES P. STEYER

ATRIA BOOKS

NEW YORK LONDON TOKYO SYDNEY SINGAPORE

ATRIA BOOKS, a division of Simon & Schuster, Inc.
1230 Avenue of the Americas, New York, NY 10020

Library of Congress Cataloging-in-Publication Data

ISBN: 0-7434-0582-X

First Atria Books hardcover printing May 2002

10   9   8   7   6   5   4   3   2

For information regarding special discounts for bulk purchases,
please contact Simon & Schuster Special Sales at 1-800-456-6798
or business@simonandschuster.com

Printed in the U.S.A.

THE
OTHER
PARENT

To Lily, Kirk, Carly, and my wife, Liz:

Who were my inspiration for writing this book and
who let me use the upstairs playroom in peace . . . well,
most of the time.

And to my mom, the indomitable Marnie:
Who made life so fun and interesting,
we never really needed a TV set.

CONTENTS

Part One   **AN INSIDE LOOK AT THE MEDIA AND KIDS**   1

One: **AT HOME WITH THE OTHER PARENT**   3

Two: **IT'S ALL ABOUT MONEY**   26

Three: **SEX SELLS**   44

Four: **MEDIA VIOLENCE: IN HARM'S WAY**   69

Five: **THE SELLING OF KIDS AS CONSUMERS**   96

Six: **THE POLITICS OF MEDIA AND KIDS**   119

Seven: **THE POWER OF CAMPAIGN CASH**   150

Part Two   **TAKING BACK CONTROL: STRATEGIES FOR CHANGE**   181

Eight: **IT ALL STARTS AT HOME**   183

Nine: **CALLING THE MEDIA INDUSTRY TO ACCOUNT**   200

Ten: **PROTECTING THE PUBLIC INTEREST**   226

Eleven: **THE CHALLENGE OF CITIZEN ACTION**   241

AFTERWORD   251

ACKNOWLEDGMENTS   253

NOTES   257

INDEX   269

Part One

AN INSIDE LOOK AT THE MEDIA AND KIDS

AT HOME WITH THE OTHER PARENT

It's 6:30 A.M. Saturday morning. Thank God, we get to sleep in. . . . All quiet in San Francisco except for the foghorn—until the padding of tiny footsteps in the hallway, followed by the creaking of our bedroom door. It's Kirk, seven years old and full of energy. He struts into the room and does his little "Shake Your Booty" routine in front of our mirror. Where'd he learn that stuff? How could my son be imitating Mick Jagger at this age? "Dad, can I get into bed with you and Mom or go into the family room and watch TV?"

"Kirk, it's six-thirty in the morning," I plead; "we want to sleep. Okay, you can watch TV . . . but *only* PBS or Nick Jr. Nothing else. Got it?"

Kirk rushes off to the family room. Uh-oh. More footsteps. Now it's four-year-old Carly. "Kirk is watching *Dragon Tales,* and I wanna watch *Barney,*" she says, crying—well, fake crying. She wants her *Barney* video. "Work it out with your brother," I grunt. "Mom and I want some more sleep. It's *Saturday.*"

More footsteps. This time it's Lily, eight years old and rubbing those big blue eyes. She wants to play *Backyard Baseball* on the computer and wants me to help install it. I want to pull the blankets over my head and hide. Why not let the TV and the computer be the baby-sitter while we grab an extra an hour or two of sleep?

Like most parents, my wife, Liz, and I find ourselves wrestling with that temptation regularly. It's so easy to let our kids tune into the media world while we steal a few precious moments for ourselves. We may be too tired, stressed, or busy to keep a close eye on what our kids are watching, but most of us assume that it's benign. After all, TV was such a big part of our own childhood experience, and we turned out okay, right?

Maybe so. But in fact our kids are living in an entirely different, much more complex media environment than we ever could have imagined at their age. The rules—and the risks—have changed radically, and many of us have been slow to grasp the difference.

In the 1950s, 1960s, and 1970s, when many of us grew up, kids lived in a much simpler and safer media environment. Back then, there were only three major networks plus PBS, a couple of key radio stations in each market, a few local movie theaters, and computers that were so big they filled a room. Media then was a lot like the "Ozzie and Harriet" type of family—safe, positive, under control— and it doesn't bear the slightest relation to the reality today. Unlike the children of the 1950s, 1960s, and 1970s, whose media choices were limited and stood out like isolated, familiar landmarks in communal life, kids today inhabit an environment saturated and shaped by a complex "mediascape" that envelops and bombards them day and night. Roaming among TVs, VCRs, the Internet, radios, CD players, movie screens, and electronic games, kids can easily spend more time in this vast mediascape than in the real world—and, not surprisingly, far more time than they spend in direct contact with their parents.

Today, as child development expert T. Berry Brazelton, M.D., warns, media is really "the biggest competitor for our children's hearts and minds."[1] According to a University of Maryland study, American kids now spend 40 percent less time with their parents than kids did in the mid-sixties. That's right, *40 percent* less time— just seventeen hours a week total with their parents, down from thirty hours in 1965. At the same time, they spend far *more than double* that amount of time—more than forty hours per week on average—staring at the tube or the computer screen, listening to the radio or CDs, and playing video games. Now, which is the parent in this picture?

It's strange that as adults we've paid so little attention to such a powerful influence on our children's lives. So many of us read armloads of books about babies and child care. We're careful to teach our kids not to talk to strangers or wander the streets by themselves. Most of us make sure we know where our children are physically and with whom. And yet, day after day, year after year, we let them wander alone, virtually unsupervised, through this other universe—almost completely oblivious to what they're seeing, hearing, playing with, and learning.

Think about it. If another adult spent five or six hours a day with your kids, regularly exposing them to sex, violence, and rampantly commercial values, you would probably forbid that person to have further contact with them. Yet most of us passively allow the media to expose our kids routinely to these same behaviors—sometimes worse—and do virtually nothing about it.

THE NEW MEDIA LANDSCAPE

I have to admit that it took me a long time to understand this new media reality and its effect on kids. That's strange, because kids have been my passion since I was fifteen, when I got my first job as a counselor at the Fresh Air Fund camp in upstate New York. It was my mom who first inspired my love for kids. She worked as a schoolteacher in low-income schools for more than thirty years, and her "lectures" about the importance of teaching were a regular staple of our dinner table conversations for as long as I can remember. When I founded the national child advocacy organization Children Now in 1988, kids became my life calling and have ever since been at the center of my professional life.

But it was only when we had our first child, Lily, in 1993 that I really began to appreciate the impact of the media on kids' lives. I can still remember how, at as early as eight months old, my baby daughter was already actively responding to images that would flicker across the TV screen. It was right about then that I started noticing, during the ball games that I so love to watch, all those sexy beer commercials with scantily clad women, and cringing when ads came on for TV shows and movies about kidnappings and gruesome crimes—wondering if I should change the channel or at least mute them when our baby girl was in the room. What had seemed perfectly normal was suddenly making me feel uncomfortable.

Like most parents, I wasn't prepared for this new media reality. Growing up, my parents didn't let me watch much TV at all, because they thought reading and active play were more important. Sports on TV or radio were pretty much the only exception to the rule, and my brothers and I occasionally went to the neighbors' to watch the *Three Stooges*. I can still remember being upset in fourth grade because most of my classmates could discuss *Batman* in intimate detail, and we weren't even allowed to watch it. Those were the days when the Smothers Brothers were considered risqué, and when parents decried the influence of the Beatles. When *All in the Family* first appeared, it was considered edgy television because it dealt with issues like racism and discrimination against women. All in all, it was a very different era.

Back then, media was also still governed by at least some semblance of public-interest policy. The broadcast networks saw their news divisions as the standard bearers of a great tradition and often operated them at breakeven or a loss. There was, for a brief time, the "family hour"—a voluntary code among programmers that they would air only family-friendly shows until 9:00 P.M. because so many children might be watching. We all knew that many TV shows could be as worthless as junk food, but for the most part we assumed they weren't a bad influence. Many of us who grew up in those days assume that the media continues to operate under those same rules today.

But while we weren't paying attention, everything changed. The implicit bond of trust between families and the media was broken. Spurred by cable competition and the relentless deregulation of the media industry during the 1980s, TV broadcasters, led by the new Fox network, abruptly abandoned the family hour and dropped the unwritten code that kept most sexual and violent content off the screen. Instead of maintaining a safe harbor for kids and families, the networks flooded channel after channel with increasingly explicit sex, commercialism, and violence. So much for voluntary codes of social responsibility.

At the same time, the reach of the mass media exploded, and it will be expanding even more in coming years. Cable channels have proliferated since the 1980s, and as industry pundits like to say, we've gone from the age of broadcasting to narrow casting. Instead of three major networks plus PBS, there are now hundreds of channels, and that number will soon multiply further with the advent of digital TV. With personal computers in more than half of all American homes, the Internet and electronic games are also competing, along with heavily marketed music, for kids' attention. As every parent knows all too well, kids are now surrounded by the clamor of media messages day and night. For millions of American kids, the media is, in fact, "the other parent"—a force that is shaping their reality, setting their expectations, guiding their behavior, defining their self-image, and dictating their interests, choices, and values.

Confronting this media reality as parents, my wife and I realized that we had to take a much more active parenting role when it came to the media and our kids. Liz and I aren't zealots by any means, and neither one of us can relate to finger-wagging moralists or fundamentalist ideologues on the topic of the media and morals. In fact, I don't even think it's practical to go as far as the American Academy of Pediatrics, which recently recommended that kids under age two never watch TV. I'm hardly a paragon of virtue—every once in a while, I can't resist showing my kids the food-fight scene from *Animal House*—but my wife and I have set pretty strict media limits for our own kids.

Still, whatever rules we have at home sometimes feel like the equivalent of sticking a finger in the media dike. At the age of five, for example—thanks to one of her friends across the street—Lily was introduced to Spice Girls videos. I'll never forget watching with no small degree of horror as our tiny firstborn child provocatively danced and lip-synched to her favorite Spice Girls tune, "If You Wanna Be My Lover"—abruptly teaching me the role-modeling influence that media has on even the youngest kids. I also noticed that most of the second, third, and fifth graders I taught at E. Morris Cox Elementary School in East Oakland, where I volunteered for ten years, don't have a clue about the names of their senators or the vice president of our country. But they know all about Bart Simpson, Kenan and Kel, the latest hip-hop artists, and the names of virtually every character on prime-time TV.

INSIDE THE MEDIA

When I started Children Now, I was convinced that if we were to reshape public policies on crucial children's issues such as education, Head Start, and child health care, we first needed to change the attitudes of the public and opinion leaders on these subjects. So from the beginning of our work as a major lobby group for children's rights, we approached media leaders for help in spreading the message.

By the time Lily was born, Children Now had begun researching and publicizing the effect of the various media, including news, entertainment, and advertising, on the daily lives, values, and behavior of children. We had commissioned national surveys asking kids to describe their experiences with mass media, and we were astonished to find that this was the first time that polls of this type had ever been conducted. Despite the incredible barrage of media that bombards kids, nobody had ever bothered to ask *children themselves* what they thought about its impact.

During the course of those studies, I spoke directly with hundreds of youngsters. Each had opinions on the media, and they all cared deeply that their views were being heard. The first thing most kids made clear was how thoroughly tuned into the media they and their friends were. They talked about how much it affected their peers and how it often left them feeling scared, angry, or depressed. I remember one ten-year-old telling me, for example, that he was "more scared watching the local news on TV than horror movies, because the news is for real."

Kids also said that the media didn't accurately reflect their reality—that media companies didn't understand what it was like to be a kid. "They think we're pretty dumb, so they just feed us a lot of sex and violence whenever possible"—that was the type of comment that I often heard. They felt alienated yet at the same time heavily influenced by what they listened to or saw. And few kids I talked to thought that media was doing much of anything positive for kids—such as modeling responsible behavior or educating them about issues that were important in their lives.

As we started lobbying in Washington, D.C., on issues like the Children's Television Act and a new ratings system for TV programming, it was amazing to see how few voices there were on the kids' side of the debate. I was also continuously frustrated to see how little serious attention was paid to the influence of media on kids by leaders from Washington to Hollywood and Madison Avenue. With rare and notable exceptions, few people seemed to be doing much of anything to make it better. So, in 1996, with my own kids squarely in mind, I decided to move on from Children Now and trade in my advocate's spurs for those of a media company leader. I was tired of trying to convince media leaders to do a better job for kids, so I had the notion that I would just do the job myself. As my mom always said, "Put your money where your mouth is." So armed with a little moxie and a terrific group of investors, I set out to build a new kids' educational media company—JP Kids—that would create high-quality content for kids on TV, the Internet, publishing, and related platforms. I had no idea what I was in for. And that's when my real education in the world of kids' media began.

In 2002, six years after launching JP Kids, we are still solidly in business, one of the few remaining independent kids' educational media companies dedicated to high-quality content in the United States. Our biggest hit series has been the very popular show *The Famous Jett Jackson*, which runs daily on the Disney Channel, and we've got a couple of new series that will hopefully be airing soon on PBS and other networks. We've also got a promising new publishing division as well as new educational media initiatives, but I'm not writing this book to promote JP Kids or Children Now. They'll succeed or fail on their own merits. Rather, this is an insider's view of the world of kids and media, from someone who's seen it up close from many different angles. As a parent, as a national child advocate, as someone who teaches constitutional law and civil liberties courses at Stanford University, and as the head of one of the few independent children's media companies in the United States, I've had a unique vantage point. And from where I stand, the world of media and children is not a very pretty picture. In fact, I'm convinced that the huge influence of the "other parent" should be a matter of urgent national concern for parents, policy makers, and responsible media executives alike.

TELLING THE TRUTH

When I first decided to write this book, my wife and some of my friends told me I was crazy. After all, it wouldn't do a lot for my relationships with some of the top executives at the big media companies that JP Kids does business with on a regular basis. And it probably wouldn't make some of my friends in the political and advocacy worlds happy either. Moreover, it would inevitably expose me as an imperfect parent who makes just as many mistakes as others do.

The stakes were made even clearer to me by author and media observer Ken Auletta. We were together at a kids and media conference in New York, and he asked me, "Jim, are you going to be honest? Are you going to tell the truth?" At first, I didn't understand exactly what he meant. Now I do.

If you want to tell the truth about today's media world, then you have to tell some pretty tough stories. And you have to name some names . . . including those of some people you like on a personal level and certainly some with whom you do business. As I said earlier, despite all the airbrushing that the media industry and some of its political allies manage so adeptly, it's not a pretty picture. There are a lot of very harmful things that are being done to kids and our society in the name of shareholder value, for profit alone. And there's not nearly enough being done to take the extraordinary potential of media and turn it into a positive force in our kids' lives and our global culture. That makes answering Auletta's question a lot easier. I'll do my best to tell the truth as I have experienced it, and let those proverbial chips fall where they may.

MONEY RULES

I may have been naive, but I originally assumed that the companies that produce and distribute kids' programming, as well as other media that kids so readily consume, have an overriding interest in children and a genuine concern for their best interests. How wrong and unaware I was. While I've met many people in the kids' media industry, both creative types and executives, who do fit this profile and care deeply about children, it's at best a minority viewpoint. What I learned the hard way is a very sobering lesson: market forces and the short-term profit goals of a few giant media corporations—not quality issues or kids' needs—dominate the media world, including nearly all the "edutainment" content produced for kids. Put simply, money rules all, not the best interest of kids or our broader society.

This lesson has been drilled home to me time and time again over the past five years by top media decision makers. During our first year at JP Kids, the head of kids' programming at the WB network, a woman who was a longtime and highly respected kids' programmer, warned me never to use the word "educational" within earshot of the individual who was head of the network at the time, unless I wanted to get our project killed immediately. Months later, I sat in the office of a top CBS executive and listened to her embarrassed explanation of why she was canceling a series order for a high-quality kids' show that she had previously raved about. "From a creative and educational standpoint, it was everything we were looking for. It's our favorite show," she told me. "But you know the reality of kids' television—it's all about the deal and the bottom line.

Somebody else just offered us an extremely profitable package deal that costs us virtually nothing, so we're going to cancel the order, even though we really love the show." In other words, no big profit potential, no sale.

Recently, the mercenary nature of kids' TV was described to me very bluntly by a colleague, the American-based head of a leading Canadian production company known for its successful deals in the U.S. marketplace. In May 2001, we were negotiating with this Canadian company to coproduce a couple of series. As this top executive explained to me:

> It's easy to buy your way onto Fox Kids. Just show Haim [Saban, the then-head of Fox Kids and Fox Family] the merchandising money, and he'll make the deal. . . . It's a lot harder to buy your way onto Nickelodeon than Fox, but now that Viacom is cutting budgets so much, it may be doable. It's all about the deal we offer them. . . . Buying your way onto PBS is pretty simple. If you can deliver one to two million dollars in sponsorships, you can usually get a weekly series. For three to five million dollars you can get a daily strip—five days a week, the Holy Grail. At PBS, they're a lot more open to, *ahem,* more "entrepreneurial" and profitable strategies now that Bush is in office.

Welcome to the world of kids' TV circa 2002. That conversation reflects the basic reality that underlies not just kids' television but nearly every aspect of the media today. From TV, music, and movies to video games, the Internet, and publishing, an unprecedented and unfettered drive for short-term profits and rising stock prices now rules America's media companies and virtually all the content they create and distribute. Let me be very clear. This unchecked commercialism and obsession with the bottom line has a very direct and disturbing effect on the images and messages that influence our kids. Today, media companies, most of which are large, vertically integrated conglomerates, encourage coarseness and routinely "push the envelope" with sex, violence, and provocative language, *not* because it makes the creative product better, but solely because it makes that "product" stand out from the clutter of competition.

At a time when mergers and acquisitions and a disturbing, relentless trend of consolidation dominate the media industry, are we really surprised that concerns about quality and the needs of children have been shunted aside? Are we truly surprised at the lowest-common-denominator nature of so much content? As we'll explore in depth in subsequent chapters, the past decade's wave of media mergers has produced a complex web of business relationships that now defines America's mass media and popular culture. These relationships offer a huge opportunity for cross-promotion and the selling of products among different companies owned by the same powerful parent corporations. Today, America's media landscape, not to mention the content that our kids consume for five or six hours every day, is dominated by a handful of massive conglomerates—only six or seven of them at most. These giant conglomerates own four of the five companies that sell 90 percent of the music in the United States. These same companies also own all the major film studios, all the major TV networks, and most of the broadcast TV stations in the largest ten markets. They own all or part of virtually every commercial cable channel. As outspoken media entrepreneur Ted Turner said recently,

> Pretty soon there won't be but two cable companies left, and there'll be only four or five programming companies left. I think it's sad we're losing so much diversity of thought and opinions to big companies like News Corporation who only care about their own power. They don't care about the good of society.[2]

These are all-purpose media corporations. And, quite simply, they look at kids as targets in this vast commercial empire they are conquering in the name of profit—or, as they like to say, "shareholder value."

MORE MEDIA, LESS CHOICE

To the casual observer of today's media landscape, it might seem that there's been a serious increase in consumer choice, especially for kids. But look more closely. As one noted author and media critic explains:

> It's the nature of the choice, and how the choices are laid out there, that is really the most striking feature. . . . The issue isn't really the amount of choice; it's the amount of commercialism that permeates all the choices. So while it seems like you have a massive range of choices, they're really underneath it girded by the same commercial logic. . . . Everything is dedicated to the idea of selling something.[3]

Harsh words perhaps, but accurate. In the struggle to attract the largest audiences and ensure the greatest profit margins, these huge media giants are often locked in a crass race toward the bottom, employing sensationalism, not for artistic reasons but as a means of exploitation—to grab, and keep, audiences' attention. This represents a fundamental shift over the past two decades. "It used to be that you stripped yourself of censorship to be honest," noted writer Larry Gelbart, whose credits include *M*A*S*H, Tootsie,* and *A Funny Thing Happened on the Way to the Forum.* Now, he told *The New York Times,* "it's not done in the service of honesty, but in the service of competition, of the marketplace."[4] Herb Scannell, the widely admired president of Nickelodeon and one of the most thoughtful and committed media leaders I know, recently observed, "There's a whole business aura to post-eighties culture that's completely different. Everybody has stock now, and I think business has impacted media in a way that says, 'What's my return?' sooner rather than later."[5]

As I travel to various places around the country, I hear three primary concerns over and over again: there's too much sex, too much violence, and too much commercialism in media. I'll address each of these issues in later chapters, but it's important to understand right up front that the roots of each of these problems are most definitely colored green. As Reed Hundt, former chairman of the Federal Communications Commission (FCC), said plainly, "Market values aren't necessarily family values."

LOSS OF INNOCENCE

For me, as a parent of three young children and as a longtime teacher, the loss of innocence at too early an age is perhaps the highest price that American kids pay in this new media environment. Ever since the Hays Office began monitoring Hollywood morals in the 1920s, Americans have worried about the media's impact on "family values." But before our mass-media culture became so explicit and so pervasive, before large media companies began to realize huge profits by pushing sex and sensationalism, things were different. Parents were much better able to control what their children learned about and when. I'm hardly a prude, having grown up in the "free love" era of the late 1960s and 1970s, but I am deeply troubled by this aspect of today's media culture. Our kids are bombarded with language, messages, and images that far exceed the most outrageous forms of pop culture we experienced. And instead of making a social or political statement, they aim to shock and titillate for commercial reasons.

Traditionally, childhood was guarded by what Neil Postman, chairman of New York University's Department of Culture and Communication and a respected media observer, calls a "sequence of revealed secrets." Kids were routinely protected from information that they were not yet ready to understand. That innocence is priceless. It's an essential element of childhood and growing up. But today, such gatekeeping is virtually impossible. In the course of a single year, the average American child is exposed to about ten thousand episodes of sexual intercourse or references to sex on television alone. We're not even talking about their repeated exposure to sex in movies, ads, magazines, music, radio shows, and easily accessed Web sites. In a recent two-week survey of TV shows by the Henry J. Kaiser Family Foundation, *more than two-thirds* of the shows that aired in what used to be the "family hour"—from 7:00 to 9:00 P.M.—contained sexual content inappropriate for kids. And this was only broadcast television, not the more extreme content routinely available on cable.

This constant and overwhelming exposure to sexual messages is coming at a time when splintered families, the decline in organized religion, and struggling public schools have left many kids without other clear messages when it comes to sexual behavior and values. Should parents be the first line of defense? Absolutely. But the media has some serious responsibility too, especially when they are using publicly owned airwaves to make billions of dollars.

If we don't start taking responsibility—as parents first, but also by demanding it from the huge media interests as well as the government officials who are supposed to regulate them on behalf of the public interest—then we put our children at continued risk. We will raise generations of kids desensitized to violence, overexposed to reckless sex, and commercially exploited from their earliest years. And our culture will pay an ever-increasing price.

RAISED ON VIOLENCE

Part of that price is a tolerance and a taste for violence. More than a thousand scientific studies have shown that over time, exposure to violence in the media results in desensitization, fear, and increased aggression. The American Psychological Association has stated it plainly: "The accumulated research clearly demonstrates a correlation between viewing violence and aggressive behavior." The surgeon general, the National Institute of Mental Health, and the American Academy of Pediatrics agree. Media industry flacks who question the evidence about media and violence are the equivalent of cigarette company executives who testify to Congress that there's no proven link between cigarettes and cancer.

Today, repeated exposure to media violence can start at frighteningly young ages. The average preschooler watches well over twenty hours of television and videos a week, and more than 90 percent of programs during children's prime viewing hours feature violence. By the time they enter middle school, American kids have seen eight thousand killings and a hundred thousand more acts of violence on TV. Again, we're talking about only broadcast television here—not violent video games, movies, music, or the hugely popular, head-banging World Wrestling Federation (WWF) excesses on cable.

For some of the most vulnerable youngsters in our society, violent media can provide a script for fantasies of mayhem. Are they the sole cause of adolescent violence? Certainly not. But they are definitely a factor. Repeated playing of violent computer games such as *Doom* can function as horribly realistic rehearsals. And unfortunately, weapons can be the far-too-easily-obtained props that kids use to put their rage-and-media-fueled fantasies into action. Other kids—those who don't shoot up their schools—can become more and more numbed to violence and tolerant of it as an alternative in life. This far more pervasive effect—what former New York senator Daniel Moynihan refers to as "defining deviancy down"—has disturbing, long-term implications for many kids and for the health and safety of American society.

CAPTIVES OF THE FREE MARKET

Commercial exploitation is another price that American kids pay from the time they are in diapers. I can't tell you how many meetings I've been in over the past few years, both with media executives and advertisers, in which kids were referred to almost exclusively in terms of their monetary value as consumers. It's nauseating but entirely routine in the media world. As we'll see in chapter 5, consumerism among kids is at an all-time high (you might say "low" if you question the values that this represents). With hundreds of companies, armed with sophisticated studies and the latest focus-group research, targeting kids from the cradle through high school,

is it any surprise that so many parents, including myself, are frequently taken aback by the consumeristic impulses of children? I
sometimes wonder, for kids left alone in the afternoon, is it worse to
watch the daytime talk-show parade of "little girls obsessed with
their looks," "one-night stands," "teens who lie about abuse," and
"sexy lingerie for criticized wives," or the endless stream of commercials that punctuate them? Both are driven by the same imperative—the media's single-minded focus on the bottom line. But that
impulse has its worst expression when it specifically targets kids,
seeking to manipulate them in the interests of corporate profits.

ABANDONED BY OUR PUBLIC REPRESENTATIVES

So who is looking out for the interests of the public and our kids?
You might be asking yourself by now, hey, where's the government,
and what's a more important national priority than nurturing the
healthy growth of future generations? The American people, after
all, own the airwaves and much of the other resources on which
these large media empires have been built. Shouldn't there be special rules that protect kids and require these huge media conglomerates to operate in the public interest when it comes to our
youngest citizens? It is more than naive to pretend that the market
alone will protect them. After all, there's a reason we require kids to
go to school until they're sixteen. There's a reason we have child
labor laws. There's a reason we don't let people under sixteen drive
cars. There's a reason we have strict underage drinking laws—
because kids are not equipped with the same capacity for judgment
and discrimination as adults. They need guidance, education, and
special rules to keep them from being damaged or exploited. We
recognize this in virtually every sphere of American life. Yet in the
media world, we have stripped away the very rules created both to
protect kids and to enhance their lives, leaving them almost entirely
to the profit-driven manipulations of a largely unregulated free
market.

It wasn't always like this, as we'll explore in depth in later chapters. During the 1950s, 1960s, and 1970s, profit motives were balanced by a belief in social responsibility as well as, in many instances, public interest obligations enforced by government. As far back as 1934, Congress awarded broadcasters the free use of the public airwaves *on the condition* that they in turn serve "the public interest, convenience, and necessity." Courts, the Congress, and federal regulators such as the FCC have consistently upheld the public-interest standard, and for decades broadcasters and other media leaders respected it.

Today, however, the public-interest standard has been rendered virtually meaningless. With the exception of some much-watered-down kids' TV regulations, broadcasters and the huge media conglomerates that own them rarely provide any fare that remotely reminds us of their public-interest obligations. Other branches of the media act as if they've never even heard of the concept. So when—and why—did the media lose sight of its public-interest responsibilities?

The trend began in the 1980s, when free-market conservatism and the culture of "greed is good" captured the country. The deregulation craze shook industry after industry, as regulatory agencies were stripped—or stripped themselves—of their authority. The media industry quickly went the way of the airlines and financial services. Regulations protecting the public interest, not to mention children and families, were scorned, and the results were devastating. President Ronald Reagan's FCC chairman, Mark Fowler, waved the deregulation flag and announced that the TV is merely a "toaster with pictures." Under Fowler, the FCC stopped requiring stations to air educational and informational shows for kids, and it stopped limiting advertising on children's shows.

Fowler also handed the keys of the television industry to financial speculators, eliminating the rule that required media owners to hold on to a station for at least three years before selling it. As a result, a rash of speculative buying, selling, and mergers swept the industry. New corporate owners—with no media experience and eyes focused exclusively on the bottom line—took over venerable television networks such as NBC and CBS. Today, Westinghouse (which merged with CBS, which then merged again with Viacom) and General Electric—the guys who really do make toasters—are in charge of television. At the same time, cable TV—which, being nonbroadcast, was never subject to "public trust" restrictions— increased competition for audiences, began "pushing the envelope" with raunchy shows to grab attention, and intensified the focus on the industry's profit margins.

The bottom-line trend that began in the 1980s accelerated in the 1990s. The 1996 Telecommunications Act, which deregulated even more aspects of media ownership, triggered cutthroat competition and massive consolidation, particularly in the television arena. In addition, as recently retired FCC chairman William Kennard describes it, the 1996 Telecom Act "defanged" the FCC, making it virtually impossible for public interest and citizens groups to challenge broadcasters' licenses. As a result, the twenty-first-century world of media, more than ever before, is now focused on market share, mergers, and vertical integration. The huge companies that make various media products today also control the financing and distribution of those products. The media is guided by the forces of free-market capitalism, and media companies are even more tightly ruled by simplistic numerical yardsticks such as quarterly profit-and-loss statements.

In an interview for this book, Steve Case, the chairman and visionary leader of corporate giant AOL Time Warner, openly acknowledged this reality, admitting that even in his view, the media industry had "become too Wall Street–centric, too focused on what the analysts are saying, and much too focused on what the stock price is tomorrow."[6] Today, shareholder returns matter far more than quality or the public interest. The resulting cost-cutting and ever-increasing competition mean that only the strongest and biggest media companies survive. This is social Darwinism in its purist form.

It does not have to be this way. We may have made many mistakes and missed many important opportunities to rein in big media and make it accountable to kids and the broader public interest. But we are at a watershed moment in our media-driven society, and we have a chance to reverse many of these trends and make the media much more of a positive force in our society. I didn't write this book (and nearly drive my wife and kids crazy in the process) just in order to *describe* the problem. I'm not merely going to explore the problems of vertical integration by huge conglomerates and how that leads to a proliferation of sex, violence, and commercialism in the various media. Instead, Part II of this book is about solutions and achieving change. We are going to look at the positive steps that parents, the media industry itself, government, and citizen activists can take to make the media environment healthier for kids. And I am going to outline a specific action agenda for each sector to pursue in addressing this most crucial issue.

Parents Taking Control

It's tempting to believe that we can trust the media with our kids, that we don't need to pay close attention to what movies or TV shows our kids are watching, what computer games they're playing, where they're surfing on the Internet, or what lyrics are coming through their Walkman headphones. It's much easier to believe—as our parents could—that we can trust the media. After all, we're only adding more work and more worry to our lives if we admit that we now need to be as wary of the media as we are of strangers accosting our children on the street. As a result, many parents are in a state of "media denial," while others feel overwhelmed and helpless.

But the fact is, we need to take as much responsibility for our children's media consumption as we do for their performance in school and their physical well-being. If we're worried about what our kids eat, then we should certainly be worried about what our kids are watching. Taking responsibility takes effort, no question, but it's achievable. I've devoted an entire chapter to the role of parents, and I've laid out practical, concrete strategies they can use to assert control over the "other parent" in their children's lives, starting today.

Calling the Media Industry to Account

I am sick and tired of hearing industry leaders and spokespeople try to evade their responsibility and point the finger at everyone else—parents, "censors," or other media companies who they claim are worse offenders than they are. It is long since past the time when the media industry itself, and particularly the top executives of these huge media conglomerates, took sustained and serious responsibility for the products and content that they are marketing to kids, for shaping our culture and values. They must be held accountable. Period.

Many of the people I know in the upper echelons of the media industry are intelligent, capable, and upstanding people. But they are leaders of companies that appear to have only one purpose: the relentless pursuit of short-term profit and "shareholder value." I believe, however, that the media industry, by its very nature and role in our society and global culture, must act differently than other industries—not least because they have the free use of our public airwaves, our digital spectrum, and virtually unfettered access to our children's hearts and minds. These are priceless assets, and the right to use them should necessarily carry serious and long-lasting obligations to further the public good.

But rather than talking about our moral and social responsibility to kids, media leaders use the First Amendment argument to stop healthy debate. By framing every criticism as a threat of censorship, they derail any discussion and action on the real, underlying issue—the need to protect kids and enhance their learning in the new media environment. Now, without question, the First Amendment is one of the most hallowed jewels of our Constitution. It stands for our nation's commitment to individual freedom of expression and to a free press so essential to a participatory democracy. But as someone who has taught First Amendment law and politics at Stanford University for more than a decade, I can tell you that the industry's application of the First Amendment to kids' media is largely a self-serving sham.

In chapter 9, we'll look at a range of proactive investments and measures—including serious funding for quality children's media as well as media literacy programs—that should be part and parcel of the huge conglomerates' operating mandates. And we'll explore how the media and advertising industries can play a critical role in realizing the enormous educational potential of the Internet and other digital technologies.

The Role of Government

As we'll see time and again throughout this book, a free, unregulated marketplace will *never* care about kids. In that Darwinian setting, only the fittest survive and only profits matter. Kids need special rules, special protections, and strong, mediating forces that will place their interests above the ruthless imperatives of short-term profit margins. The last time I checked, that was supposed to be the role of government in our democratic system. But in fact, our government has been doing very little lately to regulate the media on behalf of the best interests of America's kids and families. It's time for that to change. It's time for our elected officials to stand up to the deep pockets of the media companies and help create a healthier media environment for kids.

We'll explore further our government's far too cozy relationship with the media industry and look at the constitutional history of First Amendment law to show just how far Congress and the FCC can and should go to regulate media on behalf of kids. We'll also examine some instances in recent history when Congress, the president, and the FCC have used their constitutional powers to promote the interests of children despite industry objections. And we'll look at why, as Senator Joseph Lieberman has warned, the current FCC is failing to use its basic enforcement powers in the best interests of America's kids and families.[7] But perhaps most important, in Chapter Ten this book will set out an agenda for what government should do to help over the next decade. Given that the media is the "other parent" in kids' lives, government has a major role to play in curbing its excesses and promoting its use in the public interest.

Citizens Standing Up for Kids

In an interview for this book, former President Bill Clinton was surprisingly optimistic about the concept of forging a broad coalition to support media reforms that favor children and families. He saw possibilities for this in both Congress and among citizen advocacy groups, noting correctly that the vast majority of Americans—both conservative and liberal, Republican and Democrat—feel a deep, heartfelt concern over the current state of our media environment. Drawing on his eight years in the White House, he compared this opportunity for cooperation to the broad base of support for economic aid to Mexico and other developing countries, which came from an unusual coalition of liberals and conservatives. It even brought Pat Robertson to the White House for his one and only visit during the Clinton presidency. I think the former president is onto something, and it's a sense I've had ever since I began researching this book and giving frequent talks about this subject. I find that people of all political persuasions agree with the need and many of the strategies for media reform. People from all backgrounds and political parties share concerns about the ways in which media is shaping our kids' values and behaviors. It's not unusual for people to come up to me after a talk and say, "I'm actually very conservative, but I agree with you about these issues." In fact, I found myself agreeing with a conservative like William Bennett, with whom I'd never agreed on *anything*, when he conducted his shaming campaign against Time Warner and their profit-driven distribution of misogynistic rap music.

I do think there's interesting potential here for an unusual cross section of American citizens—and, hopefully, government leaders—to come together around these issues. In chapter 11, as in the other solutions-focused chapters of this book, I've suggested a specific, concrete agenda for citizen activists to pursue as we seek to rein in and make more positive the enormous power of the media in children's lives.

At the end of the day, this is an issue that is simply too important to ignore. We are truly at a crossroads as we enter the twenty-first century. In the shadow of the events of September 11, 2001, we are learning the power of collective action and common ground. The need is there. The media's messages are ever more pervasive in our society and ever more powerful forces in shaping our children's values, behavior, and, very possibly, their future. The "other parent" is real, and it is everywhere. The challenge of restraining it is enormous. But so are the rewards for meeting that challenge—and the consequences for failure will be equally profound.

What we need is a new model, a new contract between parents, the media industry, and our government. We do not face a Hobson's choice between free speech and a free market on the one hand and government censorship or bureaucracy on the other. Rather, the true choice is a balanced one of how best to serve the needs of American society and most of all our kids—how to direct the extraordinary powers of traditional and new digital media to be a positive force in our children's lives. That's no small challenge, but we ignore it at our peril. The wise former FCC chairman Newton Minow said recently, "If we turn away from that choice, the consequences of our inaction will be even greater educational neglect, more craven and deceptive consumerism, and inappropriate levels of sex and violence—a wasteland vaster than anyone can imagine or would care to. Let us do for our children today what we should have done long ago."[8] It's time to get started.

Two

IT'S ALL ABOUT MONEY

If there is one single theme that has dominated my learning curve about kids and media, particularly since I started to build our own kids' and educational media company five years ago, it's that *money rules all*. I simply cannot overstate how central money and the insatiable pursuit of profit is to the workings of children's media. Everything else pales by comparison. When I started JP Kids after seven years of building Children Now, I assumed that the world of kids' media would be balanced between a traditional business approach and a genuine commitment to kids and education. After all, why work in this field if you don't care about kids? But I quickly learned that there *is* no balance. Money comes first, and there is no close second.

I'm sure many readers, particularly parents, instinctively know that money and commercial imperatives are a huge driving force in kids' media, simply because it's apparent in so much of the content and marketing that our kids are subjected to. But until you see it up close and live with this obsessive "profits above all else" mentality on a daily basis, it's hard to conceive of the scale of its importance. If we want to deal constructively with the impact of the media on our children's lives, then we must restore some balance to the equation. Today, the system is completely out of whack. And kids are the biggest losers of all.

In the opening chapter, I related how the head of a large Canadian production company explained that you can in effect "buy" your way onto Fox Kids or PBS children's programming simply by guaranteeing a certain amount of money to the network. Maybe that doesn't surprise you, and it certainly is common knowledge to insiders in the media industry, but it sure isn't the way things ought to work. Bill Baker, a longtime, respected media executive who is now the president and CEO of WNET (Channel 13), the PBS flagship station in New York, almost jumped out of his chair when I interviewed him. "I've just got to tell you this story," he said. "It sums up everything I know about kids' TV." It was about his friend Pat, who had spent nearly thirty years in the television business and ran a station in Los Angeles. As Bill explained, Pat was a hard-nosed business guy, and he had pretty much seen everything there was to see in the television world . . . until one year when he went to the annual convention of NATPE, the National Association of Television Program Executives.

This convention, which I've had to attend almost every year as the head of JP Kids, is held annually in venues like Las Vegas and New Orleans. Its purpose is to exhibit new programming by all the major television and entertainment companies for individual television stations (as opposed to networks) to buy and air. This is called syndication. As at any sales convention, there are lots of scantily clad women running around trying to get you to come to their booths to see the products that their company is pitching, and there's lots of free food and drink. It's quite a spectacle. NATPE is also a place where you can meet Jerry Springer, Montel Williams, Judge Judy, and Rikki Lake, up close and personal, or get one of the "*Baywatch* babes" to pose with you for a picture and sign your program.

So Pat was at the NATPE convention when he ran into a friend in the children's syndication business. "You *won't* believe this one," the friend said. "I have a kids' show that I've sold to two hundred television stations already. Guess how many stations wanted to see the program?" Pat, a grizzled industry veteran, cynically guessed twenty or thirty—but the answer, his astonished friend told him, was *zero*. Not one of the representatives of the two hundred television stations had bothered to watch the show. The only questions they had asked were "What's the deal?" and "How much money can we make?" Not a single question about the content of the program, whether it was any good, whether it was educational, whether it met FCC guidelines, or what the themes and characters were. The only issue that counted was the money issue. The producers would actually be paying the stations a fee to air the program, since the production companies, in turn, would make their money on the tie-in toy merchandising. As Bill Baker told me, shaking his head as he recounted the story, "This is what's happened to the entire business. How much money we make, the bottom line, is the *only* measure of our business today. And frankly, that's probably going to happen with these Internet businesses too, which will also influence kids greatly. In my opinion, to aim only for the bottom line is to aim too low."[9]

Unfortunately, this story is merely one of hundreds I could recount that drive home the same point. Since average American kids spend more than five hours per day consuming media, its content has an enormous influence on their values, behavior, and self-image. And if money is the only consideration shaping that media, you can imagine the results. Actually, you don't have to imagine them, because they're right there in front of you every day—on your movie screens, coming from your stereos, on your computer monitors, in your video arcades, and on your television sets. Media is everywhere in kids' lives, and money drives all of it. As we examine the "other parent's" influence in shaping children's reality, never forget that greed lies at its heart. But things weren't always this way.

THE STRUCTURE OF MEDIA TODAY

The United States is in the midst of an extraordinary transformation of its entire media universe. We are in an era of enormous concentration and consolidation, in which a mere handful of media mega-conglomerates now dominate the global media landscape. This concentration of media and communication in the hands of a few has occurred at a dizzying pace. Indeed, in the six years since I started JP Kids, there has been an incredible spate of mergers and acquisitions in virtually every sector of the media world, from television, movies, and radio stations to publishing houses and the music industry. The stories are all the same. A handful of corporations now exert a cartel-like stranglehold on virtually all aspects of the twenty-first-century mediascape.

Back in 1983, the noted media scholar Ben Bagdikian wrote a book called *The Media Monopoly*,[10] which chronicled how approximately fifty media conglomerates had come to dominate the entire U.S. media world, including radio, television (both broadcast and cable), film, newspapers, magazines, and music. Now, two decades later, a media world run by as many as fifty conglomerates seems almost hard to imagine. As Bagdikian explains in his most recent update of *The Media Monopoly:*

> When the first edition of this book was published in 1983, fifty corporations dominated most of every mass medium, and the biggest media merger in history was a $340 million deal. At that time, the strategy of most of the fifty biggest firms was to gain market domination in one medium—to have the largest market share solely in newspapers, for example, or in magazines, or books, or movies, but not in all of them. By the time the second edition was published in 1987, the fifty companies had shrunk to twenty-nine. By the third edition in 1990, the twenty-nine had shrunk to twenty-three, by the fourth edition to fourteen. By the fifth edition in 1997, the biggest firms numbered ten and involved the $19 billion Disney-ABC deal, at the time the biggest media merger ever. But the biggest of 1983, worth $340 million, would give way seventeen years later to AOL Time Warner's $350 billion merged corporation, more than 1,000 times larger.

*   *   *

Other sources like *Forbes* have put a lower value on the AOL–Time Warner merger, more in the $150 billion range, but that hardly matters. The point is that today there are only *five or six* huge megacorporations that dominate the entire global media business. They include AOL Time Warner, Disney (which bought ABC), Viacom (which bought CBS and is the parent corporation of my publisher), News Corporation (which bought Fox, among others), Vivendi Universal, and General Electric–NBC. There are a few other large players in the media and telecommunications field, such as AT&T/TCI, Microsoft, Bertelsmann, Liberty Media Corporation, USA Networks, and Sony, which also figure in the landscape, but it is an unbelievably concentrated picture, no matter how you look at it.

Let's take the Walt Disney Company, for example. It is not just your little family entertainment company led by Uncle Walt. It's the third largest global media conglomerate, with fiscal year 2000 earnings of more than $25 billion. Theme parks and resorts produce 27 percent of its revenues, studio entertainment accounts for 24 percent, and media networks make up 17 percent. In addition to its rights to theme parks, Disney owns one broadcast network (ABC) and all or part of at least nine cable channels (ESPN, Disney Channel, the new ABC Family channel, A&E, Lifetime, E!, Toon Disney, etc.). It also owns six different production and distribution companies (Walt Disney Pictures, Touchstone, Miramax, Walt Disney Television Animation, etc.) as well as a music group with at least five labels. It owns publishing assets (including Hyperion, Disney Publishing, and *Discover* magazine) and a couple of sports teams. It owns ten different television stations, the ABC, ESPN, and Disney radio networks, and a variety of newspapers. It also controls a growing Internet empire that includes ABC.com, ESPN.com, Disney.com, and Family.com, among others. In short, Disney is everywhere.

AOL Time Warner is an even bigger leviathan. Approved by the FCC in January 2001, the merger between AOL and Time Warner is the largest media merger in history. The new company promises to offer a powerhouse of integrated communication, media, and entertainment across all platforms—computer, phone, television, and handheld wireless devices. AOL, the world's largest Internet service provider, delivers twice as much mail as the U.S. Postal Service, links over half of all on-line American homes to the Internet, and owns Netscape, CompuServe, MapQuest, and Spinner.com. AOL Time Warner has huge music assets including such famed labels as Atlantic, Elektra, Rhino, Warner Bros. Records, Columbia House, and Time Life Music. In the TV world they own distribution through all of the Time Warner cable systems (the nation's second biggest cable company) as well as the WB Television Network, HBO, Cinemax, CNN (and all its spinoffs), TBS, TNT, Cartoon Network, Court TV, and a part interest in Comedy Central (co-owned with Viacom). In the movie arena, they own Warner Bros. Pictures, Castle Rock Entertainment, and New Line Cinema. In TV programming and production, they own Warner Bros. Television, Warner Bros. Animation, Hanna-Barbera Productions, HBO Productions, among others. In publishing, they own such magazines as *Time, Fortune, People, Sports Illustrated, Money, Entertainment Weekly, Parenting*, the publisher DC Comics, and many others. And, oh, yes, like other media conglomerates, they own sports teams, including the Atlanta Braves, Atlanta Hawks, Atlanta Thrashers, and, for good measure, World Championship Wrestling.[11]

Viacom, the corporate owner of my publisher, is another mega-media giant. Its vast holdings have increased dramatically during this period of massive media consolidations. Like Disney and AOL Time Warner, it is vertically integrated, meaning that it owns both multiple means of distribution as well as many forms of content production. For example, Viacom now owns both the CBS and UPN television networks (broadcast television distribution) as well as global cable distribution outlets such as MTV, VH-1, and Nickelodeon. Viacom also owns Paramount Studios, Nickelodeon's animation studio, and a number of other production assets. And Viacom owns a huge number of radio stations, major publishing enterprises such as Simon & Schuster, and the Blockbuster video chain.

I could go on and list the assets of News Corporation or Vivendi

Universal, but I think you get the picture. To put it plainly, control of the mass media, across all platforms, is increasingly concentrated in fewer and fewer very powerful hands. I'm no left-wing radical, but we all need to be concerned in this society if most of the main media sources fall increasingly under the control of a small number of giant corporations and extremely wealthy people, especially when they may be inclined to use this media power for their own economic or political purposes.

It's critical to understand that mergers in the media business matter a whole lot more than other types of consolidation. Having five or six widget manufacturers may be all you need in the widget industry to safeguard product and price competition—the main concerns of traditional antitrust laws and economic theory. But consolidating the power to create and distribute news, entertainment, and ideas in the hands of a few giant conglomerates with a vast array of other commercial interests raises very significant issues for our society.

The hallowed American concept of a "marketplace of ideas" depends on a range of voices and owners. The fewer the sources of entertainment or information, the less we have a true, unfettered marketplace. Similarly, our entire concept of freedom of expression relies on a diversity of voices and ideas—and when ownership and control of distribution is concentrated in the hands of just a few, you start to wonder about the meaning of the term "diversity." We often hear that we all enjoy many more "choices" today as viewers and listeners and readers. But that's not necessarily the case. Beneath the surface of that apparent range of choices, there are only a handful of owners with the same commercial imperative at work. As Aurora Wallace, who teaches in New York University's Department of Culture and Communication, said recently, AOL Time Warner's incessant mandate for selling and cross-promoting "empties content of anything but a consumption message. If every part of the company has to serve every other part of the company, there's no incentive to talk about anything else. . . . It's not evil. It's logical, according to corporate logic. The problem is that we expect the media to do other things. To inform us. To provide social glue. If that glue is only about consumption, we are missing something. It creates a grand illusion of choice."[12]

I see this lack of choice every day, up close and personal, in the world of kids' and family media. Lawrence Grossman, former president of NBC News and the Public Broadcasting System, concludes, "While the number of TV channels and media outlets is burgeoning . . . a few conglomerates, which have no direct responsibility to the American public, wield extraordinary power over the ideas and information the public will receive."

Leaders of the media industry widely recognize and applaud this enormous concentration of power and resources. Ted Turner, the fabled entrepreneur who finally sold his own large company to Time Warner (before the merger with AOL), frankly acknowledged, "We do have just a few people controlling all the cable companies in this country."[13] Peter Chernin, president of News Corporation and lieutenant to Australian-born media baron Rupert Murdoch, proudly observed that "if you look at the entire chain of entities—studios, networks, stations, cable channels, cable operations, international distribution—you want to be as strong in as many of those as you can. That way, regardless of where the profits move to, you're in a position to gain."[14]

But those of us who are not among the handful of media moguls see a different side. As Pulitzer Prize–winning journalist and author David Halberstam commented:

> The object of these mergers is never to improve the service. The person [the conglomerates are] interested in is not the person who buys the newspaper, not the person who gets the broadcast in his home. The person they're interested in is the person who buys the stock. . . . [Conglomeration means] less and less real commitment to the reader of news. Disney is not a company that's interested in excellence in journalism. They just squeeze, squeeze, squeeze. It's been a disaster. The stock price becomes the only part of the report card that matters. . . . You can serve only one god.

MERGERS, MONEY, AND KIDS—A BAD MIX

You might be asking yourself how this all applies to the world of kids and family media, but the connection is simple. In the kids' television world, for example, you can readily see the effects of what media analysts call "vertical integration," in which the same huge companies that make content or programming also control the distribution channels. The Walt Disney Company, as I mentioned earlier, owns a variety of television and film production companies, including Walt Disney Television Animation, Touchstone Pictures, ABC Entertainment Television Group, among others. These programming entities in turn supply Disney's broadcast network (ABC) and its many cable channels (Lifetime, Disney Channel, ABC Family, Toon Disney, Playhouse Disney, ESPN, The History Channel, E! Entertainment, etc.) with Disney "product." Suffice it to say that there's a built-in economic bias—some might call it a corporate imperative—for those who control the distribution channels to put their own "products" on them, rather than someone else's. This is especially true in the kids' arena, where the really big bucks are made in licensed characters and merchandising.

As you might imagine, a media giant like Disney is most interested in selling retail products based on its own "branded properties," often at its very own Disney stores. As a result, there is a huge focus on that "synergy" at the expense of other creative and educational goals. Just look at the numbers. In 1997 alone, $25 billion of Disney merchandise was sold, more than twice the total global sales of Toys 'R' Us. Disney's own licensing revenue that year was $10 billion, and Time Warner's (premerger, of course) was over $6 billion.[15] No wonder that we see such products as a Mickey for Kids perfume and the zillions of other licensed products that our children beg for at the local toy store. It's just one big marketing machine targeted at kids. If you don't believe me, put a children's video from Disney into your VCR and count the number of previews and branded, licensed products pitched on the screen before you get to the beginning of the "Feature Presentation." You'll be amazed. Then you might be angry.

Another troubling outgrowth of this vast merger and consolidation trend, one that has enormous consequences for kids, is the lack of accountability created by huge corporate structures. As media conglomerates grew bigger and bigger in the past fifteen years, so did the predominance of "shareholder" values and quarterly profit margins. At the same time, accountability has dramatically declined in these very same corporate structures. Remember, we are talking about companies with tens if not hundreds of thousands of employees. It's no longer clear where the buck stops in many of these institutions, though it is very clear that "bucks" are the be-all and end-all of their corporate strategies. As we'll see over and over again in subsequent chapters, large corporate behemoths have a way of dampening accountability and of placing the pressure for profits above all other values. There's always somebody else to point the finger at or some corporate P.R. hack to try to rationalize nakedly offensive but profitable programming as an expression of "artistic freedom." In short, nobody is held accountable for anything but profits, and the results are right there for you to see on your screen. Bluntly put, the bottom line is also the lowest common denominator.

One recent experience I had in the children's television world speaks volumes. In December 2001, we met with several senior executives of the Fox Broadcasting Company (FBC) to discuss their decision to stop programming the Fox Kids program block from 8:00 to 11:00 A.M. on Saturday mornings and instead to lease it out to the highest bidder. The reason for Fox's decision? To cut costs and increase bottom-line profits. During the meeting, I asked the executives about the government-mandated FCC rule that requires all broadcast stations to air a minimum of three hours of "educational and informational" programming per week. "Oh, that's not a problem," they laughed. "We'll urge the local stations to put on some cheap or free educational stuff from 7:00 to 8:00 A.M. on both Saturday and Sunday mornings, and then we can use those sports promo shows that Major League Baseball and the NFL gives

Fox for free. Those can count as educational shows, too." These
latter programs, *In the Zone* and *Under the Helmet,* are hardly what
Congress had in mind when it passed the Children's Television Act,
but the Fox Broadcasting execs didn't seem to care. The shows
were free, and better yet, a promotion for their lucrative sports fran-
chises. This kind of cynical attitude toward children and public
interest responsibility is what results from a "profits alone matter"
mentality.

Having run JP Kids and Children Now for more than a decade,
I've gotten to know most, if not all, of the key figures in kids' media
and television. None of them was willing to go on record about the
pressures they feel to produce profits above all else. That doesn't
mean they haven't talked to me about the subject at length. It's just
that they don't want to be quoted by name. As one leading industry
executive said to me recently after extracting a promise that I
wouldn't use his name, "Today, in our huge company, all that matters is making my twenty percent growth targets. It's not about the
shows anymore. It's not about quality content. It's not about kids.
It's all about growth, cutting costs, and making the quarterly numbers."

In the six years since I founded our kids' media company, I've
seen corporate profit pressures loom ever larger in the children's
television industry. As I said earlier, it's all about "the deal." When
an independent company goes to pitch a series for television or a
series of books to a publisher or even a new Internet strategy, the
conversation initially focuses on the creative content. Is it fresh or
edgy? Is it right for their target audience? But time and again, it all
comes down to money and deal terms. If you're willing to finance
the television series yourself, for example, or come in with half the
production budget from some other source (like an international
partner or a toy company), then all ears perk up. If not, your
chances of getting something on the air are slim.

Today, as the media industry is fighting a deep slump in advertising revenues and ever-greater pressure from Wall Street for continued growth and profits, the top-level executives I deal with think

about little else at the end of the day but their financial performance. Want to know why somebody green-lit *Jackass* on MTV or *Temptation Island* on Fox or the latest violent action cartoon on Fox Kids? Just try to imagine the pressure for ratings and profits that the executives who chose them feel. I guarantee you that's the real story behind the decision, no matter what P.R. excuses they may offer. And if the "product" makes good money or gets good ratings, then that company will be willing to weather whatever criticism may come with it. As Rupert Murdoch—whose Fox and News Corporation empire has done so much to lower the quality and taste standards of media around the world—remarked about his journalism business, "All newspapers are run to make profits. I don't run anything for respectability." You could substitute the words "television networks," "movie studios," or "record companies" for "newspapers" in his declaration, and the quote would still be entirely accurate.

The implications of this "money rules all" mentality have been equally disastrous in the music industry. As a *New York Times* critic wrote a couple of years back, popular music and its related institutions, like MTV and commercial radio stations, "have become increasingly reliant on market research, primarily because ratings and circulation are so important to their advertisers. As a result, the mall rules and music is in a lull."[16] It's ironic that this blatant trend toward the complete commercialization of the music industry may ultimately hurt its popularity with the audience, but that's what media concentration and a short-term profit mindset will bring you—that and prefabricated groups like the Spice Girls, whose tunes my daughter Lily used to like. My wife and I discovered that the Spice Girls were above all a merchandising machine aimed at young girls. There were Spice Girl bomber jackets, books, potato chips, calendars, and key chains. Polaroid even created the Spice Cam as part of its line of cameras, and promoted it to nine-to-twelve-year-old girls through an advertising campaign. And our parents thought the Monkees were bad!

Music marketing to teens is more sophisticated and equally, if not more, aggressive. As media critics like Mark Crispin Miller of New York University have noted, there is very little separation between marketing and content aimed at teens. They're all part of the same commercial package. If you think about rock videos, for example, they are basically highly sophisticated and seductive advertisements for songs, clothes, and other "must have" products. Watching an ad is no longer the price you have to pay for watching the show. The ad *is* the show. There's virtually no separation.[17] And again, kids, or in this case teens, are the target.

Movies and television, too, are suffering from commercial, copy-cat attempts to lure viewers with sex and violence. Large conglomerates often discourage risk and creativity, while pushing sameness in pursuit of the bottom line. Peter Bart, the always outspoken editor-in-chief of *Variety*, recently described the movie industry in the context of its new corporate ownership:

> A movie studio is part of this huge corporate cocoon, and therefore, theoretically, a studio should be willing to take bigger risks because one bad movie or even one bad summer in all likelihood won't erode the value of the [parent company's] shares. But the way it works out, the studios are if anything more risk averse. They are desperate to hedge their bets. It's the nature of bureaucratic self-protection. Every unit of a multinational corporation has to meet its numbers. That is reflected in the kind of pictures that get made.[18]

MEGA MEDIA AND DEMOCRACY

This is a book about kids and media, not an examination of the impact of media consolidation on our democratic processes. But it's important to see the connection between this dizzying spate of mergers in the media world and the threat it poses to so many of the most important values in our society. For me that connection starts with kids—the most precious resource that we have. But it also has serious implications for the functioning of our democracy.

In an open and free society such as ours, we rely on the media a great deal for public discourse and for the expression of democratic values. The First Amendment depends on a genuinely free and diverse "marketplace of ideas," in which a wide range of individuals and organizations have the opportunity to express information and views for the rest of us to ponder. As President John F. Kennedy pointed out to a convention of TV broadcasters, "The flow of ideas, the capacity to make informed choices, the ability to criticize, all of the assumptions on which political democracy rests, depend largely on communications. And you are the guardians of the most powerful and effective means of communication ever designed."[19]

But in recent years, as huge corporations have come to own virtually all of the means of communication, critics have raised disturbing questions about the implications of ownership and the impact of mega media on our democracy. As journalist and press critic A.J. Liebling once said, "Freedom of the press is guaranteed only to those who *own* one."

The most serious concerns about mergers and consolidations can be separated into several categories:

- First, there is the question of unfair economic competition and the distortion of marketplace principles brought on by oligopoly. We are supposed to be able to rely on antitrust rules to counteract that, but they have rarely been enforced lately in the media arena.

- Second is the question of unfair competition and the restraint of information and ideas through practices like cross-marketing and elimination of competing news sources. In a related vein, critics have focused on the general deterioration and increasingly corporate slant of the news and public affairs materials communicated by big media companies.

- Finally, as we'll explore in great detail in regard to kids, is the issue of the lowered and coarsened quality of entertainment programming and the consequences for our society.[20]

As the always colorful media baron Ted Turner said about his competitor Rupert Murdoch, the owner of News Corporation:

> I worry about how much control this man is getting. Like the former Führer, Murdoch controls the media for his own personal benefit—for money and power. . . . He thinks that his media should be used by him to further his own political goals. He's also a scumbag because he "goes down market" so much in his papers.[21] ["To go down market" means to use scandal, sex, and splashy crime to appeal to the lowest level of human interests.]

What critics like Turner are concerned about, besides sheer smarminess, is the control that the new media conglomerates have over the free flow of ideas. Constitutional scholar Burt Neuborne put it bluntly when he stated:

> I'm not satisfied with a two-tier First Amendment that says that a relatively small slice of the world gets to decide what gets said and all the rest of us sit like groundlings in the audience and grunt about whether we like it or not. Because that's what we are going to do unless we can find a way to increase the ability of people without large amounts of money to either get access to the media, to get access to the political process, to in some way break through the huge screen that money creates these days so that they can get their voices heard as well.[22]

A couple of recent cases reveal the dangers of a world in which a very few companies control the most popular media outlets in our society—especially when there is an important public policy issue that could affect their corporate profits. One classic example involves what has been called "the giveaway of the digital spec-trum." Although we'll explore this outrage at length in Chapter Seven, a brief summary will illustrate my point. As part of the 1996 Telecommunications Act, our government representatives in Congress gave the broadcast industry a portion of the publicly owned airwaves—valued at about $70 billion—*for free*. Rather than auction off this public real estate—increasingly valuable, thanks to digital technology—and allow the government to use that money for the social good, our elected officials caved in to long, hard, and suc-cessful lobbying by the broadcast industry and arranged this free giveaway. In return, broadcasters merely promised to use this wind-fall of new frequencies to broadcast high-definition programs.

As unconscionable as that was, the story gets worse. During the time that this rip-off occurred, roughly a nine-month period, the three major network news shows—NBC, ABC, and CBS—aired a sum total of nineteen minutes of coverage on the entire Telecom-munications Act and *not one single minute*—not a word—about the public's $70 billion charitable gift to the broadcast industry. As I mentioned, we'll explore in a later chapter how and why this hap-pened and why kids got robbed in the process. But the point here is that the democratic process failed. The broadcasters, who are our primary source for the nation's news, effectively embargoed the story—denying the public its right to know about this outra-geous giveaway. This is a clear example of how the needs of huge media conglomerates can run squarely against basic constitutional freedoms and the American public's right to debate key issues of national policy concern. What's changed in journalism as a result of consolidation is not that there's been a shift to false reporting. The change is toward *not* reporting at all—a "broadcast black-out," in the words of former Republican Senator Bob Dole.

In a recent interview, Dan Rather, the CBS news anchor, spoke harshly about the negative changes in national television coverage. He blamed warped values for the decline in international news cov-erage—"the Hollywoodization and 'frivolization' of the news"—and pointed the finger squarely at the major networks, including his own. "Entertainment values began to overwhelm news values," he observed. Later, Rather attributed these change to the massive consolidation of the media business. "The larger the entities that own and control the news operations, the more distant they become. . . . At one time, news was an integral part of the corporation," he noted, recalling the days when CBS was run by William Paley, before it became a division a Viacom. "The person who ran the corporation was intimate with the people in news and had a dialogue with them that provided a little check and balance to the drive for profits and ratings."[23]

In another well-known example, Disney-owned ABC News canceled a 1998 story by its leading investigative reporter exposing a variety of labor and safety practices at Disney World in Florida. As the *New York Times* subsequently reported,[24] ABC News denied that it killed this investigative report because of the identity of the subject, but who's kidding whom? Indeed, in a recent interview on National Public Radio, Michael Eisner, chairman and CEO of Disney, asserted bluntly, "I would prefer ABC not cover Disney. . . . I think it's inappropriate for Disney to be covered by Disney." A few days after Eisner made these remarks, ABC canceled a report covering Disney's employment of pedophiles at its theme parks.

Reflecting on these troubling issues raised by mass media consolidation, *The New York Times* commentator R. W. Apple stated:

It's my conviction that the Founding Fathers . . . had a reason for giving journalists special privileges in the Constitution. The reason was that we were supposed to find out what's going on, here and abroad, and report it, so that the public could understand and make an informed judgment [on public issues]. It was not put in the Constitution so that publishers could make billions of dollars or so that journalists could make millions of dollars. It was put in the Constitution so we could do serious journalistic work.[25]

THE BOTTOM LINE ON THE BOTTOM LINE

For the past ten years I've seen the impact of this consolidation trend and its relentless short-term profit mentality on the world of kids and media. If you're like me and the vast majority of parents and citizens in this nation, you're troubled by what you see and hear from our heavily concentrated media industry, particularly as it shapes the lives of America's youngest and most impressionable audiences. If you share these concerns, then understand that the root cause of them is the drive to make money and profits for a few. In the next three chapters, we'll take a look at the price our kids are paying for those profits—every hour and every day of every week.

Three

SEX SELLS

From its earliest days, broadcasting has been nakedly motivated by market forces. Perhaps no one put it more bluntly than Harold A. LaFount, a member of the Federal Radio Commission. "Commercialism," he stated in 1931, "is at the heart of broadcasting in the United States. What has education contributed . . . ? Not one thing. What has commercialism contributed? Everything—the lifeblood of the industry."[26] The creators of television understood that clearly. When TV debuted in the 1950s, broadcasters aired twenty-seven hours of children's programming a week—not out of the goodness of their hearts, but to encourage parents to purchase television sets.[27] The more families they could lure to the little flickering black-and-white screen, the more products they could sell via commercials, and the more money they could make from advertisers.

Today, half a century later, little has changed. In an age of hundreds of broadcast and cable channels, HDTV, sixty-one-inch wide-screen sets, picture-in-picture, and 3D surround sound, the same principle holds true. The more people broadcasters and cable companies can draw like moths to the nation's 229 million television sets (2.2 for every household in the country), the more products they can sell, and the more money they can make from advertising. Fundamentally, television in the United States has only one purpose, concluded Cornell University professor John Condry, cofounder of the Center for Research on the Effects of Television— not to educate or entertain, but "to sell things."[28]

And when it comes to pushing products, the first rule of marketing is that "sex sells." Over the years, that's a lesson that broadcasters, cable companies, music industry executives, and many other media suppliers have learned extremely well. Struggling to compete with one another for profitable "eyeballs," the networks have, decade after decade, pushed the envelope of what they consider acceptable for family viewing. As television journalist Louis Chunovic has ably chronicled, broadcasters have increasingly followed the principle that "there's no better audience grabber than sex."[29]

It wasn't always that way. Back in the early 1950s, when the television age dawned, the words "sex" and "pregnancy" were unmentionable on TV, and twin beds were the rule even for the small screen's married couples.[30] Broadcasters voluntarily vowed to keep the airwaves free of "profanity, obscenity, smut, and vulgarity,"[31] and their 1951 code of standards ruled that "the use of locations associated with sexual life or with sexual sin must be governed by good taste and delicacy."[32] Even as late as the early 1960s, any TV image of a husband and wife in the same bed had to reveal at least one of the wife's nightgown shoulder straps; not even the subtlest hint of connubial nudity was allowed.[33]

But by the mid-1970s, as the sexual revolution exploded, traditional notions of what was permissable in movies, books, theater, and television changed rapidly. TV shows like *All in the Family* began dealing with subjects such as premarital sex, adultery, homosexuality, and pregnancy.[34] Lightly edited feature films were bringing risqué content to TV, and explicit sex was suddenly beamed, uninvited, into millions of homes through the new phenomenon of cable television. On public access cable channels after 11:30 P.M., any viewer of any age could stumble onto explicit, hard-core shows like *Midnight Blue,* featuring strippers and prostitutes and hosted by *Screw* magazine publisher Al Goldstein.[35] (I remember flipping the dial one night when I was a teenager and suddenly seeing a set full of porno stars sitting around naked on one of these channels—an eye-opening and unforgettable experience.) After harsh criticisms by Congress and the Federal Communications Commission (FCC), broadcasters voluntarily agreed in 1975 to set aside the 7:00–9:00 P.M. period every evening for shows that were considered appropriate for "family viewing." But even so, despite continued criticism from public-interest and religious groups, prime-time kept pushing the limits, as "jiggle" programs like *Charlie's Angels* and *Three's Company* drew audiences with shows packed with sexual innuendo.[36]

More than anything, however, it was the Reagan administration's deregulation crusade in the 1980s that loosened most of the remaining restraints on broadcast and cable companies, setting the industry off on a downhill race for the bottom line. Ironically, given the fact that the Reagan team was so cozy with Jerry Falwell and the "family values" fundamentalists, one effect of their policy was that new pay cable channels started bringing more X-rated action than ever into American homes. The last barriers came tumbling down in the late 1980s, when a new major television network, Fox Broadcasting, took on the Big Three—CBS, NBC, and ABC—targeting a younger audience with raunchy shows like *Married . . . with Children*. All of a sudden, the lewd, crude Bundys paraded into American homes in the prime-time 7:30 slot, taking family viewing down to a new level.

Since then, it's basically been anything goes. Today, sex is the focus and main plot device of more and more television shows, from the casual bed swapping of *Friends* to the bathroom-stall couplings of *Ally McBeal*. Shows aimed at teen audiences, like *Boston Public,* are every bit as loaded with sexual content. Episodes of that show have featured sex between high school students and faculty members and the confession of one teen that she masturbated while fantasizing about her male teacher.[37] Today, as Syracuse University media professor Robert Thompson points out, "It's commonplace to hear erection jokes on *Friends* at eight o'clock; even gentle little programs like *Everybody Loves Raymond* have the kind of stuff that, when it played on *Three's Company* twenty years ago, made the PTA go completely ballistic."[38] And remember, that's just broadcast television. Cable channels air uncut, R-rated movies, porn, and adult prime-time fare like HBO's *Sex and the City,* available to viewers of all ages in subscribing households.

Most of these shows, except for *Boston Public,* aren't targeted at kids, so why should we care about their content? The reason is that children over ten do not limit their TV viewing to *Rugrats, Scooby-Doo,* and other programs specifically produced for youngsters. Instead, most kids that age spend up to 70 percent of their television time watching adult shows,[39] where sexual content has been skyrocketing.

According to a study by the politically conservative Parents Television Council, sexual material on broadcast television jumped more than 42 percent in just two years, from 1996 to 1998; "plainly put," the report said, "television is the raunchiest it's ever been." Another recent study, released by the Kaiser Family Foundation in 2001, found that over two-thirds of TV shows, including 84 percent of sitcoms, now contain sexual content, up from 56 percent in 1998.[40] For young viewers, it all adds up to an average exposure of more than 14,000 sexual references each year, on TV alone.

TABOO-FREE ZONE

Of course, kids spend only part of their media day watching television. Preadolescents and teens are sophisticated multitaskers, routinely ricocheting among CDs, radio, videos, the Internet, computer games, television, and movies—sometimes using several types of media at once. Like water, author Douglas Rushkoff observed, the media "conducts social electricity . . . wherever it spreads, its contents are carried, too."[41] These days, much of that content is graphically sexual, and kids are steeped in that explicit brew. The

CD collection of one fifteen-year-old girl I know, for instance, contains not only Disney's *The Little Mermaid* but also *Dr. Dre 2001* (labeled PARENTAL ADVISORY: EXPLICIT CONTENT), with its track titled "Pause 4 Porno" and lyrics about fellatio and misogynistic sex, and albums by Eminem, who sings about sodomizing his mother and arranging for his sister to be gang-raped. This is the cultural environment in which our kids are growing up. "We are now dealing with a generation," remarked actor-director Keenen Ivory Wayans, "where the cat's out of the bag in every single subject. . . . Society as a whole has moved into a taboo-free zone."[42]

For many kids, that zone is also routinely free of parental supervision. It may be true that you can't control children, especially older kids, twenty-four hours a day, and you can't keep them from being bombarded by sexually graphic, demeaning messages. But it is also true that many conscientious parents overestimate the amount of media monitoring that they do. According to one recent study, for example, 85 percent of parents say they always or often pay attention to what their kids are watching on TV, but most kids—61 percent—say they watch TV without adult supervision. Something isn't adding up. The fact is, parents aren't paying nearly enough attention to their children's media consumption. We're busy and stressed out, and many of us were raised at a time when cultural wars were fought against restrictive moral standards.

Throughout the sixties, especially, freedom of speech was a potent social issue, from the UC-Berkeley campus to Chicago nightclubs and New York TV studios. Comic Lenny Bruce was considered a counterculture hero for using four-letter words in his routines, a cause for which he was arrested fifteen times. The free-speech battle was fought on the airwaves too—in 1967, Beatle George Harrison appeared on the *Smothers Brothers* TV show, exhorting his hosts to keep fighting TV censors: "Whether you can say it or not, keep *trying* to say it," he urged. As a result of the rebellious youth culture in which most of us were raised, many parents today have a greater tolerance for crude language and behavior than their parents did—but I believe that the pendulum has swung too far for commercial motives.

That's the main worry, in fact, of Scott Nash, who is one of the leading kids' illustrators and graphic designers in the country. In his view, kids are spending way too much time in a market-driven media environment that doesn't have their best interests at heart. "Media," he says, "is like my wacky Uncle Ray—a friend of my dad's who used to bring all kinds of semi-subversive things into our home, things that really didn't belong in our family." Uncle Ray used the shock effect to get attention, and that's exactly what the media is doing, for the same reasons.

THWARTING PARENTS AS GATEKEEPERS

Why does it matter? After all, most kids will probably grow up to be normal adults, even after overexposure to sexual media messages. The truth is, it matters for a lot of reasons, and those reasons change as children grow and mature from early childhood into adolescence. At the earliest ages, exposing kids to the media's sexual barrage violates what many parents feel is childhood's precious and protective veil of innocence. Neil Postman, chairman of New York University's Department of Culture and Communication, defines children as "a special class of people . . . requiring special forms of nurturing and protection." It's the parent's role, he argues, to guard them from aspects of life that they are not ready to understand, including sexual relations, violence, illness, and other potentially frightening features of the adult world. Bit by bit, as children grow older and are psychologically able to handle and understand more information, it's the parent's job to expose them to those aspects of life in appropriate and timely ways. Parents are essentially the gatekeepers, introducing children to a sequence of revealed secrets about adult life.[43]

I believe most parents understand intuitively what Postman means. We know that young children can be easily scared and confused by behavior that they don't understand, and we struggle to shelter them from those parts of life until they're older. This gatekeeping, in fact, goes to the heart of who we are as parents—and that's exactly what the media is violating. By thrusting increasingly explicit sexual imagery and language at us on television, radio, movie screens, and in advertisements, the media too often exposes our children to those secrets before we think they're ready, shattering our role as gatekeepers and protectors. Too often, parents feel blindsided by the media, surprised and sickened by what their kids have been exposed to, and helpless to control the rate at which their children are pushed into the adult world.

My friend Susan, the mother of two daughters—now both teenagers—remembers vividly when this first happened to her. When her youngest child was five years old, she rented the video of *Look Who's Talking*, a movie about a talking baby. Although the film was rated PG-13, she thought it would be harmless entertainment for her kids. After all, it was promoted by ads featuring a cute five-year-old boy and his happy parents, all wearing "official" *Look Who's Talking* T-shirts and sweatshirts (available through an 800-number, in kids' sizes small, medium, and large). As she turned on the video with her kids, Susan watched, stunned, as a man and woman luridly groped each other in an office. The film cut suddenly to shots of thrashing sperm traveling inside a vagina, talking to one another as they hunted the egg and hurled themselves against its membrane (which parted suggestively as one moaning sperm managed to penetrate). The whole sequence lasted an excruciating four and a half minutes—during which Susan realized that TriStar Pictures had now exposed her preschooler not just to adult lust but to the entire subject of human reproduction—something she had counted on introducing herself in a few years, when she felt her child was ready. "I felt sick to my stomach with anger at that studio for inappropriately marketing this movie as a film for little kids. It still makes me furious," she says.

Every day, parents of young children feel just as thwarted as movies, advertising, and other forms of media expose kids to "behavior that adults spent centuries trying to hide from children," as Joshua Meyrowitz, communication professor at the University of Michigan, puts it.[44]

TEACHING EXPECTATIONS

In this overheated cultural climate, kids are not only being exposed to sexual material very early. They are also growing up with unrealistic and distorted information and expectations about sex. Today, the media is very much a teacher—about the world, about judgment, about sexual relations. Children of all ages tend to identify with young, glamorous entertainment stars and use their fictionalized and media-hyped lives as a key source of information about sex. Despite the fact that many parents consider themselves to be their kids' main source of sex education, more and more adolescents say they rely on the media for this knowledge.[45] In fact, according to studies by the Kaiser Family Foundation, thirteen-to-fifteen-year-olds rate the entertainment media as one of the top sources of sexual information,[46] and nearly a quarter of all teens report that they learn "a lot" about birth control and pregnancy from movies and TV.[47] They're absorbing not just "facts," but behaviors and standards, too. Through the media, as psychology researcher L. Monique Ward explains, kids learn social norms and expectations about how to be sexual, who should have sex and when, as well as

> whom to have it with, and what the appropriate sequence of activities is. Through its themes, storylines, characterizations, and dialogue, [the media] provides insight into these sexual scripts, depicting various aspects about attracting and selecting partners, dating and sexual decision making. Watching is an eager audience of children and adolescents who may have little experience of their own and minimal input from other sources to which they can compare these portrayals.[48]

As Ward points out, the media's most frequent message about sex is that it's a form of recreation—a competitive, manipulative "sport" emphasizing physical appearance and "momentary, high-sensation pleasures." Many teens don't get a counterbalancing message, since parents are often reluctant to talk about sexual issues, and most schools and religious organizations don't provide these guidelines. From the stories that the media tells kids—packaged and distorted for maximum marketing effect—children learn patterns of behavior in what some researchers refer to as "stalagmite effects—cognitive deposits built up almost imperceptibly from the drip-drip-drip" of repeated exposure over time.

During early adolescence especially—an age when children go through rapid physical and emotional changes, have less contact with adults, and make the challenging transition out of elementary school—they are turning to the media for role models for behavior, decision making, and sex. Adolescence is a time, explained Dr. Jacqueline Eccles, a psychology professor at the University of Michigan, "when our children need to figure out who they are and what is their place in the larger society"—and today that perception is shaped, in significant measure, by media messages.

Those messages are confusing. Even teen magazines that steer their editorial focus away from sex lace their pages with provocative ads—like Calvin Klein's images of teens in underwear and Levi's ads showing a boy's face pressed against the crotch of a woman's jeans. Brandon Holley, editor of *ELLEgirl,* acknowledged that "this demographic is bombarded by sex images,"[49] and the influence of those images starts early. As one nineteen-year-old girl reflected, "I don't recall having sexuality pushed in my face when I was ten or eleven. But I have a younger half-sister who is eleven years old, and she's a very big fan of Britney Spears and the Spice Girls, and she tries to emulate them. . . . I see her wanting to wear clothes that I would never have considered wearing."[50]

Boys don't escape these powerful influences. While girls have long suffered from anxiety about their bodies, boys are catching up, thanks to increasingly glamorized and sexualized images of young males in advertising and the entertainment media. One recent Calvin Klein newspaper and billboard ad, for instance, featured an image of a muscled boy of about seventeen, wearing nothing but revealingly clingy white bikini underwear. Thanks in part to widely hyped media images like these, some boys are now struggling with what some call an "Adonis complex," trying to burn baby fat and build six-pack abs in order to look cool and sexually attractive. When advertisers use sexualized teenage bodies to sell products, they create images and expectations that are frustratingly impossible for most teenagers to live up to.[51]

The media's relentless emphasis on sex also shapes expectations and behaviors. In one study, teens said their top two sources of sexual pressure were television shows and music. As fourteen-year-old Rayelyn Rodriguez explained it, some TV shows "tell kids 'Everybody's doing it.' Then some kids think, 'Well, if everyone's doing it, why don't I?' " Drew Pinsky, MD, an expert who talks to a lot of teens on his popular call-in show *Loveline*, aired on radio and MTV, is convinced that extensive early exposure to sexually charged material can have a negative effect on kids. "Premature exposure to sexual material tends to be sexualizing," he has said, for children who are not psychologically mature enough to handle it.[52] The opposite is also true. Kids who get most of their information about sex from their parents, not the media, tend to be less sexually active overall.[53] Eight-to-twelve-year-old kids, in fact, would rather hear about sex and relationships from their parents and trust their parents more than other sources.

RISKY BUSINESS

A steady diet of media sex can have other troubling effects on adolescents. The fact is that while sex is pervasive in the media, it is rarely accompanied by any discussion of the risks and consequences of sexual behavior. These risks are real for American teenagers today. The rate of teen pregnancy in the United States, while it has declined in recent years, is still double that in Europe and nine times that in Japan, and sexually transmitted diseases (STDs) are on the rise. One quarter of sexually active teens—about four million kids—are infected with STDs each year,[54] and the highest rates of gonorrhea and chlamydia are among teens between the ages of fifteen and nineteen.[55] The most alarming news is that AIDS ranks sixth as the leading cause of death for young people between fifteen and twenty-four.[56] Twenty percent of those who have AIDS are in their twenties, and the majority were infected as teenagers.[57]

These are critical health issues for teens and anyone who is sexually active, but they are rarely addressed by the number-one source of sex information, the media. As seventeen-year-old Gaines Newborn of Los Angeles observed, "Shows like *Dawson's Creek* bring out a lot of sex questions that kids want to know [about], but they don't answer them." When television and movies do manage to address sexual issues in age-appropriate ways, with realistic information about choices, responsibilities, and consequences, they can help teens sort through the facts and make positive choices. Too often, though, the entertainment media use sexual content as attention-getting bait to lure viewers, with no discussion whatever of risks and responsibilities. "Surveys tell us young people get a lot of their information about sex from TV," notes Drew Altman, president and chief executive of the Henry J. Kaiser Family Foundation, a health and media research organization. "With the problems facing adolescents today, how sex is shown on TV is just as important as how much sex is shown."

The reason, points out Lynn Ponton, MD—a psychoanalyst and professor at the University of California, San Francisco—is that sex is an area of life that is fraught with risk, and "most adolescents," she notes, "don't yet have well-developed risk-assessment skills."[58] Encouraged by the media environment, teens are not only having sex earlier—at the average age of sixteen—"but they are taking greater risks in this area," she adds.[59] Continually exposed to images of unprotected sex, teens may downplay the risk of such behavior—"with consequences that include sexually transmitted disease, unwanted pregnancy, and pathological relationships, among others."[60]

In a candid article in one high school newspaper, for example, teens recently talked frankly about the pressure they feel to have casual sex. Due in large measure to the media's influence, a tenth-grade girl reported, kids are "obsessed with sex" and "aren't prepared for what they are actually getting themselves into," she said. "The emotional connection doesn't have to be there," an eleventh-grade boy added; "no one has any expectation beyond a one-night stand," reported a ninth-grade girl. Sex—especially oral sex—"is meaningless, just for fun"—like "going out and having a soda," another student stated. For some, however, there is an emotional price. One boy described parties where tenth-graders drank a lot and had casual sex in order to fit in; afterward, he'd see girls "just sitting there crying and touching their stomachs," realizing what they had just done. In a media climate that promotes recreational sex to grab audiences, teens are growing up with risky attitudes and habits that could harm them—physically, psychologically, and emotionally—down the road. "I believe we have let our teenagers down in this area," Ponton states. "We may provide condoms, but we don't offer conversations."[61] Instead, we set kids loose in a media culture that defines sex as a game. "It's all about getting what you want quicker and easier," one teenager remarked.

By undermining parents' gatekeeping role, providing unrealistic information about sex, and persuading kids that sexual risk-taking is less serious than it really is, the media is not only destroying kids' innocence too soon but is also setting them up for disappointment and dangerous choices. What's missing in this mix is adult responsibility and restraint. Parents aren't controlling, or effectively influencing, their kids' media environment. And the companies that create and distribute media for our consumption are interested primarily, sometimes exclusively, in the profitability of their commercial products. The values of the media, as John Condry argued, "are the values of the marketplace." It cannot, he said, "be a useful source of information for children. Indeed, it may be a dangerous source of information. It offers ideas that are false, unreal; it has no coherent value system, other than consumerism; it provides little useful information about the self."[62]

RATINGS ROULETTE

Although society once went too far in policing the media's morals—no one today, of course, would want to pretend that married people don't sleep together—at least there was a consensus that adults had to consider the welfare of young audiences. Take movies, for example. The Hays Office was established in the 1920s, followed by the Production Code in the 1930s, to keep Hollywood's standards on the straight and narrow. Sexual innuendo, nudity, references to adultery, and of course sex itself were banned from the big screen, on the understanding that "no picture shall be produced which will lower the moral standards of those who see it."[63] After movies won free speech protection, the Motion Picture Association of America (MPAA) eventually abandoned the Production Code in the late sixties. In its place, the industry created an age-based, self-regulated movie rating system to help parents determine what movies are appropriate for their children.[64] That's still the system that we have today—only it's gotten so "elastic" as to be almost useless, as studios, putting profits far ahead of families, push the limits of the ratings while staying technically within the rules.

G-rated movies, for general audiences, are supposed to contain no bad language, sex, or violent content, while films rated PG—parental guidance suggested—may have some of that unsuitable content. Although PG movies can't have scenes showing drug use or explicit sex, they can contain brief nudity and moderate levels of horror and violence. Things get more complicated and less clear, however, with PG-13 and R ratings. PG-13 films contain some material inappropriate for children under thirteen, and R films are deemed unsuitable for kids under seventeen—but the line between the two ratings can be extremely fine. For example, as Michael Tollin, producer of hit films such as *Hardball* and *Varsity Blues,* explains, "It's widely understood in the industry that you're only allowed to use the word 'fuck' once in a PG-13 movie, and it must be in a nonsexual context." So, in fact, there can be one syllable's worth of difference between a PG-13 and an R movie—and, Tollin adds, "many studios want you to push PG-13 movies to the max, getting them as close to an R rating as you can." In other words, include everything you can possibly get away with, and make sure that "fuck" is in there. The reason? To attract as big an audience as possible, including teenagers who like films with sexual or violent content. Since most adolescents stay away from G- and PG-rated movies, "studios see PG-13 as the perfect compromise," explained James Meigs, former editor of *Premiere* magazine, "rough enough not to alienate young teens, but tame enough for most families."[65] Still, a PG-13 movie these days can easily include enough edgy material to make many parents uncomfortable.

In fact, PG-13 movies today have a lot of content that would have been restricted to R movies in the past. Since the PG-13 rating was introduced in 1984, it's been stretched to include increasing amounts of sexual content, foul language, and violence. The reason, many in the industry point out, is economic. Studios have done extensive research on the comparative profitability of PG-13 and R movies. According to Mike Tollin, some conclude "that you're tying one hand behind your back if you release an R movie that's going after a teenage audience, because some percentage of kids under age seventeen are not going to be able to get in to see the movie." As a result, studios pack as much edgy material as possible into PG-13 movies to capture a bigger audience. "We have arrived at this condition through an erosion of the rating system," movie critic Roger Ebert observed. "Movies that would have been R, such as *Coyote Ugly*"—a film about girls who dance on top of bars to boost liquor sales—"are PG-13. The younger teenage market is served with movies that are R in their hearts but PG-13 to the MPAA bean counters."

At the same time, enforcement of the R rating is now "so porous," Ebert added, "that almost anyone who really wants to see an R movie can do so."[66] The prime ticket buyers for many of these movies are teens. Forty percent of adolescents say they "sometimes" or "often" go to R-rated movies with a parent,[67] and many kids under seventeen routinely see R-rated films without parents in theaters, on cable television, and on videos. Studies show, in fact, that R movies are the most watched type of film for high-school and college students. And, just as the PG-13 rating has absorbed a lot of formerly R-rated material, the R rating, too, has stretched to include graphic material that would formerly have earned an adults-only rating. The adult category has almost disappeared, and the R rating has become crammed with more and more explicit material that is regularly viewed by an underage audience of kids.[68] Not only are R movies graphically sexual—containing seven times the amount of sexual material as most TV shows[69]—but they are also more likely than not to contain scenes of rape and violent sexual aggression. In one study, researchers who watched thirty R-rated movies found only one that featured no sexual violence.[70]

This is the fare that many if not most teens view on a regular basis. As Janet Maslin, movie critic and mother of two has pointed out, "when kids reach a certain age, they want to see movies just because they're rated R." It's natural. As kids get older, they want to cross once-forbidden boundaries into adulthood. And they take their friends along. Moviegoing is a social activity, and there's a great deal of pressure on many kids to see movies that might give their parents pause. In a domino effect, younger siblings follow their lead and push the limits too. "As the bar gets raised for older teens," James Meigs notes, "the standards shift for younger teens, for tweens, and all the way down the line."[71]

The only force standing in the way of their exposure to this increasingly coarse content are adult gatekeepers—theater owners and, especially, parents. So far, neither of these groups have really stepped up to the challenge. Most parents may say they don't want their kids to see these movies. But when they drop their kids off at the multiscreen theater, it's all too easy for youngsters—once they're past the ticket takers—to wander into R-rated instead of PG-13-rated films. At too many theaters, the age-based ratings have been loosely, if at all, enforced.

The bottom line is that underage kids are a huge market for movies, and studios and theater owners know it. Despite the fact that teens make up only 15 percent of the country's population, they account for nearly a third of the movie audience.[72] "The big audience is teens," concluded Kansas Senator Sam Brownback, "and they are teased with sex and violence." As the Federal Trade Commission (FTC) disclosed in a 104-page report, released in September 2000, fully thirty-five of forty-four R-rated movies the agency examined were consciously marketed to and targeted to youngsters under seventeen.[73] In an especially egregious case, a studio used a ten-year-old in their market research for an R-rated movie.[74] Unfortunately, the FTC concluded that it has no legal authority, under existing laws, to stop companies from marketing adult-rated entertainment products to children. The problem is that although there are industry and state laws banning the marketing of alcohol and tobacco to young people, there are no similar laws protecting youngsters from the marketing of adult entertainment.

When the FTC report first came out, the movie industry brandished its usual claims of censorship and free speech to defend exploitative marketing practices. "We always believed," declared Warner Bros. president Alan Horn, "that both the content and the marketing of movies were protected by the First Amendment." However, the studios have been chastened by the FTC's report; and Horn, one of the most thoughtful and responsible studio executives I know, acknowledged that the right to free speech doesn't diminish his studio's "commitment to marketing our films responsibly."[75]

Indeed, since that revealing FTC study, there have finally been calls from within the industry to increase protections for young audiences. This is particularly impressive when you consider that Kurt Hall, the head of the United Artists Theatre chain, says his company gets the most complaints "from parents who are mad that we haven't let their kids in an R-rated movie."[76] The National Association of Theatre Owners (NATO) has promised not to run trailers for R-rated movies before G- or PG-rated feature films, although its members—who own twenty-five thousand screens—will decide "case by case" whether to run such trailers before PG-13 movies.[77]

The guidelines are already having some effect. In November

2000, Universal Studios changed its plans to run a preview trailer for its PG-13 release *The Mummy Returns* before the PG-rated movie *The Grinch*.[78] NATO is also urging its members to hire extra security staff to check the age of young theatergoers for R-rated movies that are especially explicit or violent.[79] In Utah if theater owners don't comply, they could conceivably face jail time, if a law proposed by State Representative David Hogue goes into effect. A theater owner or manager who intentionally, knowingly, or recklessly allows an underage child into a "patently offensive" movie could be guilty of a Class A misdemeanor. One Utah theater owner doesn't think that's a bad idea; "maybe then," he said, "they'll realize how much responsibility they have—that they're the ones with the final say of whether these kids get in."[80]

On another front, the Directors Guild of America has been urging overall reform of the MPAA rating system, including "simple, clear, and detailed rating," a marketing code of conduct for adult-rated entertainment products, and a "zero tolerance" ratings enforcement policy.[81] Studios are also beginning to provide a bit more information with their ratings. An ad for *The Mummy Returns*, for example, included the PG-13 rating as well as the more specific advisory "Adventure Action and Violence." More detailed ratings would have helped my friend Dave, who rented the movie *There's Something about Mary* for his ten-year-old daughter and a friend— despite its R rating—because he assumed that a comedy couldn't be too bad. Dave still gets tense when he remembers watching with the girls—a pained smile on his face—as Cameron Diaz moussed her hair with semen instead of styling gel. Ever since then, Dave pays more attention to the ratings.

WHERE IS THE V-CHIP?

If TV's experience is any guide, however, "improved" ratings don't always help. In 1997 the television networks instituted an age-based rating system to warn parents about prime-time programs that contained sexual material, coarse language, and gratuitous violence. Later that year, all the networks, except for NBC, enhanced those guidelines with ratings indicating the type of mature material in the programs. For example, *S* means sexual situations, *V* indicates violence, and *L* stands for objectionable language.

Lo and behold, the rating system had a big effect, but not the one that many parents had hoped for. Since the ratings were first put in place, TV shows' sexual content, coarse language, and violence have virtually exploded, and programs are depicting three times as much teenage sex.[82] According to a 2001 study by the Parents Television Council (PTC), prime-time shows are routinely dealing with topics, such as oral sex and pornography, that a few years earlier were rarely touched on even in late-night programming.[83] What's happened, according to the PTC's leader, conservative activist Brent Bozell, is that some networks saw "the opportunity presented by the rating system to insert even edgier content into their shows." The results should not be a surprise. "This is an industry obsessed with 'pushing the envelope,' " he said; networks "weren't abiding by the letter of the ratings system . . . they aren't abiding by the spirit either."[84]

So what the ratings have accomplished is to give some TV networks and producers the sense that they can stuff prime-time shows full of sexual content so long as they conscientiously tag them with a TV-14 or TV-MA rating. Consider this dialogue from the WB network's TV-14-rated *Buffy the Vampire Slayer*. One of the most popular TV shows for teens, it airs in most locales during the old "family hour":

> Faith: "I'm about ready to pop. Are you up?"
> Xander: "I'm suddenly very up."
> Faith: "Just relax and take your pants off."

Then there's this bit of dialogue from Fox's TV-14 teen show *Boston Public*. A high-school teacher named Lauren has just informed a fellow teacher, Marilyn, that she recently had sex with a former student.

Lauren: "Do you think this is too weird?"
Marilyn: "Well, he's twenty-one. He's an adult."
Lauren: "But . . . He calls me Miss Davis. I mean even during, he
  called me Miss Davis, and it was an incredible turn on."
Marilyn: "To be called Miss Davis during? . . . Lauren, you're
  attracted to this kid because he was one of your students?"
Lauren: "I admit, there was something intoxicating when he said I
  influenced his life, and that went to my teacher ego, and ego is
  an erotic zone."

Clearly, the use of ratings hasn't encouraged the networks to tone down the sexual content of their shows, including those aimed specifically at teens. Instead, it's effectively gotten them off the hook by putting the ball squarely in the parents' court. Even if broadcasters were abiding by their own voluntary guidelines, the ratings are of limited value to parents. That's because the rating system is not only confusing but inconsistently applied. A show rated V for violence, for example, may be more or less intensely violent depending on whether it's also rated TV-14 or TV-MA (for mature audiences).[85] These are shades of meaning that many parents miss. Compounding the problem is the sheer volume and complexity of the ratings task. There are more than two thousand hours of TV programming each day, and networks are responsible for rating their own shows.[86]

Unfortunately, few parents are making use of the TV ratings. The number of parents who understand them dropped from 70 percent in 1997 to 50 percent in 2000,[87] and nine out of ten parents don't know how even their children's favorite shows are rated.[88] Moreover, the TV rating system was created in the first place to work in tandem with the V-chip. Remember that breakthrough device? It was supposed to be the government's and TV industry's high-tech answer to programming excesses. Embed a V-chip in every television that recognizes the rating codes and give parents the power, via remote control, to block out shows that they deem objectionable. But the V-chip still has a long way to go to move from good idea to practical reality. The chip was to be installed in all new televisions, thirteen inches or larger, produced after June 1, 1997. By July 2001, 40 percent of American parents did in fact have a V-chip-equipped television,[89] but only 17 percent of them—and 7 percent of all parents—were using those devices, according to a study by the Kaiser Family Foundation. Although more and more parents now own TVs that have the blocking device, "a great many parents still don't know it exists," says my former Children Now colleague Vicky Rideout, director of the Kaiser Foundation's program on the entertainment media and public health.

There's no mystery about why the V-chip hasn't caught on. Basically, there's been next to no effort to promote it. How many educational TV spots have you seen publicizing and explaining the V-chip to parents? Personally, I don't think I've ever seen one. It's not hard to figure out why. It's not in the television industry's interest to encourage the use of the blocking technology, which would limit the audience and commercial reach of many shows. When you give parents the power to block programs, you also give them the power to block advertising. So why spread the word? It's not in the industry's financial interests for parents to make widespread use of the V-chip. But it's particularly troubling to me that elected officials—many of whom rely on the industry for donations—have not pushed for major funding for a V-chip public education campaign.

WORDS AND MUSIC

Second only to watching TV is the amount of time kids spend—up to four or five hours a day—listening to music,[90] on CDs, on MTV, and on the radio. Like their parents, kids today are growing up in the emotionally resonant, rhythmic, amniotic environment of recorded sound. And like their parents, kids still like music that pushes the edge, that challenges the status quo—something that artists from Elvis to Eminem have done. In fact, because so many of today's parents, myself included, grew up with music that was a defiant social statement, many of us cringe at the thought of criticizing the content of the music that our kids are listening to. After all, the last thing we want is to sound like our own parents, who were hopelessly uncool and out of touch with our youth culture all those years ago. Still, that doesn't excuse us from paying attention and speaking out when we hear our kids listening to sexually violent, demeaning, or misogynistic lyrics.

Lyrics like that are more common than many parents might think. Sex, as much as love, is a dominant theme of music today, and "the words do count," according to Stanford University's Donald Roberts, who has conducted pioneering studies on the music industry's impact on children. "Kids learn the lyrics," Roberts observes, "and part of what they learn from them is a set of expectations." Unfortunately, he adds, the more defiant, alienated, and threatening to the mainstream a music type is, the more attention kids pay to the words.[91] And when it comes to sex, lyrics are often defiantly, even sadistically explicit. Listen to these lines from Eminem's song "As the World Turns":

Go go gadget dick!
Whipped that shit out, and ain't no doubt about it . . .
Stuffed that shit in crooked and fucked that fat slut to death

Songs like these are routinely marketed to kids, who absorb, memorize, and mimic them in the media- and commercially driven environment of teen culture. It's by no means just the fringe recording groups that are churning out these graphic lyrics; nearly a third of the twenty-five best-selling albums of 2000 carried warning labels for explicit content.

Those labels—warnings adopted by the Recording Industry Association of America (RIAA) in 1990—read PARENTAL ADVISORY: EXPLICIT CONTENT. They are voluntarily placed by record companies on any of their own recordings that parents might object to. It's a system that evolved after Tipper Gore and Susan Baker, wife of former secretary of state James Baker, brought the problem of shock rock to the public's attention in the mid-1980s. Their organization, the Parents Music Resource Center (PMRC) did a lot to bring pressure on recording companies, and Tipper Gore in particular suffered a lot of derision from First Amendment advocates who viewed the PMRC as a group of schoolmarmish prudes. Once again, however, the free speech mavens—still fighting the old battles of the sixties—failed, in my opinion, to see two points. First, kids (we're not talking about adults here) should be protected from explicitly and violently sexual audio material—just as they are from printed pornography—instead of being the target of its marketing. In December 2001, in fact, a new FTC study harshly criticized recording companies for their slowness in limiting adult-themed content aimed at children.[92] Second, the graphic content of that material has less to do with "artistic expression" than it does with commercial profits. Consider what one well-known songwriter recently had to say about Marshall Mathers (Eminem), one of the most successful "bad boys" in music: "Eminem and his record label are hiding behind freedom of speech. I guarantee you if he were to scream out any record executive's or Madonna's home address in his music, he'd be banished from recording. But he's selling tickets now. It's not affecting them directly. It makes for good controversy, and it's sick."

Personally, I think Tipper Gore and the PMRC were onto something important years ahead of their time. Unfortunately, the music labeling they advocated has not been as effective a solution as it might have been. Sure, it's better than nothing—but not much. The reason is simple. How many parents do you know who supervise their children's music purchases once their kids are over the age of eight or nine? With a little money in their pockets, most kids can buy their own CDs, or they can easily trade or download recordings that they want over the Internet. The biggest effect of the PARENTAL ADVISORY: EXPLICIT CONTENT label may be to frighten parents who discover there are fistfuls of CDs branded with that warning in their children's music collections.

As for the kids, it's possible, even probable, that the presence of a warning label may make a CD purchase even more daring and alluring. And most kids can buy these CDs without any problem from most record stores. It's troubling—because lyrics *do* matter and *do* influence the judgment and expectations of young listeners, especially when they're receiving few counter-balancing messages from other sources. In one study, 24 percent of high school students ranked popular music as one of their top three sources for guidance on social interaction.[93] As Stanford's Don Roberts explains, when popular music serves as a domi-nant, often uncontested, source of information for an adolescent, the chance that it will influence his or her beliefs and behavior increases dramatically.[94] Once again, the "other parent" is shap-ing the ways kids see the world, with disturbingly little control or supervision.

SURFING FOR SEX

If verbal messages have an impact, visual images brand themselves even more directly on young psyches. And in the course of their media grazing, many kids are encountering—often unintention-ally—explicit sexual images on the Internet. A congressional study of Internet use conducted in 2000 revealed that one out of four kids from ten to seventeen stumbled across pornographic pictures while they were surfing the Web.[95] It's easy to do. One girl mis-typed the name of a teen magazine and found herself on an adult site.[96] Typing simple Web addresses like "whitehouse.com" and "teens.com" also delivers, in seconds, a prodigious display of X-rated material.

The main protector of kids on the Internet, so far, are parent-acti-vated blocking options on browsers like America Online (AOL) and software packages that parents and schools can purchase to keep kids from accessing adult sites. Some of these work better than others, according to a study by *Consumer Reports*. AOL's parental control fea-ture, which is included in the monthly subscription price and permits kids to see only sites that have been approved by human reviewers, was successful in screening out 86 percent of adult sites. The downside of this feature, though, is that it prevented kids from having access to 63 percent of the informational sites tested. This can be a problem for kids who have to use the Internet for schoolwork and find that they've been denied access to Web sites that their teachers assigned. Some of the off-the-shelf software packages, however, do a far worse job of blocking X-rated material—one package, in fact, screened out only 10 percent of adult sites. "The devices do not live up to the hype," notes Judith Krug of the American Library Association.[97] Unfortunately, they're the main gatekeeping option parents have, short of supervising their kids' on-line sessions (we'll talk more about that in Chapter Eight). And at this point, governmental solutions may be hard to come by. Although Congress passed and President Clinton signed the Child Online Protection Act in 1999, which would have prevented the distribution to minors of harmful on-line material, a federal appeals court declared that the legislation was unconstitutional.

Just as worrying for parents as exposure to on-line pornography is the possibility of direct sexual solicitations over the Net. According to the congressional study conducted in 2000, nearly 20 percent of kids surveyed had experienced one of these on-line episodes.[98] Most of these encounters occur below the radar of parents' awareness and law enforcement's, and only 10 percent are ever reported.[99] With more than 25 million kids on-line,[100] the Internet is increasingly another media environment where kids roam unsupervised at some degree of risk. While I don't want to overemphasize this problem, it's something that all parents need to keep in mind.

The result? Parents find it hard, if not impossible, to be effective gatekeepers. Over the last three decades, we've progressively let standards and protections for children erode. First, it was in the interest of free speech and artistic freedom, but along the way, the marketplace took over. Now it's exclusively commercial interests that determine the content of the media, and explicit sex is a tried-and-true formula to grab audiences—on television, in movies, in music, and on the Net. The problem is that, although most of this material is supposedly targeted at adults, it's actually marketed to and consumed by children. Roaming unsupervised in the media world, many of them are growing up with distorted information and expectations about sex. To a troubling extent, the adults—industry, government, and parents—are letting the media set commercially driven sexual standards for kids—who, more than anything, need responsible adult guidance, information, and love.

Four

MEDIA VIOLENCE: IN HARM'S WAY

By now, it's a heartsickening cliché. Alienated, disaffected youths—Dylan Klebold, Eric Harris, Kip Kinkel, Michael Carneal—vent their anger and "get famous" by shooting up a school—in Pearl, Mississippi; West Paducah, Kentucky; Jonesboro, Arkansas; Springfield, Oregon; Littleton, Colorado; or Santee, California—killing not just targeted "enemies" but innocent children and teachers in blasts of bombs or semiautomatic gunfire. In almost every case it's been a young white male. In each case, the boys "really didn't care who they killed as long as they killed," noted Bill Bond, principal of West Paducah's Heath High School, where fourteen-year-old Michael Carneal murdered three girls who were praying in a high school hallway. There are other similarities too. The young shooters all felt bullied, slighted, or inferior. All were steeped in a hyperviolent pop culture of bloody movies and video games. And many saw the massacres as a way not just to get even but to make themselves the center of the media's attention. "Getting your picture on the cover of *Time* and *Newsweek*," Bond added, "that is going out in a blaze of glory. I used to be a troubled kid myself and I can tell you, you could love me or hate me but you were not going to ignore me." Killing innocent students, he said, "is the ultimate attention getting."[101]

Eric Harris and Dylan Klebold, the high school killers in Littleton, Colorado, wanted to be media stars too, but they wanted to shape their own story. Before they came to school at Columbine High on the morning of April 20, 1999, armed with bombs and guns and planning to kill two hundred fifty kids, they filmed their own "back story" videos, explaining their aims and motives. "It's going to be like fucking *Doom!*" Harris said on one of the tapes, referring to his favorite shoot-em-up video game. "Tick-tock, tick, tick. . . . Ha! . . . Straight out of *Doom!*" The boys even discussed who would be the best director to immortalize them in a movie, Quentin Tarantino or Steven Spielberg. "Directors will be fighting over this story," Klebold bragged.

In a terrible twist on life-imitates-art, the school killers sought stardom for their live-action mayhem—which, in turn, was modeled on the movies, music, and gory videos they played over and over. Michael Carneal learned his murderous technique from the movie *The Basketball Diaries*. After he watched the film, he mused to a ninth-grade friend, "Wouldn't it be neat to go in the school and shoot people that you don't like," like in the movie.[102] Barry Loukaitis, a fourteen-year-old honor student who shot and killed two students and a teacher at Frontier Middle School in Moses Lake, Washington, was impressed by the film *Natural Born Killers*. He told a buddy it would be "pretty cool" to go on a killing rampage like the movie characters.[103] Mitchell Johnson, who killed four class-mates and a teacher in Jonesboro, loved gangsta rap, especially a song called "Crept and We Came" by Bone Thugs-N-Harmony that graphically describes a mass killing.[104] And Luke Woodham, the seventeen-year-old shooter in Pearl, Mississippi, spent so much time viewing violence-laced television and Web sites that before his rampage, his parents disconnected his computer and cable television.[105]

In an even eerier hall-of-mirrors-like multiplier effect, young shooters like Carneal, Harris, and Klebold did become media stars, with months of TV, newspaper, and magazine coverage publicizing their outrages and making them role models for others seeking the ultimate attention. Michael Carneal, for one, understands the bloody echoes of his actions. Incarcerated for twenty-five years in Kentucky, he became "seriously depressed" after the rampage at Columbine High School because "he felt a lot of responsibility for that happening," according to a juvenile justice commissioner.[106]

THE BLAME GAME

Invariably, each horrendous episode brings a backlash of finger-pointing and blame. Much of it, naturally, is politically polarized. Democrats, who accept massive campaign donations from the media, place responsibility on the lack of strict gun control laws and the excesses of the National Rifle Association (NRA). Republicans, deep in the pockets of the gun lobby, fire back that it's all the media's fault. Debate disintegrates into an either-or battle that nobody wins, and the violence goes on and on. This kind of competitive blame-casting is pointless. Are guns too easily available? Is the media too filled with gratuitous violence? The answer to both questions is yes. Violent media and access to guns are both responsible—along with broken homes, feelings of inadequacy or rejection, drugs, child abuse, poor schools, a lack of counseling services, even "spiritual emptiness."[107] There is no single answer, no single cause.

Why is it, when it comes to violence, that we let ourselves be so distracted by fake either-or arguments? For other problems, it's natural to look at a range of underlying factors. We don't blame heart disease, for instance, exclusively on genetics or lifestyle or diet. It's clearly a problem caused by a combination of these factors. Each individual may be more or less influenced by one or another of them, but they all come into play, and they all have to be addressed if a patient's condition is going to improve. The problem with the violence issue is political. Each side tries to lay exclusive blame on the other in order to deflect attention and pressure from its own constituency. The politicians don't lose. The powerful gun and media lobbies don't lose. It's only families and kids and the quality of our national life that suffers from the lack of responsible solutions.

So let's start with this basic premise: Violent media is a contributing factor to youth violence in our society. It is not the *only* factor. But this book, after all, is about media, and it's not within our scope and purpose here to explore in depth the other reasons that kids resort to violence. We are going to talk about violence in the media and what we know about its effects on kids. And the truth is that we know an awful lot. Over the last thirty years more than *a thousand* studies, by major medical and public health groups as well as the surgeon general's office and the National Institutes of Health, have concluded that media violence does have an impact on children in four particular ways:

- It can make them fearful and lead them to believe that the world is a mean and violent place.

- It can cause some kids to act violently and aggressively toward others.

- It can teach them that violence is an acceptable way to deal with conflict.

- And it can desensitize them toward the use of violence in the real world.

A MEAN WORLD

The first problem—the "mean world" syndrome—was initially described by George Gerbner of the University of Pennsylvania's Annenberg School for Communication. Gerbner, who has studied TV violence for more than three decades, concludes that media violence can create an almost paralyzing sense of fear that the world is a violent place where physical aggression is normal. Gerbner associates this syndrome with frequent television viewing. Although adults are afflicted with this fear, children are particularly apt to be seriously distressed by violent media images; their feelings of terror and mistrust can last for many years. A prime source of these images is TV news, which happens to be America's number one source of news and information. The old newsroom saying goes, "If it bleeds, it leads," and most local television newscasts are dominated by killings, assaults, disasters, kidnappings, terrorist attacks, and other stories designed to provoke a strong emotional reaction from viewers. This violence-laced local coverage is also the cheapest kind for stations to produce. It requires little thoughtful analysis and few seasoned reporters and producers—all the better for the station's bottom line.

The entertainment media deserves its share of the blame too. In her book *Mommy, I'm Scared,* psychologist Joanne Cantor recounts many examples of children who have been tormented by media-induced dread. In one case, a graduate student recalled that seeing the movie *Jaws* as a child affected her for decades after. She would suffer anxiety attacks every time she approached a lake or swimming pool. Even years later, the intense fear still caused her to suffer from panic-anxiety attacks and feelings of extreme claustrophobia.[108]

Obviously, this is an unusual case. Not everyone who sees a violent, frightening movie in childhood is plagued by adult fears of this intensity. But it *is* true that young children, who can't distinguish between fantasy and reality, can be easily and deeply scared by realistic depictions of violence and grotesque characters. "Sensationalized violence, terror, and human misery," notes Cantor, a professor at the University of Wisconsin, "can create an extraordinarily upsetting environment for children and an enormous . . . challenge for parents who want to behave responsibly."[109] Most of us, I'm sure, can remember occasions when, as children, we were terrified by something that we'd seen on television or at the movies—whether it was the attacking seagulls in *The Birds* or the flying monkeys in *The Wizard of Oz.* The fact is, though, we saw these sorts of movies rarely, not weekly or, in the case of television, daily. In recent years, Hollywood's growing taste for grotesque, graphic fare has upped the stakes, from *Friday the 13th* to *Creepshow* and *Scream.* Although these movies are not intended for young children, it is a fact that small kids are regularly exposed to them in the company of unthinking parents, baby-sitters, and older siblings. "I know parents who took eight-year-old kids to see *Boyz N the Hood*," movie producer Michael Tollin told me. "Those kids had nightmares for months. To me that's completely irresponsible parenting." In Champaign, Illinois, Katherine Hansen, a teacher of emotionally disturbed children, works with kids as young as five years old whose parents routinely take them to see violent films. "They haven't seen *Bambi*," she said, "but they've seen *Scream, Scream 2*, and Chucky," the killer doll in the gruesome *Child's Play* movies.

Unfortunately, for some kids even G-rated movies can be disturbing, a fact that's not surprising when you realize that G-rated animated films contain "a significant amount" of violence, according to a recent study published in the *Journal of the American Medical Association*.[110] The chances of upsetting and frightening young children are much greater, however, at PG-rated movies, which many parents consider fairly safe for kids. Because there are so few G movies, many parents opt for PG films as an alternative. But when Joanne Cantor and her colleagues randomly sampled a number of these movies, they found that PG films were, in fact, closer to PG-13 than to G movies in content. One recent PG release, *The Little Vampire*, actually caused some kids to sob with fear,[111] and the promotional trailer for another PG movie, *Dr. Seuss' How the Grinch Stole Christmas*, caused crying preschoolers to flee one California theater.[112] Herb Scannell, the president of Nickelodeon, experienced as a parent the unpredictable effects of movies—and script decisions—on young children. Herb recently took his little daughter to see the PG-rated movie *My Dog Skip*. "I thought it was going to be a homerun with her because it's a dog movie," he says. "But in the film the dog gets hit by a shovel, and then the boy slaps the dog. It was a very upsetting movie for both of us. As a parent," he says, "you have to be acutely aware of the violent content of these movies. You've got to think about that stuff and how it will affect your kids."

What you have less control over as a parent, however, are the trailers that are shown before a lot of PG films. I recently took my eight-year-old and seven-year-old to see the PG-rated *Dr. Dolittle 2* and found it fun and harmless—but before the movie started, the three of us had to sit through eight previews, including disturbing promos for PG-13 movies like *Final Fantasy* ("Parents Strongly Cautioned: Sci Fi Action and Violence") and *The Fast and the Furious* ("Parents Strongly Cautioned: Violence, Sexual Content, and Language"). These clips were totally inappropriate for my kids and many of the other children in the audience, as are so many ads on daytime and sports television.

NOT JUST FAIRY TALES

Why does all this matter? Haven't kids always dealt with scary, gory, and violent stories, even in fairy tales? Isn't exposure to that kind of material just part of the process of growing up? The standard bedtime stories certainly have their share of frightening and violent plots—Little Red Riding Hood's grandmother is gobbled by a wolf, while Hansel and Gretel, abandoned by their parents to starve, are threatened by a witch who wants to eat them. At the end of the story, they shove her into an oven to burn her alive. These stories have been common fare for little children for generations, but as psychologist Bruno Bettelheim explained in his book *The Uses of Enchantment,* fairy tales "should be viewed as symbolic renderings of crucial life experiences. The child understands this intuitively, though he does not 'know' it explicitly." What the child learns from Little Red Riding Hood, Bettelheim argues, is that not everyone is trustworthy. And while these stories can increase a child's anxieties, they also resolve them, teaching them that resourcefulness can help them overcome scary situations. Among the advantages of fairy tales, Bettelheim contends, is that by "hearing them, the child comes to believe that [inner] transformations"—and the mastery of challenges—"are possible."[113]

The most important phrase in Bettelheim's statement, however, is "hearing them." The reason young children can listen to these stories and go easily to sleep is that fairy tales are read to them by caring adults and leave much to the imagination. Grownups can alter and soften their tones of voice, according to the child's response, and they can give physical and verbal reassurance as they read. Clinical psychologists Andre Derdeyn and Jeffrey Turley have noted that young children, with their capacity for imagination and magical thinking, need little in the way of graphic or literal images to produce a sense of overcoming adversity. "In fact, a more graphic or realistic presentation," they state, "would likely flood the young child with fear and make a mastery experience impossible."[114] That *flood* of fear is what the lifelike visual violence of film and television can produce, particularly among young children, and it takes a toll. According to a 2001 study by Sesame Workshop, creators of *Sesame Street,* two-thirds of children aged six to eleven—and three-quarters of nine-to-eleven-year-olds—suffer from intense, vivid anxieties about violence, guns, and death.[115]

As any parent who experienced the events of September 11, 2001, knows, helping your child cope with real-life, televised images of death and destruction is no easy task. That is why continued responsibility on the part of television news programs and executives, on the local and national levels, is a terribly important children's media issue. Most network news coverage of the September 11 attacks proved to be reasonably responsible. What's far more troubling, however, is the steady stream of violent images in local and national TV news programs, including the torrent of sensational TV newsmagazines, that leave many children feeling fearful and depressed.

SCHOOL FOR VIOLENCE

There are other ramifications of visual violence. Study after study has shown that children who watch violence on the screen act more aggressively and violently toward others. In one landmark experiment, conducted in 1956, twelve four-year-old children viewed what would now be considered a fairly benign Woody Woodpecker cartoon that featured lots of animated violence. Another group of twelve young-sters watched the "Little Red Hen," a nonviolent cartoon. After-ward, the kids who had seen the Woody Woodpecker cartoon acted far more aggressively—breaking toys and striking other kids—than those who had watched "Little Red Hen."[116] Since then, decades of research have produced similar results, most focusing on the links between violent television and aggression. One long-term study tracked the behavior of eight-year-old boys until they turned eigh-teen. The conclusion? The more TV violence a boy watched at the age of eight, the more aggressive his behavior would be—not only at age eight but ten years later, at eighteen.[117] In fact, the aggression of eighteen-year-olds, rather than eight-year-olds, was most closely correlated with violent television viewing at the younger age. A sim-ilar study followed the behavior of boys until they turned thirty. Those who had viewed the most televised violence at age eight were convicted of more serious crimes, punished their own children more violently, and were considered more aggressive by their wives than other males examined in the study.

The effect is not limited to this country. Researchers in western Canada looked at the behavior of first and second graders after tele-vision was first introduced into the region. They found that, in just the first two years, there was 160 percent more hitting, shoving, and biting among youngsters.[118] The direct link between media violence and aggression was reinforced in a 2001 study by a team of Stanford University researchers. When children at one elementary school spent less time watching television and playing video games, they were 50 percent less likely to be physically aggressive with each other, and the most aggressive children showed the most improvement.[119]

NO CONSEQUENCES OF VIOLENCE

Longtime researcher George Gerbner explains the connection this way: "We are dealing with the formula-driven mass produc-

tion of violence for entertainment—what I call 'happy violence,' "
he contends. "It is swift, painless, effective, and always leads to a
happy ending." These stories tell people that this is the way life
works. And, he adds, "there is no more serious business for a culture or a society than the stories you tell your children."[120]
Gerbner is right. Today, on TV and in the movies, there are rarely
any consequences for violent acts. In cartoons, TV wrestling, and
many movies, no one really gets seriously hurt. There's little
agony and bloodshed. No one is left grieving, and no one is punished for acting violently. The hero, in fact, is often the one who
turns to violence to solve a problem. The overwhelming message,
note education professors Nancy Carlsson-Paige and Diane
Levin, is that "violence is fun, violence is exciting, violence
doesn't hurt," and people can use violence "to solve problems
with others."[121]

That's a message that was heavily promoted on kids' TV beginning in the 1980s, when the Reagan administration eliminated
restraints on sponsors and producers of children's programming.
Not only did violence flood Saturday morning shows—in beat-'em-
up animated programs like the *Teenage Mutant Ninja Turtles*—but
the "violence is fun" theme was heavily marketed through the merchandising of related action figures and other tie-in toys to kids.
Although, with the notable exception of TV wrestling, television
violence has been on the decline since Congress began monitoring
it again in 1993, the marketing of media violence-themed toys continues. Just check out the aisles in your local toy store. Graphic
violence is a staple of child's play, from Gundam action figures
with long rifle cannons, gatling guns, and "giant attack scissors
included!" to X-Men the Movie Sabretooth action fighters, packaged with security-guard dolls whose severed heads dangle from
their necks.

"The lessons children learn from a movie or TV show are much
more powerful when the toys take over their play," Professor Levin
says. "It's like a double whammy because children's play becomes
the place where they try out and learn to use the violence they saw

on the screen." The fact that a number of these toys are linked to R-rated movies and mature-rated video games makes this kid-targeted merchandizing even worse. "The entertainment industry," Levin argues, "is marketing violence to children knowing it is harmful, in the same way that tobacco companies market cigarettes to children, knowing that it's harmful to their health."[122]

Of course, it's nearly impossible to get many media people to acknowledge that violent entertainment is a problem. When they aren't shifting blame onto other causes of youth violence such as the need for stricter gun control laws, they're hiding behind the time-worn protections of the First Amendment and "creative freedom." Typical is the reaction of actor-director Kent Dalian: "I think the whole issue is ridiculous," he countered. Wars, rapes, and killings "have existed since the beginning of time. A film is nothing but art. And art has no responsibility except to be true to itself. It's not there to educate, set a good example, or change the world. It might do those things, but it has no responsibility to."[123] Even Rob Reiner, a terrific filmmaker who has been a leading advocate of child-friendly public policies and who has worked extensively and effectively with Children Now and others on behalf of key children's initiatives, can dodge a bit when it comes to the issue of entertainment violence. "I'm not saying that . . . movies can't affect a child's behavior," Reiner told Terence Smith of *The News Hour with Jim Lehrer.* "But to deal with the problem," he said, we have to "start dealing with the root causes of violence . . . and not just point the finger at Hollywood or point the finger at guns."[124] Now, Rob Reiner is a truly committed and effective child advocate whose heart and political activism are definitely in the right place, and he's correct that we need to deal with all the root causes. But that still sounds a little too much like passing the buck—"we're not the only ones who are to blame." Countless others in the media—in the movie, television, music, and electronic games industries—continue to make far worse, diversionary arguments and to do less than they should. They have stonewalled, with straight if not entirely sincere faces, all the way to the bank.

PROFITING FROM VIOLENCE

What it all comes down to, as usual, is money. Some inside the industry see that more clearly than others. "It's a complex world, and you see actors and directors doing certain things because it's a paycheck. You make choices. You adjust your moralities," commented the actor Bryan Brown. "Producers and directors want to make movies. They want to make movies people watch. If violence sells, these pictures will be made, regardless of all the B.S. otherwise."[125] As a result, moviemakers and networks will produce bloody, gratuitously sadistic fare that they would never want their children to see. It's a money-driven double standard made worse by the increasing consolidation of the media industry. As one example, Les Moonves, former head of Lorimar Studios and now the widely respected president of CBS Entertainment, pointed to the pressure on television networks to deliver higher profits to their corporate owners. There used to be, he said, "a public trust of social responsibility." But now there's a new, bottom-line-focused agenda. "Network presidents don't keep their jobs based on the number of Emmy Awards. Let's face it; there is more sensation and violence because it works. The movie of the week has become the killer of the week story."[126]

But if the only problem was money, the situation might even be tolerable. The problem is that, for some troubled kids in some situations, the heavy saturation of media violence—driven by commercial greed—can help push them over the edge of rationality and into a real world of mayhem of their own making, modeled on media portrayals. The school shooters were simply the most famous of these lost kids, bred on violence and unable to separate reality from the blood-spattered commercial fictions they consumed. It's happened too often, in too many terrible ways, to ignore. In Greenfield, Massachusetts, an eighteen-year-old girl was stabbed to death by a nineteen-year-old boy whose room was filled with nearly a hundred violent horror films, a machete, and a goalie mask like the one worn by Jason, the teen murderer in the *Friday the 13ᵗʰ* movies.[127] In Los Angeles, a man was arrested for robbery and murder sporting a fedora and bandana just like Freddy Krueger, the slayer in *Nightmare on Elm Street.*[128] I want to be very clear on this point. *Of course,* there were other factors in these killings; movies didn't "pull the trigger" any more than poverty or access to guns or childhood trauma did. But they were certainly, unquestionably, a contributing factor. The media, remember, is the storyteller that kids are growing up with. As adults, and as a society, we need to listen to the stories and understand the lessons that they're teaching—about anger, about humanity, and about the use of violence as a first resort.

The great majority of kids don't watch a violence-drenched movie like *Natural Born Killers, The Matrix, Scream,* or *Nightmare on Elm Street* and then commit acts of violence themselves. Most kids can tell the difference between fantasy and reality and keep them separate. But some kids can't. Some kids believe the stories that the media tells them. Just as they look to it for facts and knowledge about sex, they look to it for guidance about how to deal with the world when you feel oppressed, about the nature of glamour and fame, and about the likely consequences of violence. Young kids, especially, don't often understand the link between actions and consequences—a disconnect that's worsened by media that rarely show realistic results of violent acts. It was tragic but not outside the realm of comprehension when a thirteen-year-old boy killed a six-year-old girl using moves he'd seen on television wrestling shows. Harder to fathom is the amazement of a young gunshot victim in Boston that his bullet wound actually hurt. Deborah Prothrow-Stith, MD, Dean of Harvard's School of Public Health, who treated the injured youth, remembered thinking, "He's really stupid, anybody knows that if you get shot, it's going to hurt. But it dawned on me," she added, "that what he sees on television is that when the superhero gets shot in the arm, he uses that arm to hold on to a truck going eighty-five miles an hour around a corner . . . and shoots a couple of hundred people while he's at it."[129] We need to face the fact that, as a model for experi-

ence, the media is creating a set of strange, distorted, and dangerous expectations for some children.

SELLING VIOLENCE TO CHILDREN

Clearly some kids—because of their collection of risk factors and
their inability to move safely between fantasy and reality—are in
more danger than others from violent media. These children are
literally being placed in harm's way by media companies whose
sole priority is to make a buck. In fact, in too many cases, they are
being actively targeted by media companies, who see their taste
for violence as a lucrative market to nurture and exploit. In
September 2000, the Federal Trade Commission reported that 80
percent of violent, R-rated movies were aimed at children *under*
the age of seventeen. In subsequent testimony before the Senate
Commerce Committee, Mel Harris, president of Sony Pictures
Entertainment, actually admitted test-marketing a violent PG-13
movie, *The Fifth Element,* to children as young as nine years old. It
was, he said, "a judgment lapse,"[130] but it was not by any means
unique. According to marketing memos to executives at
Columbia TriStar, the studio planned to test the slasher movie *I
Know What You Did Last Summer* with ten- and eleven-year-
olds.[131] Other industry memos discussed market testing the R-
rated movie *Disturbing Behavior*—with its "strong violence,
sexuality, language, and drug content," as MGM warns—to children only ten and twelve years old. These are some of the clearest
examples of the industry's callous, inexcusable exploitation of
young children for profit.

After the horrific school shooting at Columbine High School,
many moviemakers and TV programmers did do a little soul-
searching, at least for a few months, acknowledging that their products might have played some role in promoting a culture of
violence. Some thoughtful decisions were made. A movie about a
high school cheerleader called *Sugar and Spice and Semiautomatics*

was retitled *Sugar and Spice*. The Bravo cable channel killed a segment called "Teen Suicide School" from the show *The Awful Truth*. CBS canceled a *Promised Land* episode about a schoolyard shooting in Denver, and the WB network postponed an episode of *Buffy the Vampire Slayer* that featured a school massacre. Similarly, after the terrorist attacks on September 11, 2001, a number of networks and studios tentatively questioned their reliance on violent images and themes. "Violence is part of the world," responded Sherry Lansing, chairwoman of Paramount Motion Picture Group, "but it's our responsibility not to trivialize violence, not to glamorize violence, not to make it look cartoony."[132] Nice words, but time will tell if this new sense of responsibility translates into long-term, concrete change. I, for one, am pretty skeptical.

Recently, too, the TV and movie industries have improved some of their parental warnings, adding more information about the content of many shows. And in response to the 2000 FTC report, many theater owners have tightened their restrictions on admitting children under seventeen to R-rated movies. In the process, however, it's become clear just how dependent these movies have been on underage audiences. After the restrictions went into effect, R-rated films like *The Mexican* and *Freddy Got Fingered* had lower box-office takes, and some movies may have lost as much as 40 percent of their opening week earnings because of the new policies.

The recent restraint shown by some television executives, movie studios, and theaters has hardly been matched by the music industry, however. After the school shooting in Littleton, Interscope Records released Eminem's *Marshall Mathers LP,* deciding merely to blank out two words—"kids" and "Columbine"—from these lyrics in the rapper's song "I'm Back":

> *I take seven kids from Columbine, stand 'em all in line*
> *Add an AK-47, a revolver, a 9/A Mach II, and that ought to solve*
> *   a problem of mine*
> *And it's a whole school of bullies shot up at one time.*

Here is a song that glamorizes and glorifies the schoolyard blood-letting, but it's art, right? Eminem has defended his kill-thrill lyrics, claiming that some people "think that if you tell a kid to put a gun to his head that he's going to do it, but kids are a lot smarter than we give them credit for."[133]

Not all kids, unfortunately—as the parents of fifteen-year-old Elyse Pahler discovered. Elyse was "sacrificed" by three teenage followers of the death-metal band Slayer, whose music celebrates "carnage, Satanism, and torture." In their song "Altar of Sacrifice," for example, Slayer's lyrics describe

. . . High priest awaiting, dagger in hand
Spilling the pure virgin blood
Satan's slaughter, ceremonial death.

That was more than just a song to Joseph Fiorella and his buddies Jacob Delashmutt and Royce Casey; it was a summons. As Fiorella stated in a court report, "It gets inside your head. It's almost embarrassing that I was so influenced by the music. The music started to influence the way I looked at things." He told his friends that he'd "be down for sacrificing . . . a virgin." Two months later, after specifically selecting Elyse for sacrifice, they choked her, stabbed her multiple times with an antler-handled knife, stomped on her neck, and let her bleed to death. The boys were sent to prison for terms of twenty-five years to life. Meanwhile, Slayer—whose records celebrating serial killers such as Jeffrey Dahmer have sold hundreds of thousands of copies—are really "nice, conservative people," maintains a spokeswoman for their label, Columbia Records. "It's a matter of opinion," she said, "how you take the music."[134] The opinion of scholars like Stanford University's Don Roberts is that the music should be taken seriously, because its words and images affect how adolescents are socialized."[135] And the recording artists who are most listened to by kids include those with the most graphically violent and sadistic lyrics—from Grammy-winning Eminem to the multimillion-album-selling band Limp Bizkit. Kids who are already feeling alienated and angry are especially responsive to lyrics that glorify hostility and violence. For many in the music industry, feeding and fueling that adolescent rage is a fast way to profits in the large and lucrative teen market. What the industry is all about, according to Jimmy Iovine, co-chair of Interscope Geffen A&M, is "how you evoke and provoke emotion in people."[136] Specifically, what recording companies are stoking is "anger and fear," according to another industry executive.

Now I happen to like Jimmy Iovine. He's an intelligent, talented, and very successful figure in the music business, but I totally disagree with much of what he and Interscope Records produce. Tapping into—and blowing the lid off—the angst and turmoil of disaffected youths is a thriving industry, and it's the stock in trade of bands like Slayer, who—according to their publicist—are just posing for the benefit of their death-metal audiences. In a *Frontline* segment for PBS, media critic Douglas Rushkoff explored the explosive phenomenon of rage rock among mainly white teenage boys, who favor lyrics that spew violent threats against "others" such as women and gays. Kids who feel spurned by the mainstream, Rushkoff says, defiantly claim this music as their own, thinking that it's part of an underground culture that's repellent to the commercial media. They couldn't be more wrong. The truth is, this music is about as commercial as it gets. "Rage rock is a double-dog dare to the mainstream marketing media—just try to market this," he says. "And the thing is, that's exactly what they've done." It turns out, Rushkoff asserts, that "the nastiest expressions of youth culture are manna to an industry ravenous for anything authentic to sell," igniting fans with incendiary lyrics and driving enormous profits for the music industry and their conglomerate owners.

The rage rock band Limp Bizkit is a case in point. At the 1999 peace and music "Woodstock" event in Rome, New York, the band helped fuel a riot with their lash-out number "Break Stuff":

> . . . I pack a chainsaw . . .
> I skin your ass raw

And if my day keeps going this way
I just might . . . break your fucking face tonight.

A woman was reportedly raped during Limp Bizkit's performance, and by the end of the event there had been alleged gang
rapes as well as widespread fires, looting, and destruction. Band
member Fred Durst says that the song "Break Stuff" was "a mistake."[137] But the publicity didn't hurt Limp Bizkit's record sales.
Pushed by Interscope and MTV, its second album hit number one
on U.S. charts, and Durst is now a senior vice president at
Interscope Records. "One part authentic rage, two parts marketing,
sprinkle with cash, and place in a preheated oven called Woodstock
'99," Rushkoff remarked—it's a perfect recipe for a commercial hit.
"The success of Limp Bizkit and rage rock was all but preordained,"
he concluded. Teen rebellion itself became "just another product."[138]

Jimmy Iovine defends the musicians—after all, rage rockers like
Limp Bizkit and the platinum-selling Eminem are only artists.
"What I'm saying is, where do you draw the line with this shit?" he
asks. "I don't know what influences and what doesn't influence. . . . But the musicians get blamed for whatever."[139]

Maybe. But the disgrace is that few critics are blaming the
"adults" who make all the profits in the industry—Interscope,
Vivendi Universal, Columbia, and the other corporate distribution
giants who are fueling and packaging this wave of adolescent rage
solely for profit motives. *They simply don't have to do it.* Sure, the
CDs they peddle to millions are labeled with the nearly useless PARENTAL ADVISORY warning. But as the FTC study revealed,
the music industry routinely ignores its own cautions. Every single
one of fifty-five "explicit" music recordings the FTC examined
were deliberately marketed to kids *under* the age of seventeen.[140]
Then, of course, there are the spinoff toys—like the Eminem action
figure sporting a hockey mask and carrying a chainsaw, with the
words "cut here" emblazoned on its neck.[141] MTV, the network
with the highest ratings for twelve- to thirty-four-year-olds,[142] fully
understands the marketing power of adolescent anger. "The word

'edge,' while it's loaded with implications, has always been an important part of the brand promise of MTV," said Brian Graden, the network's head of programming. Today more than ever, he added, "the edge, the attitude, is expressing . . . an undercurrent that is harder, that seems to be angry."[143]

According to one artist, comic-book creator Gerard Jones, this upwelling anger is just a natural part of adolescent expression. It's something that violent lyrics, stories, and images bring to the surface, enabling kids to integrate "the scariest, most fervently denied fragments of their psyches into fuller schemes of selfhood through fantasies of . . . combat and destruction." All children, Jones contends, experience this anger. "Even the sweetest and most civilized of them, even those whose parents read the better class of literary magazines, will feel rage. The world is uncontrollable and incomprehensible; mastering it is a terrifying, enraging task. Rage can be an energizing emotion, a shot of courage to push us to resist greater threats, take more control, than we ever thought we could." By identifying with a violent protagonist, he argues, "children engage the rage they've stifled, come to fear it less, and become more capable of utilizing it."[144] That approach certainly worked for Eric Harris and Dylan Klebold. The two Columbine shooters not only engaged the rage, they deliberately and explosively stoked it so that they'd have the courage to do the unthinkable. "More rage. More rage. Keep building it on," Klebold chanted in their homemade video.

The point here is that media companies are playing with fire, for profit motives alone. Violence sells, like sex. It's a marketable commodity that tunes into the inner angst and insecurities of adolescents—especially white, suburban, adolescent males. Sure, death-metal music gives voice to teens' anger, frustration, and desire to get back at others who don't treat them with respect. But it also feeds that anger—a dangerous game for kids who, due to a variety of other reasons and risk factors, are already on the edge. Unfortunately, the number of kids who fit that description may be growing. According to Dr. Alan Unis, a psychiatrist at the

University of Washington, the rate of mood disorders, depression, and suicide has been climbing among young people, and the number of seriously depressed kids under fifteen years of age may be as high as three million, reports the Amercian Academy of Child and Adolescent Psychiatry. For kids whose perception of the world is distorted and darkened, it's all too easy to take to heart the hate-filled, murderous solutions mouthed by their music idols, who are rocketed to fame and glamorized by recording companies and MTV. As one youth minister, the Reverend Chris Perry, put it, "there is a profound cultural influence, like gravity, pulling kids into a world where violence is a perfectly normal way to handle our emotions."[145]

NOT JUST A GAME

If movies and music can provide the script for some kids teetering on the edge of violent action, then video games—especially the "first-person shooter" bloodfests like *Doom, Quake,* and *Diablo*—provide plenty of rehearsal opportunities. Since they first came on the scene in the 1970s, video and electronic games have developed into a $6 billion-a-year industry, and violent games are some of the most popular with kids. According to a 2001 survey from the Harvard School of Public Health, 64 percent of video games considered suitable for kids as young as six contain intentional violence, and 60 percent rewarded players for hurting or killing other characters.[146] The favorite games of nearly half of all fourth- through eighth-graders, another study found, featured violent action,[147] and the popularity of games with extreme violence has increased steadily. They range from *WWF Attitude*—a beat-'em-up PlayStation wrestling game that offers bloodshed as an option—to *Carmageddon,* in which a driver mows down innocent pedestrians, their blood spattering the windshield (an ad for *Carmageddon* boasts that the game is "as easy as killing babies with axes").

A breakthrough development has been the introduction of "first-person shooter" games like *Duke Nukem,* in which players see and *experience* firsthand the sensations of killing enemies with guns, missiles, and grenades. *Doom,* for example—one of the games favored by the Columbine shooters—lets you kill human opponents using shotguns, saws, and submachine guns and thrill at the kill as heads, bodies, and bits of flesh explode around you. "Feel the sensation. Feel the vibration. Feel the mutilation," invites an ad for one of these hyperviolent games. Does the violence sell? You bet. *Quake* and *Doom* combined have sold more than four million copies.[148] The hyperreality of these games can be mesmerizing, even intruding on day-to-day reality. "I've been walking around in a grocery store and I heard grenades bursting around," remarked one computer gamer; "weird things like that [happen] when you spend so much time doing it."[149]

This transfer effect and the realistic shooting practice that these games provide worry many people, including Dan Huck, a police officer who organized a turn-in of violent video games in Wilmette, Illinois, just as police officers in other communities have arranged turn-ins of weapons. After playing many of these games at arcades, Huck said, "I've seen these kids shoot, and they're doing better than I am, and I've trained with real weapons."[150] Not only do shooter games provide what one judge called training for snipers,[151] they may also increase the acceptance of violence as a solution and the propensity of an individual to kill. That is a key concern of retired Lt. Colonel Dave Grossman, a former Army Ranger who taught psychology to cadets at West Point. Grossman, the author of *On Killing: The Psychological Cost of Learning to Kill in War and Society,* found that as many as 80 percent of American soldiers in the Second World War never fired their weapons due to the innate "resistance to killing your own kind." Thanks to psychological training that makes killing seem normal—including lifelike, simulated situations—the fire rate climbed to 95 percent by the time of the Vietnam war.[152]

Even more than violent television and movies, violent video games have been shown to increase aggression among those who play them. According to a 2000 study reported in the *Journal of*

Personality and Social Psychology, even brief exposure to these games can temporarily increase aggressive behavior. Most vulnerable to these effects were young men who were "habitually aggressive"—in other words, those who are already on the edge of violent behavior. "Violent video games," the researchers found, "provide a forum for learning and practicing aggressive solutions to conflict situations," priming aggressive thoughts and practicing "new aggression-related scripts that can become more and more accessible for use when real-life conflict situations arise." In one disturbing revelation after September 11, 2001, Western journalists visiting Al Qaeda safe houses in Kabul discovered packaging elements from the popular Microsoft *Flight Simulator*—a computer game that allowed users to simulate flight takeoffs from the world's largest airports and crash them into skyscrapers, including New York's World Trade Center.[153]

Nevertheless, there has been little research on actual, direct links between electronic games and real-life violence. The latest Surgeon General's Report, released in 2000, reported no clear connection, noting that the subject has not yet been adequately studied. But the recently released Stanford University study showed that restricting video game playing as well as television viewing reduced the aggressiveness of children. And many experts—citing, among other evidence, the well-known effects of television and advertising on behavior—say that common sense points to a link. The research on television, says Kansas State University developmental psychology professor John Murray, translates directly to video games; "the only thing that's different and more worrisome is that," in the games, "the viewer as player is actively involved in constructing the violence."[154]

It is this interactivity—and the sensation, repeated over and over again, of committing extreme violence against others—that especially worries some professionals. The more often kids rehearse violent acts, some argue, the more likely they are to commit them in real life.[155] This is what makes electronic games qualitatively different from more passive experiences of violence, in movies and on television. Through practice, the use of violence can become a learned response—a scripted reflex like the trigger rate effectively cultivated by the army. At the very least, there can be intense physiological effects from playing interactive electronic games. Some researchers have noted changes in heart rate and blood pressure; in some cases, the games have even triggered epileptic seizures.[156]

Others have compared the sensation of playing intense video games to the effects of taking certain drugs. During violent or frightening simulations, the player's heart races from anxiety and fear. When the scene is over, they experience heightened feelings of relief, pleasure, and excitement.[157] This neurophysiological cycle is so enjoyable for some that they repeat it over and over again—gradually needing new, more frightening scenarios to get the same rush of anxiety and pleasure. That level of addictive play is exactly what game designers go for. As one of them put it, "A video game is all about adrenaline, and the easiest way to trigger adrenaline is to make someone think they're going to die."[158] What some researchers worry about, says Kansas State's John Murray, "is whether repeated rushes of stimulation cause the memory to store away ever-more-violent images, to be recalled later as a possible response to frustration."[159]

The most violent games, according to developers, are not intended for children. There is, after all, a game-rating system, much touted by the industry and subscribed to by 100 percent of video game and 85 percent of computer software providers. Similar to the MPAA ratings for movies, the system was developed by the Entertainment Software Ratings Board (ESRB) and alerts video game purchasers to violence, coarse language, and sexual content. One of six ESRB rating icons appears on the packaging of most video games. There is the EC (Early Childhood) rating for games appropriate for children aged three and up. The E (Everyone) rating is for games approved for general use. From there—based on the level of violence, realistic blood and gore, suggestive themes, and other "content descriptors"—games are rated for increasingly older players: T (Teenagers) for kids thirteen years and older, M (Mature) for players over seventeen, and A (Adult) for those over eighteen years of age.[160] "The purpose of the rating system is to empower the parents to make an informed choice," stated Douglas Lowenstein, president of the Interactive Digital Software Association.[161] Indeed, the industry won passing marks—a B—for its rating system from the fifth annual report card on video and computer games released by the National Institute on Media and the Family, and the FTC applauded the system for being the "best and most informative in the entertainment industry."[162]

The trouble is that fewer than one out of three parents understands the video game ratings—and underage kids have virtually unrestricted access to mature games because very few retailers enforce the rating codes.[163] In one sting operation conducted by the office of Senator Herb Kohl of Wisconsin, Washington, D.C., retailers sold hyperviolent M-rated games, including *Duke Nukem,* *Quake,* and *Grand Theft Auto,* to fourteen- and fifteen-year-olds.[164] In another case, kids aged thirteen to fifteen were able to purchase M-rated games in thirty-two out of thirty-two cases.[165] Although Sears says it will not stock M-rated games, and a number of national chains—including Target and FuncoLand—say they actually enforce the ratings policy, most video game retailers do not monitor sales. This doesn't seem to trouble Lowenstein. "It is presumptuous of us," he said, "to tell retailers how to run their business."[166] Talk about passing the buck! The FTC, however, pointed the finger directly at Lowenstein's video game industry for irresponsible and reckless practices. According to its 2000 report, marketing plans for more than half of the M-rated games it studied specifically included children under seventeen.[167] "Practically everybody in the industry still markets inappropriate games to kids," Senator Kohl reported. "Practically every retailer regularly sells these games to kids and practically all parents need to know more about the rating system."[168]

So once more, with a wink and a nod and a few self-serving

statements, large media companies are busily peddling extreme violence to children while touting their rating system and criticizing parents for not being more responsible. "Violence sells," says one computer game developer matter-of-factly.[169] And in a market-driven media culture, profits count far more than other considerations. Besides, there's always the free-speech flag to hide behind. "Video games," Lowenstein argues, "are a modern form of artistic expression that have the same level of First Amendment protections as films, records and books. Indeed," he states, "each game represents an extraordinary combination of narrative story line, music, and graphic design worthy of the highest constitutional shield."[170] That position has been challenged by several lawsuits—most recently one filed in April 2001 by the family of slain Columbine teacher Dave Sanders. Their suits seeks $5 billion in punitive damages from media companies including Nintendo of America, Sega of America, id Software, and GT Interactive Software for inciting Harris and Klebold's acts of murder. So far, similar suits against entertainment companies have been unsuccessful, and it may be that this one fails as well. But it's clear from recent FTC reports that the extraordinary "artistic expression" of many of these games is matched by the industry's extraordinary greed and reckless, cynical exploitation of kids for profit.

THE COST TO COMPASSION

There is no question that most kids who play violent video games will never commit real acts of violence. But this extremely popular form of media is one more factor that can help push a troubled kid over the edge. "Each thing may be a drop in the bucket, but the bucket is full," comments Eugene Provenzo, education professor at the University of Miami.[171] It's like the tobacco effect. Most people who smoke don't get lung cancer—but 150,000 Americans do die from the disease each year. Most people who have a steady diet of violent media do not commit violence—but there are real costs to society in the levels of aggression and a cultivated tolerance for violence. As time passes and researchers focus more on the effects of new hyperviolent electronic games, we'll know more about their short- and long-term influences. But my guess is that the teen culture of rage—fueled by violence-glorifying movies, music, and addictive first-person shooter games—may have painful, long-term implications for all of us. We are raising kids on violence, and as a culture, we may soon reap even more troubling rewards.

The price of all this is more than explosive violence by a handful of troubled kids. It may, in many ways, be the future that all of us face, as a generation that's been repeatedly exposed to intense, realistic violence grows up with more acceptance of aggression, less resistance to brutality, and less compassion. There can indeed be a numbing effect. In one study, for example, boys who routinely saw a lot of TV violence were less aroused by new violent programs than boys who did not watch as much violent television.[172] Physical aggression becomes normal and tolerable—and, in fact, it is far more widespread among young people today than it was two decades ago. The number of violent acts committed by high school seniors has climbed nearly 50 percent, and arrest rates for aggravated assaults by young people have jumped nearly 70 percent since 1983[173]—about the time, interestingly, that President Reagan's deregulation policy was unleashing violent programming on kids' television.

We may not yet be at the point where kids boast, like the *South Park* character, "I did it! I did it! I finally killed something!" But a disturbing number of young people do, as Maureen Dowd of the *New York Times* reflected, laughingly treat "death as virtual entertainment." At one screening of the movie *The Matrix*, she reported, "people began yelling out 'Columbine!' " and cheered as Keanu Reeves walked through a metal detector, pulled out his guns, and blew away a building full of cybercops.[174] Disconnected from real life and fueled by the relentless pressure for corporate profits, media violence may, as George Gerbner claimed, rob us of "the tragic sense of life necessary for compassion."[175] And a compassionless society is something that we all should fear. "Somehow," said William Dodson, superintendent of the school district in Pearl, Mississippi, where two girls lost their lives, "we are not getting that across to young people, that life is not a movie. There *are* consequences."[176]

Five

THE SELLING OF KIDS AS CONSUMERS

I was reaching for a cup for my then two-year-old daughter Carly when she yelled, "No, Daddy, no!" She pointed her chubby finger at the shelf where she saw her favorite plastic cup, branded with a picture of her favorite Teletubbies character, and said, 'Po!" That moment, I recognized, was the end of Carly's babyhood and the beginning of her new lifelong career as a "consumer cadet,"[177] as marketing expert James McNeal dubs little shoppers-in-training. She wasn't even out of diapers yet. Yet Carly not only could easily tell Po apart from the other rotund Teletubbies—Laa-Laa, Dipsy, and Tinky Winky—but she had emotionally bonded with the character and its commercial tie-in products. She and the Teletubbies brand had, as McNeal puts it, "become good friends."[178]

I've got nothing seriously against the *Teletubbies* from a purely content point of view. It's an okay show, and we used to let Carly watch it on videotapes once a week. But the program does bother me—a lot—for a couple of other reasons. First of all, it's aimed at children as young as one, the very first show targeted to an audience of infants. That by itself is troubling, especially when the American Academy of Pediatrics urges parents to keep kids away from television until the age of two.

The other thing that troubles me about *Teletubbies* is that it is a blatantly commercial program. Developed in Britain, the series had already spawned a line of best-selling tie-in toys and merchandise in that country before it debuted in this country in 1998. Teletubbies dolls, pajamas, bedsheets, books, and games have flooded toy stores, marketed by Ragdoll Productions and its U.S. licensing and merchandising partner, itsy bitsy Entertainment. This retailing push, aimed at least indirectly at kids who are crawling and toddling, has really lowered the bar on children's marketing, but some plainly see it as a profitable opportunity. "The one-to-two-year-old niche hasn't been filled very well," pointed out Carol Lowenstein, head of the product licensing company Character World. Teletubbies, she added enthusiastically, is the first brand "to come along for this age group on a very large scale, with not only the programming, but all the spin-off products and other marketing elements that will come out of that license."[179] What's next, one TV critic quipped, "The In Utero Channel?" Where do we draw the line when it comes to marketing to kids?

But just as troubling as this toddler assault is the fact that our own public broadcaster has to play this merchandising game in the first place. *Teletubbies* was brought to the United States by none other than the originally noncommercial Public Broadcasting System. But Norway considered the show so mercenary that it refused to air the series. The country's preschool programming head, Ada Haug, called it the most marketing-focused children's show that she had ever seen. And at an international children's television conference that I attended a few years ago in London, Alice Cahn, then the head of PBS's children's programming, was actually booed by other attendees for agreeing to pick up the show. But that didn't stop PBS, which felt it needed the merchandising-related windfall from *Teletubbies* in the face of persistent budget cuts from the U.S. Congress. As usual, money talks in media, and Congress essentially told PBS that it had better start selling.

Thirty years ago, public funds made up 70 percent of the budget for public broadcasting, as they should. By 1998, however,

Congress in its infinite wisdom had slashed that percentage down to 11 percent.[180] As a result, since 1990, PBS has had to turn to merchandising to help plug the gap, hawking products tied to characters on *Barney & Friends, Shining Time Station,* and *Lamb Chop's Play-Along.* But *Teletubbies* is a much bigger play than any of these other ventures. Even though the more than two hundred Barney products raked in $500 million in sales in 1993 alone, PBS only received a small fraction of those product licensing fees, most of which went to the producers and marketing companies. The *Teletubbies* deal is a much richer one for PBS, which gets a cut of merchandise and video sales as well as fees from licensing.[181] The big question we should all be asking is why our nation's only *public* broadcaster is forced to behave in the same mercenary manner as the commercial broadcast networks, which are owned by big conglomerates.

LITTLE KIDS IN THE CROSSHAIRS

It's pretty clear that the goal of this multinational, sophisticated marketing scheme is not to benefit young children—who shouldn't be watching a lot of TV anyway—but to sell products and enrich the network, manufacturers, and producers. Disturbingly, the target of this huge, manipulative campaign are kids like my then two-year-old daughter Carly. The aim was to encourage her attachment to the TV characters so that she'd ask for the licensed products. And of course, we permitted it—to a limited extent—because like most parents, we found it hard to resist our toddler's pleas and the pleasure she so clearly derived from her Po cup, a *Teletubbies* board book, and a stuffed Po doll that giggles when you push its stomach. Our baby daughter was already brand-aware, like millions of her peers in the one-to-five-year-old demographic segment. Michael Cohen, a psychologist and one of the nation's leading experts in kids' media, confesses that he's uncomfortable with this. "This is an area that has changed radically over the last decade," he says. "Ten years ago, two-to-five-year-olds did not have that intensity of affinity for licensed, branded characters. It's an emotional relationship with the character, whether it's Po or Winnie the Pooh. My concern is that if you use those beloved characters to sell things directly to children, it's unfair and manipulative. You shouldn't do it. That's really clear."

I'd go even further. To me, the idea of fostering the emotional attachment of little children in order to sell them things is not just manipulative, it's exploitative and morally unethical. But in the media business today, that's been the rule, not the exception, for nearly twenty years. Probably the worst chapter in the history of children's television was written during the 1980s' deregulation spree. As commented on earlier, the ending of broadcasting restrictions unleashed a wave of sexual content designed to grab viewer attention in the ramped-up race for ratings and advertising. What was even more scandalous is what happened to kids' television. Deregulation knocked down the barriers that separated sponsors of TV programs from producers. As a result, a huge crop of animated children's shows hit the air with the explicit purpose of hawking tie-in toys. Toy companies actually funded and helped develop the shows as direct advertising vehicles for their products. From *The Smurfs* and *Strawberry Shortcake* to *GI Joe*, the *Transformers*, *He-Man*, *GoBots*, and *ThunderCats*,[182] these "kiddiemercial" cartoons promoted toys and an endless range of tie-in products and "collectibles." The formula was so successful that it was copied by movie studios such as Disney, whose animated features became increasingly linked to elaborate and extensive merchandising campaigns. Once again, the targets of these powerful marketing campaigns were not sophisticated adults—who, one can presume, are able to tell when they are being exploited—but little kids under the age of eight.

Deregulation, in effect, "allowed the marketplace to determine the definition of children's programming," based on economics, not the public interest, contends Norma Odom Pecora, telecommunications professor at the University of Ohio.[183] She points to the Care Bears as a prime example of the scope and power of these market-driven shows. The Kenner toy company introduced the Care Bears toy line in 1983, with nine collectible characters including Birthday Bear, Friend Bear, Wise Bear, Tender-Heart Bear, and Good Luck Bear. At the same time, it produced and sponsored a Care Bears television special. Soon after, *The Care Bears* miniseries debuted, along with the Care Bear Cousins toy line—and *The Care Bears Movie*. From stuffed animals to backpacks and even kids' cough medicine, Care Bears products were pitched relentlessly to little kids using the huge, manipulative power of the media.[184]

"Children are in the crosshairs of advertising and marketing," says Gary Ruskin, the head of the consumer group Commercial Alert. Advertisers, he adds, "see children as economic resources to be exploited like timber and bauxite."[185] Make no mistake about it—there's nothing benign about techniques for marketing to kids. They're specifically designed to prey on children's natural weaknesses and vulnerabilities. As Nancy Shalek, the president of a Los Angeles ad agency, explained, "Advertising at its best is making people feel that without their product, you're a loser. Kids are very sensitive to that," she observes. "If you tell them to buy something, they are resistant. But if you tell them that they'll be a dork if they don't, you've got their attention. You open up emotional vulnerability, and it's very easy to do with kids because they're the most emotionally vulnerable."[186]

There is something so ethically objectionable about this predatory practice that sixty psychologists and psychiatrists sent a letter urging the American Psychological Association to discourage its members from providing their consulting services to advertisers. As one signer, psychology professor Timothy Kramer, explained, child marketers are not just selling Barbies and Nikes and jeans to vulnerable kids; they're selling "a set of messages that say to the child that what's important in life is buying things." In fact, he notes, the truth of the matter is just the opposite. Research shows that materialistic individuals suffer more depression, have poorer relationships, and use more drugs, alcohol, and tobacco than other people.[187]

CONSUMER CULTURE

It's true that commercialism has just about always been a part of children's media in this country. Back in the mid-1950s, for example, there was an early children's television show, *Winky Dink and You*, that encouraged kids to buy Winky Dink kits enabling them to color in cartoon characters on the TV screen and add other elements to the program's animation. Commercials during the show, delivered by host Jack Barry, pitched the kits directly to the kids. "Of course, you can watch the program without a kit," Barry admitted to his TV audience of children, "but you can't really be a part of the program without 'em. And you can't have the fun that the other boys and girls who have their Winky Dink kits do have," he said, before instructing them where to send their money for the kits. Other products in those days, from Mickey Mouse watches to Davy Crockett coonskin caps, sold millions thanks to their links to popular television shows and movies.[188] In the 1980s, however, the scale and scope of these tactics grew spectacularly when the FCC relaxed policies forbidding broadcasters to air shows that were too closely linked to merchandised products. "It used to be that toys were an outgrowth of a television show, but now it's all part of one gigantic marketing scheme," observed Kathryn Montgomery, who heads the Center for Media Education. Thanks to deregulation of the airwaves in the 1980s, Saturday morning television, in effect, became "nothing more than program-length toy advertisements."[189]

The *Mighty Morphin Power Rangers* is one of the most notorious examples of this genre. Produced by Saban Entertainment and aired on Fox Television, *Power Rangers* is a live-action show about a band of teenagers who turn into kicking, fighting superheroes battling evil forces from outer space. The show is linked to a fortune in licensed merchandise worldwide, including action figures, videos, CD-ROMs, and a feature movie, all funneling to the children's media empire of Haim Saban, who is profiled in chapter 7. However, the show is also selling violence along with commercial products. According to a number of early-childhood specialists, *Power Rangers* is the most violent television show ever created for young children, featuring an array of two hundred violent acts per hour. After watching a single episode, kids in one study committed seven times the number of aggressive acts as kids who did not watch the show. Canada deemed the program so violent that its broadcasters stopped airing it in the mid-1990s. Canadian kids, though, are still able to see the show on American television channels.

Margaret Loesch, a widely respected programmer who was then president of Fox Children's Network, tried to defend the program at the time of its initial airing. "We are trying to present fantasy," she said. "We drive home the point that this is not real, and we tell children not to play karate at home."[190] But despite her best intentions, my opinion is that the Saban-Fox machine was flexing a vast amount of marketing muscle to shake down kids, with very little sense of responsibility for the messages it was sending. It was the perfect exercise of the free market. The only problem, as psychologist Mike Cohen points out, is that the free-market model breaks down once you're dealing with kids, because they do not possess an adult level of maturity and judgment. "We're talking about kids," he says. "They need nurturing, they need to be cared for, and they need guidance." What they're getting, in the case of shows like *Power Rangers,* is a cheaply produced, often irresponsible show designed for the enrichment of its marketing partners. As usual, when the free market wins, kids lose. But in the world of media, some adults can and do get richly rewarded for their skill in manipulating children.

DEMOGRAPHIC DREAM

What's fueling this marketing mania and rising consumerism? The increase in the number of children in the audience—and in their disposable income. In 1998, four-to-twelve-year-olds were responsible for some $27 billion in discretionary spending—about four times the amount they spent a decade earlier.[191] Even more important, they directly or indirectly influenced some $500 billion in spending by their parents, up from $5 billion in the 1960s and

$50 billion in 1984.[192] Children, marketing guru James McNeal declares, are "consumers in training"; each year, some four million of these "rookie" shoppers enter America's marketplace for the first time, "freshly socialized into the consumer role by parents, with help from educators and business."[193] When marketers think about children, he advises, "they should think of KIDS—Keepers of Infinite Dollars"—whose income has been growing 10 to 20 percent a year, *much* faster than that of their parents.[194]

The media hasn't missed this lesson. Today, marketers spend $3 billion a year on advertising targeted to kids, some twenty times the amount they spent a decade ago.[195] And since the 1980s, when kids' product-linked TV programs began proliferating in the newly deregulated marketplace, shows have been segmented to targeted micro markets—from the one-to-two-year-old audience of *Teletubbies* and two-to-five-year-old fans of *Barney* to the six-to-eight-year-olds, nine-to-twelve-year-old "tweens," and teens.[196] I see this increasingly aggressive niche marketing every day as we evaluate properties at JP Kids. As media industries target younger and younger kids, small children all over the world, even preschoolers, are increasingly assaulted by commercial pitches. What's so disturbing about this, as McNeal himself admits, is that "kids are the most unsophisticated of all consumers; they have the least and therefore want the most. Consequently, they are in a perfect position to be taken."

That's especially true in the age of accelerating corporate mergers. As a result of vertical integration, a company such as Disney, as we've seen, owns not only its movie studios, theme parks, and cable TV channels like the Disney Channel, ABC Family, and ESPN, but also a consumer-products division as well as the broadcast network ABC. All of these interests combine to present potent cross-marketing opportunities, amplifying the marketing punch of Disney products. When a Disney movie opens, the company saturates the market with related merchandise, from key chains and sunglasses to backpacks and toys for McDonald's Happy Meals. Disney will even push its movies and merchandise in thinly disguised "documentaries" on ABC, which, according to Disney chairman and

CEO Michael Eisner in a recent shareholder letter, "provides a promotional platform for all of Disney." Its movie *The Lion King* earned over $1 billion in licensing revenues, and Eisner characterizes the company's consumer-products division as an "immense" business. All of this leads noted film critic Janet Maslin to ask, "Have the characters in a film's story been created for dramatically legitimate reasons, or are we merely watching a prospective action figure with a pulse?"[197] Certainly, Disney is not alone in the multimedia merchandising game. In 2000, retailers sold some $7.6 billion worth of toys and video games based on movie and television characters.[198] In 1997 Time Warner raked in over $6 billion in licensed merchandise.[199] George Lucas's *Star Wars* movies, of course, have also been worth a gold mine in licensed products. Thanks to a lucrative licensing deal with Hasbro Toys, Lucas had earned back the $115 million he spent on his film *The Phantom Menace* before the film ever opened in theaters. Most recently, *Harry Potter*—a terrific book series and, in my opinion, an excellent film—has been Hollywood's latest licensing cash cow. Indeed, Warner Brothers began planning its wave of licensed products related to the movie in January 2000, nearly two years before *Harry Potter and the Sorcerer's Stone* premiered in theaters in November 2001.[200]

The result for kids—and the parents whose spending they influence—is a tidal wave of media-linked merchandise that's virtually impossible to ignore and which is, in effect, commercializing many aspects of children's daily life, from eating (promotional toys at fast-food restaurants) to bedtime stories (tie-in books) and sleep (character-covered bed sheets and comforters). Never before, one critic wrote, have the stories that adults told kids been so shamelessly "stilted and unsupple, and ultimately self-serving." It's even affecting the quality of play. In one marketing study, five- and six-year-old children were at first only moderately interested in a line of prehistoric "stone people" toys—until they watched *The Flintstones* movie. All of a sudden, the kids gave the toys names and personalities, all scripted by Hollywood. They were engrossed, repeating scenes from the film and imitating the voices, dialogues, and interactions of the movie characters.[201] The most significant worry with this type of play is that kids are bypassing their own imaginations, substituting prepackaged, commercial characters and story lines for their own creative efforts. As one mother put it, "a generic doll can be a cowgirl one day and an underwater explorer the next, but Pocahontas will always be Pocohantas." Not only is the media the storyteller, but it's also supplanting and perhaps inhibiting the ability of children to tell stories of their own.[202]

Carole Stoller, a kindergarten teacher in Colorado, sees the effects of this intense commercialism in her classroom. "Twenty years ago, for show-and-tell," she noted, "children were bringing interesting things from home. Parents were a little more involved in picking it out. Maybe a piece of petrified wood that they'd picked up on a special trip, or pictures from travels. Show-and-tell sessions now," however, "are things they've seen on TV, action figures from the movies, stuff they get from McDonald's and Burger King." Even when they draw pictures, she adds, "intertwined with it will be advertised products, especially around Christmastime." If the child draws a picture of Goldilocks and the Three Bears, for example, chances are that they'll be sitting around playing Nintendo.[203]

There is, of course, another price that kids and parents pay for this wall-to-wall media consumer culture. It's the "gimme factor," and it's the principle that child marketers prize above all. "My girls see a toy they recognize from television and movies, and right away they're asking for it. If their friends have it, they want it even more," one mother complains. James McNeal has even quantified the influence of "little naggers." Children aged five to twelve, he reports, "make around fifteen requests in a typical visit to a shopping setting with parents, around five requests a day at home, and on a vacation approximately ten requests a day—in all, around three thousand product/service requests a year."[204] This "pester power" is much sought-after by marketers, whose conferences actually include such sessions as "The Fine Art of Nagging."[205] Indeed, toy company executives now speak of a category of low-priced "shut-up toys"—

inexpensive products that parents can buy to keep their kids from pestering them in stores.

Three-through-seven-year-olds, especially, tend to "want it all," according to youth-marketing expert Dan Acuff; they love to accumulate stuff—and thanks to the fact that their "critical/logical/rational mind is not yet fully developed," they're easy targets for consumer messages.[206] Evidently, many parents are also easy targets for the "gimmes"—especially in two-income families, sales experts point out, where Mom and Dad feel guilty about not spending a lot of time with their kids and lavish extra money and presents on them instead. As child-development expert T. Berry Brazelton puts it, "We are in a very permissive era today in parenting. Parents are so busy and away so much, that it's easy to give in to the 'I want' syndrome."[207] All of this adds up to a cultural environment that seems far too often to be all about "stuff." What we have today, Mike Cohen observes, are "generations of kids who are very materially oriented. They feel entitled to these things. Even more, they actually feel troubled and anxious if they don't have them. And they don't understand that 98 percent of the world doesn't live this way."

It's true: kids in this country are growing up so surrounded by consumer messages—hustling them to buy, own, and accumulate—that they're not even aware of the level of commercial noise. It's only when, and if, they experience its absence that it all sinks in. I remember when a seventeen-year-old girl I know came home after spending a summer volunteering in a little village in Costa Rica. She walked into her room and stared for an hour or so at the huge quantities of stuff that she had somehow managed to acquire—clothing, CDs, books, drawers full of random junk, old toys—things that she never used or looked at more than once a year, if that. She told me that she felt disgusted. For the first time, she understood that none of this stuff was necessary or even helpful for a happy life. She had lived richly for nearly two months without it, and her village friends would never have been able to conceive of having so many possessions—the majority of which, frankly, were pretty useless. Of course, within a few months, my young friend was back in full teenage consumer gear, accumulating as much as ever. It's a powerful drive that is taught, literally, in the cradle and reinforced every day and everywhere kids turn. It is perhaps my single biggest concern with my own children.

Material World

The commercializing effects of media culture have been dramatically demonstrated in remote regions where television, for example, has only recently been introduced. In a fascinating account, Todd Lewan of the Associated Press documented the transformation of the Gwich'in Indian tribe in Arctic Village, Alaska, after a tribal council member brought the tribe's first TV—a black-and-white Zenith—into the village in 1980. Within fours years, the village had video games, a satellite dish, and a VCR. Since then, the tribe has abandoned much of its ancestral culture, based on hunting caribou, in favor of instant coffee, bubblegum, Nike sneakers, M&M's, microwave ovens, and Bart Simpson.

"The TV teaches greed," observed Sarah James, a Gwich'in artist. "It shows our people a world that is not ours. It makes us wish we were something else." One family's home, Lewan reported—a 480-square-foot plywood A-frame—was equipped with three television sets, two VCRs, and a Sony PlayStation. The parents put a television in their son's room so he could watch his TV shows while he played video games. Now, they said, the boy has a regular routine when he comes home from school—he eats, plays Nintendo for a couple hours, watches TV, then watches a video movie and goes to bed. It's been difficult for native stories and traditions to compete with a medium so seductive and powerful that, as one forty-three-year-old Gwich'in recalled, "I wanted to watch it and watch it and watch it . . . When I went out in the country to hunt," he acknowledged, "all I could hear was the TV in my head."[208]

ON-LINE AND OUT OF CONTROL

As media has rushed onto the Internet frontier, so have the hordes of children's marketers. In 1996 the Center for Media Education released a groundbreaking study, "Web of Deception," which highlighted the growing use of Web sites to capture the loyalty and spending power of the "lucrative cyberkid category." The study revealed two disturbing trends: the invasion of children's privacy through the solicitation of personal information and the tracking of on-line computer use; and the exploitation of vulnerable youngsters through new, deceptive forms of advertising. By offering kids free T-shirts and other gifts if they filled out on-line surveys about themselves, marketers hoped to accrue enough personal information to "microtarget" individual children. Moreover, by using popular product "spokescharacters," such as Tony the Tiger, in interactive games and other advertising tools, companies were blurring the line between advertising and play. The Internet "is a mechanism for advertisers that is unprecedented," noted the director of Saatchi and Saatchi Interactive. "There's probably no other product or service . . . that is like it in terms of capturing kids' interest."[209]

Targeting children as young as four, on-line advertisers were grabbing kids' attention and getting them to disclose a range of personal information. An FCC survey of 212 Web sites found that 96 percent asked for children's e-mail addresses, 74 percent asked their name, 49 percent requested their mailing address, 46 percent solicited their age and birth date, and others collected information on their gender, phone number, and interests. Such disclosures were often required when a child wanted to enter a contest, join in chat, play an interactive game, or even gain access to a Web site. But kids don't understand the privacy implications of these disclosures, and they're easy victims for these marketing techniques.

On the *Batman Forever* Web site, for example, kids as "good citizens of the Web," were urged to "help Commissioner Gordon" with the "Gotham Census"—in reality a survey that pinpointed kids' buying habits and video preferences.[210] Other sites have used sophisticated tracking technology that records kids' on-line activities. After children register at many of these sites, they begin to receive unsolicited marketing e-mail messages, promoting product contests and other purchasing incentives.[211] These deceptive and intrusive sales pitches are like the junk e-mails that adults receive, except that they specifically target vulnerable children. As Marc Rothenberg, director of the Electronic Privacy Information Center, explained, "Instead of doing a commercial that's roughly targeted at boys five to seven, which is a lot of the advertising on Saturday morning TV, now you're targeting a particular boy, who has a particular interest in a particular program . . . whose parents have a certain income. . . . We've never really existed before in an information environment where the TV could reach out to your child and say, 'Bob, wouldn't you like to have this new action figure, just like in the movie you saw last week?' "

As a result of these marketing abuses, Congress passed the Children's Online Privacy Protection Act (COPPA) in 1998, and its restrictions went into effect in April 2000. COPPA requires sites that gather personal information from kids to have a clear link to a privacy policy, revealing what information they collect and how they use that data. Parents have the right to review their child's personal information and to ask that no further data be collected from their child. COPPA was a good start, but truthfully, I'm critical of certain aspects of the legislation. The government jumped into the dot-com arena without fully understanding the implications of what it was legislating. Strict compliance, as it turns out, can be very expensive and burdensome, and COPPA was one of the factors that led to the disappearance of virtually all of the positive and educational kids' Web sites.

Still, Congress's concerns were real, and there's been little change in the percentage of kids' sites that solicit this type of data—85.6 percent in 2001 compared to 89 percent in 1998.[212] Typical, in some respects, is CapnCrunch.com, a site whose motto, perhaps fittingly, is "online and out of control." Kids have to register to use the site, supplying data on their state, gender, age group (including the age category "5, 6, 7"), and favorite Cap'n Crunch flavor. They're invited to share the e-mail addresses of friends by sending them electronic greeting cards and their scores in on-line games. Clicking on an icon produces a questionnaire that asks kids to name their favorite song on the radio and favorite movie star and reveal what they do when they get home from school. All of this is useful marketing information for consumer products companies.

On some sites, such as KidsCom, which explicitly gathers consumer data from children, parents now have to agree in writing before their kids can participate in surveys that "help other companies learn about kids." Although Circle 1 Network, the owner of KidsCom, has the stated mission of giving "kids a voice in the world and to each other through a variety of engaging activity," that voice may be of most interest to its corporate clients. It's clear that even though COPPA has imposed some restraints on on-line marketers, they still see the Internet as a new way to extract information from kids and develop their loyalty to consumer brands and characters. As long as there's a way to make money from children, overly commercialized Web sites will make the most of it, even while staying technically within the legal boundaries. Childhood media experts and advocates need to pay a lot more attention to on-line marketing to kids as well as the COPPA regulations themselves. We need to help this new medium live up to its extraordinary potential for enriching children's lives, instead of allowing it to be another tool to commercially exploit them.

COMMERCIAL CARPET BOMBING

No wonder that, in our culture, where kids are so steeped in commercial media, a teenager in San Francisco admitted that she can't imagine a world without marketing and advertising. "I've grown up," she said, "surrounded by television and radio commercials and billboards. I know that 'Where's the beef?' is a slogan that belongs to Wendy's and that 'I love what you do for me' belongs to Toyota. *Sesame Street*," she adds, "was even brought to me by the letter K."[213]

Teens also know that, to a great extent, their self-images and expectations are molded by the commercial media. "They set the images that we have to live up to," said one eighteen-year-old, "whether it's a physical image or lifestyle—being beautiful or having a gorgeous home and perfect kids. Magazines talk about the perfect diet plan and show pictures of people with perfect legs and stomachs, and at the same time run articles about how girls should be comfortable with the way they look. You can recognize how the media's selling to you," she said, "but you still buy into it." The messages can be overwhelming, confounding, and at least for some teens, disillusioning. "For really the first time in a decade or so, from my experience," says University of Illinois communications professor Robert McChesney, "we've seen young people, not just college students, having a real concern that their entire culture is this commercial laboratory."[214]

Tweens and teens, in particular, are targets of the media's marketing juggernaut. Known as Generation Y, they command a hefty slice of discretionary spending, about $140 billion a year,[215] and they're rich prey for consumer marketers. The number of teens will grow 7 percent by 2010 to a record 33.9 million,[2162] and, as parents of teenagers know, they're avid consumers. According to the International Council of Shopping Centers, teens go to malls fifty-four times a year and spend an hour and a half there every time—compared to all shoppers, who go to malls thirty-nine times a year and spend only seventy-five minutes there each visit.[217]

With no worries about rent, mortgages, and health insurance and plenty of spending money from allowances and part-time jobs, teens are great accumulators, and their shifting likes and dislikes are studied in detail by clothing and footwear manufacturers; health, beauty, cosmetic, and fragrance companies; movie studios, music companies, ad agencies; and the sports and electronics industries.[218] Today, MTV's programming president, Brian Graden, declares, "you have the most marketed group of teens and young adults ever in the history of the world."[219] The whole point of marketers' relationship with teens, McChesney reminds us, "is to turn them upside down and shake all the money out of their pockets."[220]

Teenagers have been a prime commercial target since the years after World War II, when consumer-goods companies began recognizing the buying power of this growing demographic group, flush with their allowances and part-time jobs. By 1956, there were 13 million teens in the United States, and their spending, by the end of the decade, had reached $10 billion.[221] As *Life* magazine commented in 1959, "What Depression-bred parents may still think of as luxuries are looked on as necessities by their offspring."[222] Teen magazines, thriving on this advertising market, flourished in the fifties, selling Clearasil, soft drinks, and snacks. A teenage girl, promised *Seventeen* magazine, "won't take no for an answer when she sees what she wants in *Seventeen*."[223] Today, there are some 30 million teenagers, the most since their parents' baby boom generation shattered the demographic records. And, more than ever, they are hotly pursued and closely studied by marketers seeking to spot teen trends and turn them into profits. There's even a name for teen-trend scouts hired by corporations. They're called "cool hunters," and they prowl teenage social networks—from ravers and skaters to hip-hoppers and goths—in search of adolescents who start and spread new trends.

"Cool is valuable to marketers," notes *The New Yorker* writer Malcolm Gladwell, and to uncover it, cool hunters cultivate a network of thousands of kids. In the case of the cool-hunting consulting firm Look-Look, five hundred of those teens are corporate correspondents, equipped with laptops and digital cameras, who, like foreign correspondents, file regular dispatches from the exotic landscape of youth culture.[224] In fact, teens are to many companies "like Africa" in the nineteenth century, McChesney says. "They look at the teen market as part of this massive empire that they're colonizing." To put it bluntly, he states, "it's all about commercial-izing the whole teen experience, making youth culture a commercial entity that's packaged and sold to people. . . . And it has worked."

Media producers, too, have turned the spotlight on the lucrative teen market, tailoring TV shows, movies, and music to the taste of thirteen-to-nineteen-year-olds. It's a marketing target they redis-covered in the mid-1990s, when Kevin Williamson wrote the teen slasher movie *Scream,* which grossed $103 million. *Scream* spawned a slew of profitable copycat flicks, including *Urban Legend* and *I Know What You Did Last Summer,* as well as many in other genres aimed at adolescent dollars, including *Cruel Intentions, Road Trip, American Pie,* and *American Pie 2.* Meanwhile, TV jumped on the teenage bandwagon, with series such as *Party of Five, Dawson's Creek, Felicity, Popular,* and *Roswell.*[225] Advertisers climbed on too—Procter & Gamble, in fact, was a coproducer of the television shows *Clueless, Sabrina, the Teenage Witch,* and *Real TV*[226]—while the music industry catered to the teen craze with the Spice Girls, Hanson, the Backstreet Boys, and Britney Spears. MTV, especially, retooled its marketing research to hit a bull's-eye with its demo-graphic group of sixteen-to-twenty-eight-year-olds. People in that age group, notes author John Seabrook, "haven't quite made up their minds yet about which brands they are going to spend the rest of their lives buying. And there's a certain amount of research which suggests that, if you get a young person at that age when their minds are still unformed commercially, you can brand them, as it were, and then have their allegiance for the rest of their consuming life-times."[227]

Hit with a ratings slump around 1997, the music video network immersed itself in market research—not just your standard surveys and focus groups, but detailed, anthropological, ethnographic stud-ies of its youth audience, a third of which is under the age of eigh-teen.[228] As teen marketing executive Rob Stone explained, "If you don't understand and recognize what they're thinking, what they're feeling, and then be able to take that and come up with a really pre-cise message that you're trying to reach these kids with in their teens, you're going to lose. You're absolutely going to lose."[229] To cultivate that valuable relationship with young viewers, marketers at MTV go to extraordinary lengths. Researchers "rifle through their closets. We go through their music collections. We go to nightclubs with them," explains the network's strategy and planning senior vice president Todd Cunningham. "We shut the door in their bedrooms and talk to them about issues that they feel are really important to them. We talk with them about what it's like to date today; what it's like dealing with their parents; what things stress them out the most. . . . We have them show us their favorite clothing outfits, what they wear to parties, some things from their photo albums and things that really mean something to them."[230]

What do they do with all of this intimate personal information? It's captured on video, edited, set to music, and presented to senior corporate executives. The purpose, Cunningham says, is to get MTV "in the hearts and minds of the viewers."[231] But more truthfully speaking, the purpose is to get into their wallets and pockets. The name of one of these MTV studies, "Sources of Gold," speaks volumes about the network's real objective. The definition of MTV's bond with teens, Cunningham reflects, is "a great brand relationship." The goal is to get teens to see the network and its products as "my brand," an emotional "extension of themselves."[232]

READING, WRITING, AND RETAILING

The reach of child marketers is extending into every possible "habitat," including the formerly commercial-free environment of the schoolyard. According to a September 2000 report by the U.S. General Accounting Office, companies are exploiting schools as a marketing arena more blatantly and extensively than ever. By targeting the 55 million American kids under age eighteen[233] in the captive environment of schools, they can get more bang for their advertising buck. Outside of schools, teens are exposed to three thousand ads every day. "It's hard for a company to cut through the clutter with its message," says Kathleen Williamson, marketing professor at the University of Houston–Clear Lake. But in the school setting, she explains, where there are relatively few marketing messages competing for the youngsters' attention, consumer messages can be much more potent and effective.[234]

The prize for many marketers is worth the effort. Teens spend some $90 billion on food and drink a year[235] and considerably more on footwear and clothes.[236] As a result, as schools have tried to cope with shrinking budgets, companies have jumped at opportunities to exchange equipment and cash for commercial promotions. More and more children are seeing their schools turned into massive ads and billboards for snacks, soft drinks, and consumer products. The roof of one school in Texas was painted with the Dr Pepper logo, and around the country, yellow school buses are plastered with ads for Burger King, Wendy's, Kmart, Old Navy, Speedo bathing suits, and 7Up. Computer mousepads, daily planners, gym banners, scoreboards, classrooms, and hallways are all coveted advertising space.

Hungry for cash, some schools even serve as sales forces for their commercial sponsors. In Colorado Springs, for example, School District 11 helped solve the problem of underfunding by turning its schools into marketing tools for more than three dozen corporate partners. The district's deal with Coke was especially enticing, promising it $8.4 million over ten years, provided the district met a commitment to sell seventy thousand cases of Coke products annually.[237] To help meet the target, its contract administrator sent a letter to district principals urging them to do their best to push Coke sales. "If 35,493 staff and students," he wrote, "bought one Coke product every other day for a school year (176 days), we would double (130,141) the required quota needed." When a school official aggressively sells "liquid candy" to students—who are increasingly at risk for a variety of obesity-related problems—something is seriously out of whack. As John Hawk, a Colorado Springs social studies teacher commented, "Students and teachers need basic training on how to deal with the corporate invasion of every aspect of life.

Schools used to be the one safe haven where kids weren't exposed to a constant barrage of advertising. Now even that's gone."[238]

The media, of course, is part of this onslaught on schools. Publisher McGraw-Hill and more than a dozen other publishers attracted widespread criticism in 1999 for textbooks that were filled with images of consumer products and references to brands including Nike shoes, Oreo cookies, Cocoa Frosted Flakes, Barbie dolls, and Sony PlayStation. Although publishers stated that they received no payment for the product mentions[239]—claiming that they were only trying to make the textbooks "meaningful" to students[240]— they gratuitously promoted commercialization in the schools.[241]

Perhaps the biggest media lightning rod in this debate has been Channel One, a company founded in 1989 to bring kid-friendly newscasts into the schools. It's actually an effort that, on balance, I support. Channel One wires schools with satellite dishes, classroom television sets, and VCRs and delivers a daily ten-minute broadcast, along with two minutes of commercials by sponsors such as Mars candy, Clearasil, Polaroid, Gatorade, Pepsi, and McDonald's. The ads have attracted a flood of criticism from consumer groups, but a former executive vice president of Channel One—now owned by Primedia—compared the company's business model to that of newspapers and commercial television. "To provide this international coverage, we are advertising-based," he said, "just like the *Houston Chronicle* or any other news service."

I personally think that Channel One is worth it. Most kids don't read the newspaper or watch television news, and Channel One gives them consistently high-quality information about the issues in the world around them. The company's reporting on the AIDS virus, for example, earned Channel One a Peabody Award. I'm certainly no defender of commercialism in the schools, and I wish that Channel One did not have to resort to advertisements to fund its efforts. But the fact is that our public schools are so desperately underfunded that they cannot pay for quality, informative current events programming. That to me is a far bigger threat to schools and our kids' education than a couple of minutes of ads that they know to expect on Channel One.

Less tolerable, however, is the use of media in schools to conduct subtle "stealth" marketing to kids. One company that was harshly criticized for this practice was ZapMe! Corporation of San Ramon, California. ZapMe! offered to wire every participating school with a $90,000 computer lab, each containing fifteen Compaq PCs, a laser printer, and roof-mounted satellite Internet connections, plus installation, training, and support. In exchange, schools promised ZapMe! that the computers would be used at least four hours a day, and students using the equipment would see commercial ads floating on the bottom-left-hand corner of the company's computer screens. ZapMe! also collected user profiles of the students, including their ages, genders, and ZIP codes, enabling sponsors to "document up-to-the-minute data on the efficiency and effectiveness" of their ads.[242] According to the ZapMe! contracts, the company intended "to monitor the network and compile statistics and demographics with regard to the habits, viewing preferences, and other nonpersonal information about the network's users."[243] By December 2000, ZapMe! had wired 2,300 schools in forty-five states, with some 2 million students in its user network. But it had also run into a major backlash from those concerned about commercial inroads into the schools. ZapMe!'s on-line ads alarmed critics and consumer activists. Ralph Nader called ZapMe! a "corporate predator," declaring that schools do not exist to conduct surveillance on behalf of the corporate marketers of the world."[244] The criticism took a toll. Although ZapMe! went public in October 1999,[245] it was essentially out of business a year and a half later as a result of poor publicity, financial losses, and declining stock price.[246]

The lesson of ZapMe! is that we can stop the marketers at the gates and influence the targeting of consumer messages to kids—provided that we recognize the powerful commercial manipulations of the media. We don't have to take it. In countries such as Sweden, Norway, Greece, and Ireland, for example, there are strict rules governing television advertising to children. In this country, as we will see, all the political clout has been on the side of advertisers.

Some twenty years ago, when the Federal Trade Commssion's staff wanted to ban advertising to kids, Congress barred the agency from issuing those regulations and rescinded much of the FTC's authority. But advertisers can be sensitive to public pressure. The power of parents and other advocates for children lies in understanding advertisers' marketing agenda when it comes to kids and letting them know, loudly, when we've had enough.

Six

THE POLITICS OF MEDIA AND KIDS

"We neglect discussion of moral responsibility by converting the public interest into an economic abstraction, and we use the First Amendment to stop debate rather than to enhance it, thus reducing our first freedom to the logical equivalent of a suicide pact."[247]

—*Newton Minow, former chairman of the Federal Communications Commission*

If you stop and think for a moment about the extraordinary influence that the media has on people's lives—most of all on the lives of children—it is obvious that this influence is a matter of great public interest and concern. And as we've seen, how media intersects with violence, sexuality, commercialism, and basic values is an issue that affects every person and every family's life in our society—an issue that literally cries out for governmental leadership and responsible policies. This is the kind of issue that government has played a role in shaping since the founding of our country, generally exerting a moderating, regulatory influence on behalf of broader public interests.

Yet when you look at government's role vis-à-vis the media, particularly in the last fifteen to twenty years, you see an almost complete abdication of leadership, a near total absence of any real responsibility for the public interest. You also see politicians supporting the needs of private media concerns over those of the broader public, whom they were purportedly elected to represent. It's the classic old fairy-tale scenario; the fox is guarding the chicken coop. In this updated version, the government officials who are supposed to be protecting the public's interest have, for all intents and purposes, been deep in the pockets of the large media and telecommunications companies they are supposed to be regulating.

The bottom line for kids is pretty simple and pretty sad. Our political leaders have largely abandoned the youngest and most needy Americans because of the overwhelming lure of money and media influence. The big losers in this equation are America's families. So how did it come to be this way and what can we do to change it?

Before we explore the current status of politics and the media in these first years of the twenty-first century, it's important to know how our national media policies originated. It was in the 1930s, when radio broadcasting first emerged and began to reach large numbers of Americans, that the government took on a more important role in shaping the media's influence on our society. The first major law designed to govern broadcasting was the Communications Act of 1934, written when Franklin Roosevelt was president. This critical law set up a system to give broadcasters the free and exclusive use of various broadcast channels. However, there was one major provision attached to this free gift of publicly owned property. The landmark 1934 law explicitly required that broadcasters serve the "public interest, convenience, and necessity." This very same legislation also established the Federal Communications Commission (the FCC) to oversee these new communications and broadcast channels and develop policies to govern their proper usage. Along with Congress and the president, the FCC is responsible for representing the public's interest in most key media issues.

THE INSIDE STORY ON THE FCC

The Federal Communications Commission is perhaps the most powerful yet least-known government agency in our entire nation. This low-profile regulatory body shapes the country's approach to all major forms of media and telecommunications policy and wields enormous power on a host of issues that affect our daily lives. Among its numerous responsibilities, the FCC has the power to

- grant (and take away) broadcast licenses from television and radio stations

- regulate any political speech in the U.S. involving the media

- ensure a diversity of media viewpoints

- approve mergers like that of AOL–Time Warner and Viacom-CBS, which now dominate our media's economic structure

- regulate the cable television industry

- ensure good service and reasonable rates for all cable subscribers nationwide

- regulate all wire communications, such as telephones, so as to ensure that consumers have rapid and efficient service at reasonable rates

- manage all domestic regulations of wireless devices, such as cellular phones, pagers, beepers, and two-way radios

- define and regulate "indecency"

- control the amount of advertising on various media outlets

- regulate much of the development of the Internet

- and finally, as we will see, to develop rules and regulations to promote quality media for children and families in the United States

In short, the FCC is perhaps the one government body that most affects the everyday life of all Americans. Why? Because ours is a communication-driven society, and we consume enormous amounts of media. Most of us use telephones, television, radio, and the Internet. As the primary policy-making body overseeing all of these areas, the FCC is the one government agency that has a dramatic effect on what we can see and hear on a daily basis. So, you might be asking yourself, why do we know so little about the FCC, and what is the structure of this very powerful agency?

While the FCC technically reports to Congress, which authorized its existence in the Communications Act of 1934, the current president and his political party by and large control it, making it a very political body. There are only five FCC commissioners, and these are five powerful although fairly anonymous people. Typically two are Democrat; two are Republican; and the fifth and most important is the chairman, who is appointed by the current president. The structure of the commission makes the chairman the key power player in all these crucial government actions. The chairman is the chief executive officer of the agency and has a direct reporting relationship with the staff of the FCC, consisting of a couple of thousand people. The other four commissioners have very small staffs, so generally it is the chairman who dominates and puts major issues and decisions to the other commissioners for an up-or-down vote. Thus, for your and my purposes, it is the chairman of the FCC, appointed by the current president, who wields the greatest clout in this incredibly powerful but little known agency (and to whom you ought to address your phone calls, e-mails, and letters when you finish reading this book and see what the FCC is currently doing—or not doing—on your behalf).

Every day, the FCC commissioners make hugely important judgments that affect our daily lives. They are supposed to be acting as our public representatives, and they are supposed to be protecting the public interest against the monopoly powers of the media giants. But they do very little to fulfill this mandate—a problem rooted in the origins of the FCC in 1934 and the nature of our current political system.

The most knowledgeable person I know about the history and actual workings of government and the media industry is a remarkable gentleman and lawyer from Chicago named Newton Minow. Minow is a true American hero—successful lawyer, successful businessman, respected civic leader, and, most notably for the purpose of this book, the chairman of the FCC under President John F. Kennedy. He not only chaired the FCC for two years in the 1960s, but he also coined the famous phrase "vast wasteland" when referring to television in a famous speech to broadcast executives in 1961. That phrase, "vast wasteland," became our first enduring sound bite about the modern age of television, and unfortunately it remains far too accurate a description of the medium today.

Since stepping down as FCC chairman, Minow has remained an important figure and lawyer in media and government circles, serving on the boards of several major media companies such as CBS and the Tribune Company and continuing to emphasize the media's public-interest responsibilities. Today, he is nearly seventy-five years old, a compactly built, white-haired grandfather and a commanding presence. He is perhaps most proud of his three daughters and three wonderful grandkids, and he still sees media as a huge influence in the lives of every American child. Newt was a great friend and adviser to me when I was running Children Now, and he continues as an adviser and inspiration to JP Kids. He is also the author of an excellent book on kids and television, *Abandoned in the Wasteland,* which was published in 1995 and gives a thorough history of the U.S. government's role in media.

As he frequently points out, the Communications Act of 1934 caused problems that continue to this day. Nobody in Congress ever defined what the phrase "public interest" was supposed to mean in 1934, and it remains vague even now, some seventy years later. The term "public interest" had previously been used in regulating the American railroad industry and telephone services—businesses that, like media, had a huge impact on the public. But these companies, which, like broadcasters, had been given public assets for free, were defined as public utilities and thus subject to extensive rate and public-service regulation. Unfortunately, the 1934 Communications Act did not hold broadcasters to be public utilities, so the media industry got the best of all possible bargains. They received all the benefits of a public utility monopoly, but none of the specific rate or public-service obligations. What a deal! The broadcasters got the exclusive, free use of the publicly owned airwaves without any specific, clear definition of their public-interest responsibilities. As Newt Minow says, the media "had the quid . . . without the quo." And so it remains today.

From the point of view of American children and families, the 1934 Communications Act and its almost seventy-year life span have been a disaster. Because Congress never defined "public interest" or imposed specific requirements, broadcasters and other media entities have gotten a largely free ride, at your and my and every American taxpayer's expense. In the absence of such specific requirements, Congress, the courts, and the FCC have struggled to define the media's public-interest responsibilities. And, as we will see, it's been largely a free-market free-for-all for much of the past twenty years. Why? Because politicians, who are supposed to regulate the media on behalf of you and me and the kids of America, have basically been in the hip pockets of the industry that they are specifically empowered to monitor and regulate.

Since the early 1920s, media companies have, in fact, believed that the term "public interest" can best be defined in the language of dollars and cents. However, until the past two or three decades, that market-driven attitude (some might call it a "greed is good" philosophy) was balanced against a different view, held by government leaders and citizens groups, that "public interest" involved meaningful social responsibilities. Since our government gave the publicly owned radio and television airwaves to broadcasters for free, the public interest actually requires media companies to make a variety of pro-social efforts and to consider the needs of their audience and the broader society as much as their own profit margins. This kind of public-interest reasoning is especially important where children are concerned.

As we all know, children don't have the same set of skills and level of judgment as adults, certainly not until they reach their mid-teens at the earliest. But America has largely abandoned the interests of our kids and families when it comes to policies and regulations affecting media. Instead, it has left the media to the largely selfish interests of the marketplace and the service of corporate priorities. And, left to the mandates of quarterly profits and the marketplace alone, children and families will receive very bad service or none at all. That's been the story behind kids, media, and politics in the United States for nearly seventy years.

No other Western industrialized nation has so willingly allowed the educational and developmental needs of its kids to be exploited in the pursuit of profit as we have. No other democratic country has so willingly allowed its children to be seen as "markets for commercial gain" and ignored their moral, intellectual, and social growth as we have. How and why could we have been so shortsighted and motivated by greed over other values? Once again, it's instructive to look back at the history of media and politics in this country to see how we got here in the first place.

WE USED TO DO BETTER

Media companies, and their broadcast divisions in particular, used to acknowledge that their exclusive and free use of the public airwaves (remember, it is *publicly owned* property) gave them unique access to America's children and youth. And with that unique and free access to our kids' intellectual, moral, and social development came a clear set of moral and social responsibilities and obligations. Both politicians and media leaders understood and honored this concept. During the twenty or so years following World War II, the TV set was actually seen as a positive agent of family unity.[248] Television was viewed as a wonderful new way to bring families together, and the programming and promotion of this medium followed suit. Large manufacturers like RCA promoted this family-friendly theme throughout the 1950s, as they sought to make this new mass medium an essential consumer appliance.[249]

During the 1950s, programmers offered a range of quality kids' offerings. At a time when Dr. Spock and *Reader's Digest* were offering parents regular advice on child-rearing practices, media companies made programs such as *Captain Kangaroo, Howdy Doody, Lucky Pup,* and *Kukla, Fran and Ollie* into longstanding children's classics. In 1951, for example, the broadcast networks' weekly schedules included twenty-seven hours of such family-friendly fare, most of which were broadcast after school and in the early evening. In addition, local stations developed their own kids' programs, many of them encouraging art, drawing, puppeting, or other positive activities for kids. Even such unabashedly commercial programs as the Walt Disney Company's *Mickey Mouse Club* and *Disneyland*—which were clearly designed to promote the theme park and various Disney merchandise—had a wealth of pro-social themes and won an Emmy Award as well as a Peabody Award for educational value.[250] During this time, America recognized that the media's influence on children, especially the impact of television, was something that needed leadership from politicians and media companies alike.

Industry Used to Take the Lead

The National Association of Broadcasters (NAB) is the principal lobbying and policy group representing the needs of television and radio broadcasters. I have seen their influence and power since my early days as a child advocate at Children Now. In fact, I have worked with the NAB staff and its president, Eddie Fritts, on several occasions over the years. They are as cordial and smooth as most Washington lobbyists. Make no mistake about their mission, however. Their sole purpose is to promote the needs and interests of broadcasters, which almost always means their financial needs. And the NAB is very effective indeed, often at the direct expense of kids and families.

Back in 1952, however, the NAB recognized the nascent concerns about the impact of television on America's children and families and issued a standards and practices code. This code would remain largely intact for nearly thirty years, up until the disastrous deregulation era of the 1980s. More important, this early NAB code included an entire section on children's programming. The words of the code seem ironic in this day and age, particularly coming from the industry's leading lobby group:

> Television and all who participate in it are jointly accountable to the American public for respect for the special needs of children, for community responsibility, for the advancement of education and culture, for the acceptability of the program materials chosen, for decency and decorum in production, and for propriety in advertising. This responsibility . . . can be discharged only through the highest standards of respect for the American home, applied to every moment of every program presented by television.[251]

Once American industry succeeded in putting television sets into the majority of American homes, however, broadcasters began to lessen their special programming efforts directed at kids and instead focused on creating programs that would sell products for advertisers. As a result, the late afternoon and early evening hours (4:00 P.M. to 7:00 P.M.) on television no longer featured as many quality kids programs. Instead, local broadcasters featured reruns of cop shows or sitcoms and frequently dumped higher quality but more expensive children's shows for cheaper, low-quality cartoons. The race to the world as we know it today was on.

The 1960s and 1970s may not have seen such an emphasis on quality kids and family media as the 1950s did, but throughout this period, there were a number of positive public-interest developments for media in general and for the kids and family audience in particular.[252] The 1970s, for example, saw the rise of numerous public challenges to television licensees, as increasing numbers of citizen viewers became disaffected with media practices and programs. The FCC intervened in a number of cases, and by the mid-1970s, this critically important regulatory body actually published standards governing negotiations between citizen groups and broadcasters.[253] Public advocacy organizations recognized that their views were part of the public-interest standards to be applied to various media entities, and up through the 1970s their voices were clearly heard and acted upon by government and industry officials alike.

THE MEDIA INDUSTRY CRIES CENSOR

Supreme Court Justice Potter Stewart once observed that we confuse the right to do something with whether it is the right thing to do.[254] When it comes to children and the media industry, Justice Stewart could not have been more right.

There is nothing that makes me angrier about the way that the media industry and many of their political allies respond to issues concerning kids and quality media than their persistent and intentional mischaracterization of the First Amendment. As a longtime advocate of civil rights and civil liberties, I am sick of the bogus cries of "censorship, censorship" from the media world. Moreover, I am offended by the repeated efforts to use our legitimate constitutional guarantees of free speech and press as an excuse to exploit children rather than as a means for serving and protecting them.

In fact, the First Amendment is for liberal media executives what the Second Amendment is for right-wing conservatives and the National Rifle Association. In each case, they have twisted a vague constitutional provision—in the case of the Second Amendment, the phrase referring to a "militia's right to bear arms"—dressed it in misleading garb, and told the public and political leaders, "you have no right to regulate us."

Time and again, media leaders defend their profit-driven motives and actions by falsely hiding behind their First Amendment rights. Practically without exception, anybody who gets up and questions television, radio, or Internet content is shouted down as a censor. Rather than seriously examining how to improve the quality of television or Internet or radio content for kids, our leaders argue to a meaningless stalemate about broadcasters' rights and government censorship. I am amazed at the way even the most progressive media industry thinkers as well as their political allies blatantly misuse the First Amendment as it pertains to kids. I wholeheartedly support the First Amendment and its guarantees of freedom of speech, press, and religious conviction. I teach courses on civil liberties to hundreds of students at Stanford University each year, and I always remind them to cherish and protect this first freedom of ours. The First Amendment is romantic. It is aspirational. Its guarantees suggest a world in which people can speak freely and equally to one another and to society at large. It is without doubt the basis of much of the freedom we enjoy in our great democracy.

But the First Amendment is not absolute. And it is simply not (and never has been) true that any and all regulations to improve media for kids and to limit specific types of content in certain situations are unconstitutional under the First Amendment. The blanket censorship argument so frequently trotted out by spokespeople for large media interests—that any efforts to promote positive media for kids or to limit their exposure to harmful messages equals government censorship—is a cruel and dishonest joke. Let's take a closer look at the constitutional facts.

Any reasonable analysis of the historical and legal treatment applied to children's issues in American constitutional jurisprudence makes clear that we view children and youth differently from adults in our society. Dozens of Supreme Court cases make it abundantly clear that children have a special status under our Constitution and that they accordingly receive special protections and societal care. In the context of the First Amendment, whether we are talking about school newspapers or access to dial-a-porn services, kids are treated differently. American courts have repeatedly held, for example, that the government can require certain magazines on open newsstands to be sold in brown paper wrappers. The government can zone certain kinds of stores away from residential neighborhoods. The government can forbid radio and television shows from broadcasting indecent material until after 10:00 P.M., when most kids are or ought to be in bed. None of these government actions are inconsistent with the First Amendment. And reasonable steps to use the airwaves in a specific, concrete way to provide public-interest programs for kids are also permitted by the First Amendment. Put simply, children are legally a special class of people, and they are entitled to special protections under the U.S. Constitution.

There are two main ways in which government can act as a positive regulatory force. The *first* method I'll call *enhancement of media speech*. Enhancement regulation has been repeatedly upheld by our nation's courts under the First Amendment, because they recognize that the scarcity of certain publicly owned assets (such as broadcast licenses) allows government to require certain types of media behavior on behalf of the public interest. Into this category fall such examples as the 1990 Children's Television Act and the constitutionally sound but now politically defunct Fairness Doctrine, which long guaranteed equal time for opposing political viewpoints. This concept, formally introduced into FCC regulations in 1949, goes to the heart of the notion that the nation's airwaves are public property and can thus be regulated by our government in the public interest. The Fairness Doctrine was actually pretty simple and logical. In essence, it required that broadcasters (a) offer reasonable time (i.e., use of the public airwaves) for the discussion of important public issues, and (b) present both sides of an issue fairly and provide airtime for opposing points of view. After the Fairness Doctrine was written into law by the FCC in 1949, it was upheld by Congress in 1959 and ultimately upheld by the U.S. Supreme Court in 1969, in the celebrated case of *Red Lion Broadcasting v. The Federal Communications Commission*.[255]

The Fairness Doctrine is perhaps the most dramatic and effective example of our government's involvement in programming since the advent of broadcast television. Not surprisingly, the media industry hated it and tried to get rid of it almost from the beginning.[256] The controversy came to a head in 1969 in the aforementioned *Red Lion* case, which involved a Pennsylvania radio station that aired a regular "Christian Crusade" series. On one occasion, the program attacked the author of a book critical of former Arizona senator Barry Goldwater (the radio program called the author "a shirker, a liar, and a communist"). To nobody's surprise, the author asked the station for the right to respond to these accusations under the FCC's Fairness Doctrine and personal-attack rules. When the station refused, the author appealed to the FCC, which found in his favor. That decision was appealed all the way to the U.S. Supreme Court, which handed down its landmark decision supporting the FCC and the constitutionality of the Fairness Doctrine in 1969.

Writing for a unanimous Supreme Court, Justice Byron White reviewed the entire history of the Radio and Communications Act and concluded that "as far as the First Amendment is concerned," the technological limitations of broadcasting impose special obligations on broadcasters who use the public airwaves for free:

> A license permits broadcasting, but the licensee has no constitutional right to be the one who holds the license or to monopolize a radio frequency to the exclusion of his fellow citizens. There is nothing in the First Amendment which prevents the government from requiring a licensee to share his frequency with others and to conduct himself as a proxy or judiciary with obligations to present those views and voices which are representative of his community and which would otherwise, by necessity, be barred from the airwaves. . . . It is the right of the viewers and listeners, not the right of broadcasters, which is paramount.[257]

This unanimous U.S. Supreme Court decision affirms that government has the power to regulate proactively and enhance various forms of media, (e.g., broadcasting), especially where public property (the airwaves) has been given away for free to licensees. This type of enhancement regulation is clearly constitutional under the First Amendment in the political and public issues arena and equally valid when related to children and family media issues as well.

This very same legal and political framework applies to positive government actions designed to improve or enhance the quality and amount of positive media for kids. The First Amendment says, "Congress shall make no law abridging freedom of speech and the press." In contrast, the same First Amendment says, "Congress shall make no law respecting the establishment of religion." The difference between the words "respecting" and "abridging" is generally understood to mean that government can't do anything to help or hurt religion, whereas it *can* help or enhance speech and media content. This distinction is extremely important to the whole area of kids and media, as well as the role that government can and should play on behalf of America's children and families.

The Children's Television Act (CTA) is a good example of this concept. In 1990, Congress passed the Act over President George Bush's veto and intense opposition from his many friends and political allies in the media industry, led by the NAB. Big media interests publicly challenged the CTA on the grounds that it was unconstitutional because it told broadcasters what to do. The broadcasters cried "censorship," just as they always do, and as usual they said it violated their hallowed First Amendment rights. And, as usual, their challenge was bogus and rejected by the courts.

It is very important to remember that the U.S. Supreme Court has consistently upheld a variety of government efforts to positively enhance and improve media in the public interest. One example is the Public Broadcasting Service (PBS), which carries many different kinds of kids, arts, and documentary programs that are in the public interest and that commercial media interests often fail to fund. Government funding of PBS is clearly constitutional, although conservatives like Newt Gingrich and Tom DeLay made careers out of trying to cut PBS's budget.

Under the same constitutional reasoning, numerous examples of pro-kids legislation by Congress, the president, or the FCC are all clearly constitutional. The bottom line is simple: The media industry opposes government efforts to promote and enhance media on behalf of kids or the broader public interest because they wish to protect their self-interested pursuit of profits, not lofty constitutional principles.

The *second* type of constitutionally permitted rules and regulations on behalf of children are what legal scholars call *"reasonable time, place, and manner restrictions."* In certain cases, government and society in general can actually *restrict* certain types of media or speech that have unique accessibility to children. Our history is full of examples of this form of First Amendment-sanctioned regulation on behalf of kids. They range from laws that regulate billboards and soundtracks to a variety of government restrictions on the location of X-rated movie theaters. A famous test of this principle was the famous *Pacifica*[258] case involving comedian George Carlin and his comedy monologue "Filthy Words," recorded on his album *Occupation: Foole.*

The *Pacifica* case is another clear example of how government can and should regulate the media on behalf of kids, while still protecting First Amendment freedoms. In the early 1970s, George Carlin's "Filthy Words" monologue[259] was broadcast during the middle of the day on a New York radio station owned by the Pacifica Foundation. A father driving in the car with his son complained about the fact that his fifteen-year-old boy heard it and that the dirty language offended him. The father's complaint went to the FCC, which ruled that in the future, if those kinds of words were used again during the day, they would fine the Pacifica radio station. The case subsequently went all the way up to the U.S. Supreme Court on appeal. The Supreme Court majority upheld the FCC's action and said that the FCC could continue to fine the radio station for playing those words because broadcasters had to take special care not to air material that might offend or shock children. As the majority opinion said, "Of all the forms of communication, broad-casting has the most limited First Amendment protection," because it extends "into the privacy of the home and is uniquely accessible to children." Thus, the Supreme Court ruled that indecent pro-gramming over the airwaves, while not entirely prohibited, could indeed be constitutionally restricted to hours during which kids were unlikely to hear or see it.

The Pacifica station and the dissenting justices argued that the words were not obscene and that they were protected speech, which could not be regulated by the FCC. And you might even agree that the routine wasn't really vulgar but rather a form of political satire. However, the U.S. Supreme Court still held that it was constitu-tional to fine, punish, and restrict the speech of the station because it was important to protect children who would be in the audience.

Over the years, there have been a number of cases in which the FCC has used its power to restrict certain types of offensive speech and punish those who use them, including the controversial radio per-sonality Howard Stern, among others. In recent years there have also been a series of cases, collectively known by the name of *Action for Children's Television,* in which U.S. courts examined whether the FCC could find ways to protect kids while permitting adults to have access to certain media. The decisions in these cases represent a careful bal-ancing act. The courts have usually upheld FCC restrictions on radio or television content during times of day or evening when kids are likely to be in the audience, up until 10:00 or 11:00 P.M. in most cases.

It is true that some respected First Amendment scholars argue against these "reasonable time, place, and manner" restrictions, but the bottom line is clear: the courts have affirmed that government may restrict various forms of media in instances where large num-bers of children may be watching or listening. The real question, then, is why our elected government leaders don't do more to pro-tect kids from damaging content, as they are able to do under the law. The answer, once again, is money, politics, and the enormous power of media business interests.

It's important to note, however, that there have been different rulings depending on the medium involved. For example, pay cable channels such as HBO or even "adult" channels such as Spice can legally air offensive content. But that's because adults have to sign up and pay for those channels, and the courts have held that parents can (or should) control that access because they have the credit cards to pay for it. The same goes for 900 numbers that people can call to get phone sex. The key factor is the type of media and whether it has "unique accessibility to children."

ACTIVISM FOR CHILDREN'S MEDIA

To help prod government into working for positive children's media, a number of citizens groups have emerged over the last few decades. In 1968, for example, the pioneering group Action for Children's Television (ACT) first began challenging exploitative practices in kids' programming. This advocacy group was started by five mothers from Boston, most notably the longtime children's television activist Peggy Charren, who were alarmed by the steady diet of violence and commercials that they saw creeping into children's programming. ACT first lobbied successfully for a special children's unit within the FCC and then began fighting to reduce the extraordinary number of deceptive commercials aired during children's programs and condemning the overall lack of quality in children's media. Their efforts received a big boost in 1972 with the announcement by the U.S. surgeon general that there was a clear link between television violence and aggressive behavior in kids. As a result of this announcement, the government actually responded with concrete action. First, the FCC and government officials forced broadcasters and their lobbying voice, the NAB, to reduce the number of advertising minutes in children's weekend television from 16 minutes per hour to the 9.5-minute limit observed in prime time. The NAB and the broadcasters also agreed to reduce the number and type of commercials in weekday kids' programs as well. These actions show clearly how advocacy groups and government can force positive changes in the world of children's media.[260]

In 1975, FCC Chairman Richard Wiley (who had been appointed by Republican President Nixon) prodded the major networks to set aside the first two hours of prime time for "family viewing time." The purpose of this "family hour" was to create a safe haven for kids and younger viewers and was another response to the surgeon general's study on violence and television. Unfortunately, the policy meant that a number of mature programs such as *M*A*S*H* and *All in the Family* were pushed to later hours of prime time, and shortly thereafter, the Writers Guild of America sued the FCC on behalf of writers and producers, saying that family-viewing time violated their rights of free expression. The writers won the lawsuit, forcing the FCC to abandon the formal "family hour" policy and leaving it up to the networks to provide this "safe haven" voluntarily.[261]

The activism of the FCC and groups like ACT in the late 1960s and most of the 1970s shows how government and citizens can effectively work together on behalf of children. But unfortunately, much of the story of the past twenty years in children's media has been dominated by weak-kneed politicians who sold off the interests of American kids and families to the highest bidder or, more accurately, the largest campaign donor.

The 1980s were basically a disaster for concerned parents, teachers, and everyone else who cares about media's impact on children. Indeed, those years mark a watershed in the growth of vast media conglomerates in our society and the abandonment of government's regulatory power over the media interests that shape our lives and society in so many ways. In 1981, a new political administration took over in Washington. For the free-market, supply-side economists of the Reagan administration, deregulation was a consuming passion. This ideological commitment to free-market ideals, unfettered by the balancing hand of government, shaped all forms of social and economic policy, affecting everything from airlines to environmental protection and health care.

Perhaps no industry was more affected by this deregulation fever than the media companies. And their champion in this headlong rush to free-market ideology was none other than the chairman of the FCC himself, Mark Fowler, who was appointed to this role in 1981 by President Ronald Reagan. I have never met Mark Fowler, but colleagues of mine who know him say he is a cordial, pleasant man, though something of a conservative ideologue. But however pleasant he may be personally, his tenure as FCC chairman was a disaster for America's kids and families. For Chairman Fowler, the only kind of regulation that was legitimate came from the market itself, and he made this clear to gleeful industry executives from his earliest days in office. In the *Texas Law Review* in 1982, he characterized the role of broadcasters in our society:

> The perception of broadcasters as community trustees should be replaced by a view of broadcasters as marketplace participants. Communications policy should be directed towards maximizing the services the public desires. Instead of defining public demand and specifying categories of programming to serve this demand, the Commission should rely on the broadcasters' ability to determine the wants of their audiences through normal mechanisms of the marketplace. The public's interest, then, defines the public interest. And in light of the First Amendment's heavy presumption against content control, the Commission should refrain from insinuating itself into program decisions made by licensees.[262]

The FCC chairman and his ideological compatriots were saying that the free market rules all, and that public interest and civic responsibility all take a distant backseat to profits and markets. Responding to the inconvenient fact that the public owns the airwaves, Chairman Fowler suggested that maybe the government should have auctioned off the airspace back in the 1930s, but that such a move would be far too disruptive now. So Fowler proposed giving the broadcasters "squatters rights" in their assigned frequency. In effect, said the public's chief media regulator and "advocate" during the Reagan era, broadcasters should be free to renew their licenses without any concerns about challenges. Moreover, since they owned the airwaves now, they should be free to sell their licenses to whomever they wished, whenever they wanted. Incredibly, the publicly owned airwaves were now being called the private property of media companies by the public official whose sworn duty was to regulate and speak on behalf of the public's interest.[263]

The end result of this ideologically driven deregulation policy was devastatingly swift. It transformed broadcasting virtually overnight from a public trust into one of the hottest businesses on Wall Street. The media industry had a field day, rapidly dismantling or abandoning many of the positive features for which the public had admired them most—quality news divisions, children's programming, and even standards-and-practices departments. The number of commercials and infomercials increased. More important for kids and families, broadcasters adopted the now familiar "anything-goes" policy in programming. The media landscape has never been the same since.[264]

DEREGULATION FRENZY

Mark Fowler came to his job as FCC chairman with one principal objective: to deregulate the media and communications industries and let market forces rule. Fowler's FCC believed that the marketplace would serve children and families. In fact, that very same marketplace quickly drove quality children's programming off the air.

As part of its deregulation agenda, Fowler's FCC withdrew regulations that required broadcast stations to air "educational and informational" programs. The results were immediate and predictable. In 1980, the three major networks were airing more than eleven hours each week of such quality kids' programs as

Schoolhouse Rock and *In the News.* By 1983, however, such pro-gramming had dropped to four and a half hours per week, and all after-school programs were eliminated. A year later, CBS dumped *Captain Kangaroo,* the well-known educational program that had served more than two generations of children. That was the last weekday morning offering for youngsters on a commercial broad-cast network. By 1990, the average number of network educational programs had dropped to fewer than two per week.[265]

At the very same time as quality children's programming was dis-appearing, toy-based television programs for children suddenly boomed. These programs, funded largely by toy manufacturers themselves, went from about thirteen in 1980 to more than seventy in 1987. This was another result of FCC deregulation. Not only had the government dropped the requirement for commercial networks to air informational and educational programs for children, it had also repealed the limits on commercial time. By 1987, kids saw some 40,000 commercials on television each year, double the num-ber they were exposed to in the late 1970s; 80 percent of these advertisements were for toys, cereals, candy, and fast food. The time given to war-based cartoons jumped from about one and a half hours per week to twenty-seven hours, and the sale of war-related toys increased in an equally dramatic fashion. In a mind-boggling decision, the FCC ruled in 1985 that these toy-based TV programs were now by definition in "the public interest" on the basis of their phenomenal sales success.[266]

In a world where profits and dollars ruled all, advocates for chil-dren and families were simply shut out. Efforts to continue the strides made in the late 1960s and 1970s were ignored and aban-doned. In fact, in December 1983, when the FCC was forced by a federal court to continue the previous era's rulemaking regarding children's programming, Chairman Fowler issued a report saying there was no need for further action on kids' programming prac-tices. With Congress and the president turning an equally blind eye to this outrage, it was left to FCC Commissioner Henry M. Rivera to offer a dissent to this disgraceful report:

I wish I had the eloquence of Marc Antony for this eulogy. Our federal children's television policy commitment deserves no less at this, its interment. Make no mistake—this is a funeral and my colleagues have here written the epitaph of the FCC's involvement in children's television. . . . The majority has dishonored our most treasured national asset—children. It has set the notion of enforceable children's programming obligations on a flaming pyre, adrift from federal concern, in the hope that the concept will be consumed in its entirety and never return to the FCC's shores.[267]

Let's be very clear here. Every time you as a parent or citizen are disgusted by what you see on television or hear on the radio or view in a video game, remember where it all started to go downhill. It began with these contemptuous, misguided policies that deregulated media in the 1980s. Remember that name, Mark Fowler. Remember how the Reagan administration sold kids and families down the river. Remember that our national values and many longstanding traditions of public interest and civic responsibility were totally sullied by greed and a mad rush for profits for a few. And children, who have never been and will never be protected by a free-market ideology, came out on the bottom of the heap. Remember this lesson as you watch the current Bush administration and current FCC chairman, Michael Powell, pursue many of these same misguided policies at our national expense.

As I sit here in California, having watched an absurd state energy crisis unfold that led to rolling blackouts, frequent power outages, and the bankruptcy of our utilities, I see the same ill-conceived ideas that drove the disastrous policies of the FCC in the 1980s. The current energy crisis and much of the Enron scandal were created by a blind, ideological commitment to deregulation and free markets, which leads to a world where a few are the winners (those who get rich quick) and the rest of us are clearly losers. The reality of the deregulation movement has been felt far and wide, and one of its most eloquent observers is industry veteran Bill Baker. Now president of WNET, the public television station in New York City, Baker spent many years as a top-level broadcast executive, working for Westinghouse Broadcasting, among others. He also wrote an excellent book on television called *Down The Tube,* which I highly recommend to anyone interested in a more in-depth look at this topic. As he says,

> For media companies, the rules have changed. There is now no reason to do anything but achieve the bottom line, because there's no potential pressure on you from the government or any other entity to do more than that. At least before the 1980s you had to pay lip service to keep your license, so you had to display some concern about what you were broadcasting, because you knew in some fairly soft way you were going to be measured on service to the community. Now the concept of public service is really a non-concept. The only measure that matters is ratings because they translate immediately to the bottom line. There is no governmental entity that is asking the right questions anymore. The only audience that matters is your shareholders. And that's why there's great fear among media industry veterans that the children's television arena is going to get even worse. And that television programming in general is going to get worse.[268]

By the way, Bill Baker made these comments to me before anyone had ever heard of *Temptation Island, Jackass,* or *Who Wants to Marry a Multi-Millionaire?*

So where did the mass deregulation of the media industry in the 1980s leave us? And why are Bill Baker and other experienced media players so pessimistic about the future—particularly government's role and responsibility in the area of kids and family media? The fact is, the 1980s changed the rules so fundamentally that even after a decade of some earnest attempts to right the ship and restore some sense of responsibility and obligation, we're still in an environment where money rules all.

SOME SIGNS OF PROGRESS

Nevertheless, there was some good news about kids and media over the past ten years or so. In 1990, Congress actually did something about the abysmal quality of children's television. Outraged by the abandonment of children by the Republican-led FCC and pressured by groups like Action for Children's Television, Congress passed the Children's Television Act (CTA). Although a number of politicians, most of whom had done next to nothing, tried to take credit, the CTA is actually a fairly simple and minimal piece of legislation and hardly a great triumph. Henry Geller, the former FCC general counsel who helped draft it, called it a "stopgap" effort and admitted that it was an insufficient response to the powerful economic forces acting against quality kids programming. The CTA requires broadcasters (not cable channels) to air an unspecified amount of "educational and informational" programming, but it makes no provisions for when these programs should air and how long these programs should be. However, the CTA still represented the first time that Congress specifically recognized kids as a special audience and that TV has the power to "assist children to learn important information, skills, values, and behavior." The law required the FCC to consider the extent to which broadcasters had served the educational and informational needs of children when reviewing the broadcasters' license renewal applications—but that was about the extent of Congress's grand pronouncement. It was left to the FCC to determine exactly what this new law actually meant and issue regulations for its enforcement. Thus, it was squarely in the hands of the FCC to determine whether this tiny but positive first step would actually have some teeth in it.

At first, broadcasters ignored the law. A famous study by the Washington-based lobby group the Center for Media Education revealed that those kid-friendly media executives at television stations throughout America were claiming that cartoons like *The Jetsons* and *The Flintstones* and old episodes of *Leave It to Beaver* qualified as "educational" programming for license renewal purposes. It would be comical if it weren't true. Moreover, the few good programs that really were educational and informational—not counting the ones on PBS like *Sesame Street, Ghostwriter,* or *Mister Rogers' Neighborhood*—were being shown at 5:30 A.M. by a lot of stations, when no one, including children, would be watching.

Unfortunately for the profit-obsessed media industry and the powerful broadcast lobby in particular, President Bill Clinton appointed an intelligent activist, Reed Hundt, to be his first chairman of the FCC. This may have been bad news for the media barons, but it was good news for millions of American parents and the small group of kids' advocates—including my organization, Children Now—who cared about children's media issues. Once Reed Hundt came on board as chairman of the FCC, things changed very quickly. Blessed with confidence and a sharp intellect, this media-savvy lawyer was never intimidated by the corporate media chieftains. I often thought that he delighted in taking them on intellectually and bluntly challenging their free-market viewpoints. Hundt was just as smart as the media barons were, and unlike them, he was driven by a real sense of mission and public-interest responsibility. He also recognized the power that he could potentially wield on behalf of American citizens. He decided, among other things, to make children's media a top priority during his term. And he made it clear to industry players and advocates alike that he was actually going to put some muscle behind this vague Children's Television Act that Congress had passed in 1990.

The FCC began developing a process for implementing the Children's Television Act and held public hearings about how the rules would be enforced. The hearings were a real eye-opener for me. My friends from the Children's Television Workshop (now called Sesame Workshop) brought Elmo to testify. Longtime advocates such as Newt Minow and Peggy Charren spoke eloquently about past traditions and responsibilities. Newer groups like Children Now and the Center for Media Education argued for the need to improve kids' programming and documented past abuses. Nickelodeon president Geraldine Laybourne came and talked about the success of her kids' cable network and spoke out in support of the new rules, even though cable networks were not subject to them.

Finally, it was the broadcasters' turn, and what I remember most is that they were uncomfortably defensive. We were all sitting in a semicircle around a wooden conference table in a stately old Washington hearing room, like one of those wood-paneled congressional hearing rooms you see on television. The five FCC commissioners were up on a dais looking somewhat like judges as all these broadcast media titans became red-faced and stammered away, one after another. They all had a little story to tell about some wonderful little community program they had supported or some local kids' program they had experimented with. And they all kept talking about how their network or station group was "deeply committed to the future of our nation's children." But after all was said and done, their conclusions were always the same: "We don't make enough money at kids' programming, particularly if it has to have some semblance of educational value."

Tellingly, the media barons *didn't* say they couldn't make *good* money by providing quality kids programming. How could they make that claim sitting in the same room with the creators of Sesame Street (a multibillion-dollar franchise) and the president of the enormously profitable Nickelodeon? No, the broadcast executives merely said they couldn't make *as much* money by creating quality kids programs as they could by, say, running daily episodes of *Jerry Springer* or creating violent, noneducational cartoons like *Power Rangers*.

There followed many months of memos and commentaries and briefs, but in the end, Reed Hundt and the FCC held pretty firm against the profit-obsessed pleas of the media industry and instituted a requirement that every broadcast station in America air a minimum of *three hours* of "educational and informational" programming *per week*. (That's right . . . the broadcasters were kicking and screaming about *three hours per week*, not three hours per *day.*) In addition, the FCC said that the broadcast networks and individual stations couldn't air these programs at 2:00 A.M. or 5:30 A.M.

They actually had to air them between the hours of 7:00 A.M. and 10:00 P.M. Moreover, the FCC even went so far as to try to define the elements of what the Children's Television Act meant by "educational and informational programming," since it was clear that the broadcasters were confused if they were trying to pass off *The Jetsons* and *Leave it to Beaver* as "educational." Finally, the FCC rules included proposals to better inform parents and the public about the shows that broadcasters air to fulfill their CTA obligations.

By the way, it took nearly three years for these rules and regulations to be finalized, and, as you will see in a minute, they are fairly easy for broadcasters to finesse. But the Children's Television Act is still a good example of how our government can positively shape media programming and practices for kids, and how Congress and the FCC should use the powers that they have as the public's elected and appointed representatives.

Now, how have the FCC regulations played out in practice? Well, it's a mixed bag. But there is absolutely no question that these rules—combined with the effective use of the bully pulpit by Reed Hundt and his successor as chairman, Bill Kennard, as well as the then president, Bill Clinton—have had a genuine impact on kids' television in the U.S., despite the fact that at the same time there was massive industry consolidation and huge cutbacks by U.S. media companies in their budgets for children's television.

The impact of the FCC regulations, which are known within the industry as the "three-hour rule," depends on which network and/or broadcast station we're looking at. Obviously, PBS airs more than three hours per week of educational and informational programming for kids—about ten times more! As for the other networks, there are a couple of bright spots. CBS now airs programs developed by Nick Jr. (the preschool block of Nickelodeon) in order to fulfill its obligations to kids' educational and informational needs. We should all have some serious concerns about the Viacom-CBS merger, but this isn't one of them. As we'll see later in the book, Nickelodeon and Nick Jr. are run by terrific, kid-oriented executives, Herb Scannell and Brown Johnson, respectively. Johnson and her team have developed a number of pioneering, successful new shows—*Blue's Clues* being perhaps the most notable—and all of them are built on a solid foundation of learning curriculum and positive values. Even though, as a cable network, Nickelodeon is not required to meet the FCC three-hour-per-week requirement, the Nick people have long been committed to kids and education. The Nick Jr. shows that now air on CBS (a broadcast network) are quite good and clearly within the better spirit of the FCC mandate. So, while all concerned parents should be very troubled by the overall consolidation trend typified by the Viacom-CBS merger, the Nick Jr. programs are good news for kids' programming on CBS.

The second broadcast network that has made somewhat of a commitment to the new FCC regulations on kids' programming is ABC, which is also part of another huge media corporation, the Walt Disney Company. Once again, while I have very grave reservations about this merger-and-consolidation trend and its broader impact on kids' media, the Disney executives, led by Anne Sweeney and Rich Ross, have done a pretty good job in helping ABC meet its three-hour programming requirement by helping to oversee the programs for ABC's Saturday morning lineup.

But the other networks . . . where do I begin? Since my day job is as chairman of a kids' educational media company, which produces programming for these big distribution companies, I should probably choose my words carefully. But the truth is pretty simple: The other major networks aren't really committed to the spirit of the FCC regulations. They just get by with the least possible effort and expense they can. Remember the cynical Fox executives who proposed using sports promos to meet the FCC requirements? Basically, the media companies view these regulations as a money loser (or to be exact, less of a moneymaker) for them. So most of them either air cheap and tired old reruns of shows like *The Magic School Bus* (Fox Kids), or they create new cheap programming like *Histeria* (Kids WB), or they air six different versions of the same silly teen-angst drama or comedy (NBC, which is now leasing its teen block to the Discovery Channel).

To be honest, however, the FCC hasn't enforced the act very stringently, which is a big part of the problem, and the current Mike Powell-led commission has done nothing for kids' TV. But as I look back over the years since the regulations were finally passed, over the industry's strenuous and repeated objection, I have to say that they have definitely had a positive and measurable impact. Industry executives now know they have some vague obligation to the children and families out there. In a world where the drumbeat of profit, profit, and more profit wipes out all but the loudest of intrusions, the FCC regulations for the Children's Television Act symbolize a legal responsibility, however minimal, that they cannot fully ignore. After a number of years of complete failure to do anything meaningful with the public airwaves on behalf of kids, that's not too bad. And if they try to skirt the regulations or fulfill them in the least expensive and least imaginative way, at least the regulations are on the books.

Now, if the FCC would only *deny* a few license reapplications on the basis of failure to comply with the kids' programming requests, that would really make a difference. But the FCC license-renewal rules were changed as part of the Telecommunications Act of 1996, making it much harder for citizens' groups or anyone else to challenge licenses. Former FCC Chairman Bill Kennard has characterized this as a "serious error" that in effect gives broadcasters a free ride. License denial would really hit large media companies where it hurts, but to do so would take political courage that we've seen very little of in Washington.

BACK TO THE BAD OLD DAYS?

Now that President Bush has appointed Secretary of State Colin Powell's son, Michael Powell, as the FCC chairman, I fear, however, that whatever progress chairmen Hundt and Kennard made on behalf of kids will now be lost. Indeed, the early signs are frightening and signal a fundamental shift in telecommunications policy.

Mike Powell's first speeches as FCC chairman called for a major new focus on deregulation. Criticizing the various public interests of his Democratic predecessors, Chairman Powell called for a loosening of restraints and regulations on the media industry. Sounding a lot like the old Reagan-era mantra, "What's good for big business is good for America," the Powell-led FCC has already begun to dismantle critical elements of our regulatory systems. For example, in April 2001 the FCC approved changes that allow the huge Viacom corporation to own both the CBS and UPN broadcast networks simultaneously. As the *Wall Street Journal* said at the time, "the FCC has shown increasing willingness to abandon long-held regulations designed to prevent cable and broadcasting companies from growing too large."[269] The FCC seems to be encouraging massive consolidation in the satellite, cable, and wireless industries as well.

Recently, the FCC has begun reviewing rules that ban TV broadcasters from owning stations that reach more than 35 percent of the nation's population. It is also planning to loosen or repeal twenty-six-year-old regulations that prevent companies from controlling broadcast stations and newspapers in the same market. Moreover, the FCC under Powell seems likely to abandon long-standing regulations that forbid giant media conglomerates from owning both a cable system and a broadcast television station in the same market. And Chairman Powell said recently that broadcasters alone should regulate violence on television, dismissing any role for government in this process.

Certain elected officials—most notably Senator Ernest Hollings of South Carolina, who heads the Commerce Committee—have been sharply critical of the Bush administration and the Powell-led FCC for abandoning these historic safeguards. Indeed, at a hearing before his committee in summer 2001, Senator Hollings accused Chairman Powell of failing to fulfill his duty to apply the law in the best interest of the public. In an interview for this book, Senator Joseph Lieberman, too, repeatedly criticized the current FCC's failure to use its legitimate enforcement powers on behalf of America's children and families and hoped that more parents, voters, and concerned advocates would pressure the FCC and their elected representatives to reverse this troubling trend.

As we have seen before, this "free market rules all" approach will be a disaster for consumers and families. In supporting the profit-driven motives of a handful of media giants, the current FCC is basically undoing sixty years of policy dedicated to the principle that multiple sources of news and information provide crucial protections in our democracy. These misguided decisions are already reducing the diversity of entertainment and news available to the viewing and listening public. In addition, smaller companies as well as talented, creative people with new programming ideas for kids, or a different perspective on an issue, will have a much tougher time getting their content on the air. How can this possibly be good for anyone except a small handful of wealthy media barons and their shareholders? The rest of us will end up with less quality and diversity of voices in what we see and hear. And the reason, as usual, is colored green.

Seven

THE POWER OF CAMPAIGN CASH

"There are two things that are important in politics. The first is money and I can't remember what the second one is."
—*Mark Hanna, U.S. senator, 1895*

SCENE #1: HOLLYWOOD MOGUL'S HOME

I drive up the long circular driveway and wait in line in my rented Ford Escort behind a string of Mercedes and Jaguar convertibles and a few Range Rover SUVs. The beautiful people are arriving. They get out of their cars in sleek clothes that you and I would only dream of, almost all of which are black. They give their car keys to the red-jacketed valets, turn to wave at one or two friends still waiting to emerge from their pricey Jaguars, then air-kiss their host and hostess, who are waiting for them at the pillared front entrance of this stately Bel Air mansion.

I finally reach the front of the line and hand over the keys to my shabby white subcompact. The valet sniffs, and I look to see if there's anyone I know well enough to walk in with. Our hosts actually greet me kindly and say to another couple standing there, "You know Jim, he does that great work with children." Having been properly anointed, I thank them for including me in such a special evening without having to pay the requisite $25,000-per-couple donation and enter the cavernous front hall. The ceilings are massive—fifteen to twenty feet high. The lovely white columns and furniture in the living room are spotless. The paintings on the wall are grand. They are probably by famous modern artists, whose names I've long since forgotten from Art 101 in college. I ease through the living room and cross through the book-lined study and out onto a marble patio that leads to an enormous backyard space. There is a tennis court on the left and a mammoth, oval-shaped swimming pool on the far right. Next to the pool are the screening room and guest "cottage" (which is bigger than most of my friends' houses). There are beautiful, carefully sculpted hedges and a string of lights, which twinkle in the soft evening. "Not too shabby," I think, just as a white-coated waiter walks up to me with a tray carrying white wine and sparkling water, and I turn to watch more black-bedecked guests sipping their drinks and air-kissing madly with new arrivals.

I venture back inside the house and locate a massive buffet table. It's laden with a terrific selection of cheeses, exquisite seafood canapés, and a variety of beautifully arranged vegetables and "caviar bars" at each end of the table. This is always the best part of Hollywood fund-raisers—the amazing food—very little of which seems to be eaten by anyone but me and the overworked staffers of the prominent senator who is the guest of honor at tonight's event.

That's why we're all here. Our hosts have opened up their spectacular home to welcome Senator (insert your favorite name here), who just happens to be in Los Angeles this evening, consulting on weighty policy matters with this knowledgeable crowd. And, oh, yes, trolling for dollars for the Democratic Party Victory Campaign, of which he'll be a major beneficiary. After about an hour of mingling, cocktails, and trips to the buffet, our hosts clap their hands for silence and introduce the guest of honor. All guests gather obediently on the lawn near the tennis court, and our esteemed senator begins by profusely thanking our hosts and acknowledging both a number of Hollywood dignitaries ("my good friend Mike Ovitz," "my great supporter Jeffrey Katzenberg," "our longtime friend Jeff Berg," and so on, and so forth) as well as several California politicians, who are also working the local crowd for cash for their own campaigns.

Next, the senator talks about all the great challenges we can overcome with this great show of support from America's leaders. As the senator lists some of these programs and future accomplishments, he makes it clear that "government will never act as a censor in any way" and adds that he looks forward to partnering with this esteemed group of media dignitaries to further our nation's global leadership role in the media and entertainment world.

Polite applause follows, and then we have more handshakes and air kisses and cocktails. Everyone goes home happy. Let me explain why.

The senator and the other politicos in attendance go home happy because they've got a nice new chunk of change for their campaign coffers, probably in excess of one million dollars. The Hollywood leaders go home happy because they know that this group of political leaders will never try to "censor" their movies or television shows or offer any significant legislation that might limit their business goals. Moreover, they are on personal, "buddy buddy" terms with key Washington and California political leaders who apparently have the greatest respect for their political wisdom and knowledge. And I go home happy because, as always, the food was incredible, and because it can be fun watching Hollywood and Washington fawn all over each other once again in such a spectacular Beverly Hills setting.

SCENE #2: THE TECHNOLOGY MOGUL'S HOME

I drive up the long, winding, tree-lined driveway to the beautiful Atherton estate. It is dusk, and I see two horses grazing in a pasture to my left. The tennis court area on the right is lit for a festive gala and set with chairs, tables, and other accoutrements. The main house looms in the foreground, its white columns glistening in the evening light. Welcome to the new Hollywood—Silicon Valley!

I drive up to the entrance of the main house, where I'm greeted by an army of white-coated valets. Since I live in San Francisco, I'm driving my own Jeep and hand over the keys to a young, fresh-faced valet, who whisks it off to a makeshift lot near the stables. Looking around, I notice that there are mostly other SUVs and station wagons in the area, along with a couple of Mercedes and BMWs.

This is Silicon Valley—not the real Hollywood—but still, it's none too shabby. I step to the corner of the driveway to observe the arriving crowd. Though Silicon Valley has been swamped with cash and power in the past few years, it is still a lot less glitzy than its neighbor to the south, particularly since the crash of dot-com mania. People dress differently too. There's a lot less black (except for Larry Ellison wanna-bes). Very few shirts are buttoned to the top; a number of male guests arrive in rumpled khakis and open-necked shirts. A few wear jeans and T-shirts, usually with a sport coat. And, yes, a number of the men actually wear coats and ties. I even spot a few dark suits. You're very unlikely to see those down in Hollywood.

As for the women, the dress is also more casual than glamorous. You see more pantsuits, more plain blouses, and far fewer revealing outfits. It's a Banana Republic and J. Crew crowd, and there's very little star quality. Like their male counterparts, a number of Silicon Valley women are in business dress—far more than would be at a typical Hollywood affair, because here women are more likely to be working as top execs in a high-tech company than to be married to an entertainment industry honcho. And, oh, yes, there are a lot more Asian faces in this Silicon Valley crowd, including several that are Indian. High-tech land has a very different demographic from La La Land.

This particular fund-raising event is a very big one. There are nearly four hundred guests, and our hosts are a young couple, thirty-four and thirty years old respectively, who survived the crash.

Though they've been working "the Valley" for nearly eight years, they look young enough to be Stanford grad students hosting an early evening beer bash.

I'm attending this party courtesy of a couple of friendly investors in JP Kids who also happen to be key leaders in Silicon Valley's relatively new lobbying association, TechNet. It was put together several years ago by some leading venture capitalists—notably John Doerr of Kleiner Perkins fame—and some politically savvy executives like former Netscape CEO Jim Barksdale, who saw the growing need to influence legislation and regulations affecting the high-tech and Internet industries. After hiring a couple of political operatives who had formerly worked in D.C., TechNet quickly rose to prominence as the Valley's leading bipartisan voice on key issues affecting the broader world of technology.

As I enter the huge main house, it's hard not to wonder what a young couple with no kids is doing with all this money and all this seeming influence. Our host is a preppy-looking man of medium build who wears black glasses and has carefully groomed, short hair. By his looks, he could easily be confused with a million other prepsters attending their fifteenth high school reunion at Hotchkiss or St. Paul's. He seems very self-assured as he greets the steady stream of guests. Since I don't really know him and am there on a comp ticket, he barely nods as I walk past him into the house. In the entrance hall, there's a table staffed by three perky young women who are checking off each entering guest's name on alphabetized lists and directing us to the gathering area in a different part of the estate.

Once inside the main party area, I'm pleased to see that one thing's similar to the Hollywood fund-raisers . . . the food. There's a huge buffet table, and we're not just talking carrot sticks and broccoli. There's a raw seafood bar, an entire cheese table with a mix of Europe's finest, as well as an excellent assortment of little sandwiches in various shapes and sizes. In addition, I'm immediately set upon by white-coated waiters serving drinks and hors d'oeuvres. It's clear that once again, we won't be going hungry. After all, for $10,000 a pop, you ought to be eating pretty well.

The event itself is depressingly familiar. After a fair amount of schmoozing and chitchat among the newly anointed Silicon Valley barons, we are asked to assemble on a grassy area near the enormous pool, where the organizers have set up several hundred chairs in front of a podium. We have two main speakers at this event—two prominent senators, one Republican and one Democrat. Our host gets up, fixes his thinning, light brown hair several times, and then welcomes us all to "the new power capital of America . . . a land where there is a bipartisan belief in the importance of the technology and communications industries as the centerpiece of the global economy in the twenty-first century." With that, he turns it over to the two guest speakers. Each senator goes on and on about the importance of this extraordinary group in front of them. Each is at pains to remind us that their party is the true defender and leader of this miraculous new industry. As one puts it, "you have my word that government will never stand in the way of or tinker with this amazing new technology by imposing burdensome regulations or taxes on its main engine."

Blah blah blah. These are the fat cats of the new media world. Just as in the old media world, they are being catered to and kowtowed to by the leading government officials in our society. It's all so friendly and warm . . . just one big bipartisan love fest.

But where's the talk about kids and families? Where is the discussion of legitimate taxes on Internet commerce? Where are the questions about the massive consolidation and mergers in the technology and telecommunications industry and their impact on consumers and average families? Here we have two of America's most prominent senators decrying any legislation or regulations that might curb the excesses of the high-tech industry. These guardians of our political storehouse are waxing eloquent about the powers of the free market and keeping government out of the "regulation business," in the very same state that is trying to recover from rolling blackouts and massive power shortages due to the similar shortsighted deregulation of California's utilities. The parallels are eerie, but nobody will think to raise them here on this glorious evening in Silicon Valley—just as nobody raised them at the sparkling event for entertainment industry moguls a few weeks earlier. The politicians—our elected leaders—are in bed with these guys. Indeed, it's a very comfortable and cozy little world to which most need not apply.

MONEY, POLITICS, AND MEDIA

How did it get this way? How did the titans of media and telecommunications, the kings and queens of Hollywood and Silicon Valley, come to wield such enormous power and influence over the very government leaders who are supposed to represent the interests of kids and families like yours and mine?

To understand the power of the media industry in our national politics, there's no better way to start than by examining the longstanding relationship between Hollywood and Washington. The relationship may seem complicated, since our nation's capital and our entertainment industry capital are separated by three thousand miles.

Despite their wildly different fashion trends, totally different weather patterns, and other seeming differences, the two capitals, not to mention many of their leading power brokers, are oddly similar and are driven by three primary obsessions—money, vanity, and power. Hollywood has two things that Washington politicians so desperately need these days: the cold hard cash needed to finance ever more expensive campaigns and the celebrity-driven fame that can make even the nerdiest politician seem glamorous. On the other hand, for the large Hollywood studios, television networks, and music industry powerhouses, what happens in Washington is absolutely crucial to their bottom lines. It's true that the success of an individual movie is largely decided at the box office, and oftentimes by the first weekend's gross. But the media industry's long-term profitability, particularly in these days of mega-mergers, is largely determined by what happens on Capitol Hill and at the White

House, where telecommunications bills, tax laws, and trade agreements with foreign entities are negotiated.

The close nexus between Hollywood and Washington is a longstanding one, and media industry executives have always seen Washington as a highly visible arena in which to further their causes. This attraction is nothing new. It dates back to at least the early 1900s when President Woodrow Wilson screened the Civil War epic *Birth of a Nation* at the White House in an attempt to improve his political support in the South. Just about everyone in our country has heard of the Kennedy family's entanglements with Marilyn Monroe, Frank Sinatra, and other high-profile media types, and the "Camelot Era" marked a time when the Hollywood-Washington love affair seemed in full bloom. Ronald Reagan literally came from Hollywood, having launched his political career as head of the Screen Actors Guild. More recently, President Clinton welcomed numerous stars and media executives into his White House world. His old pals, the television producers Harry Thomason and Linda Bloodworth-Thomason, produced the memorable *The Man from Hope* video introducing him at the 1992 Democratic Convention and subsequently advised him on numerous matters. His Republican detractors couldn't get enough of those stories about Tom Hanks, Steven Spielberg, and other industry titans sleeping in the Lincoln Bedroom, although George W. Bush also has welcomed his own media and entertainment pals to the White House.

I've seen this partnership of Hollywood and Washington many times over the past dozen years, and at first it was pretty surprising and a bit weird to me. When we first launched Children Now as a national children's advocacy group back in 1988, I spent several years commuting regularly to our office in Los Angeles. Everywhere I went, I would see the Washington political connection. I remember our first small fund-raiser, where we were introducing children's issues to a group of well-heeled Los Angeles donors. The audience of fifty at a friend's home in Pacific Palisades was split almost evenly between Hollywood power players and Washington insiders.

After the event was over, a couple of well-known senators showed up at our host's house, apparently to rendezvous with a couple of young starlets whom they were dating. It seemed strange and actually a bit embarrassing to me at first. I mean, what were two of our nation's most powerful senators doing with a couple of twenty-five-year-old actresses? Yes, of course I know . . . but still. . . . Anyhow, after a few more such parties, I soon came to see this as pretty typical. Most of our events in Los Angeles featured a mix of Hollywood and D.C. types, and they sure seemed to know and like each other. More striking to me was the marked similarity in the personalities of the members of the two cultures. Both seem to be dominated by power-driven and often insecure people, and both have given rise to worlds where ruthlessness and sometimes dishonesty can be the norm for doing business.

But much more important than the similarity in personality types, the most powerful connection between our nation's capital and the media and entertainment industry's capital is money. And its impact can be seen everywhere these days . . . from Hollywood to Washington to New York to Silicon Valley. Perhaps the entertainment industry's best-known political face is that of Jack Valenti, the debonair president of the Motion Picture Association of America. Valenti, who worked as a top aide to Lyndon Johnson, is a fixture on both coasts, representing the interests of the movie studios in Washington. You've probably seen him on TV defending the movie business and saying that it has no responsibility for violence in America. He's that short, silver-maned gentleman who seems to know all the senators and representatives by their first names.

It's pretty clear that Valenti has never let his Democratic Party ties interfere with business. "We've got good friends on both sides of the aisle," he says. "You don't survive in Washington for thirty years by being brutally partisan." Right. You survive and thrive for thirty years in Washington by handing out lots of favors, lots of celebrity attention, and most of all, lots of cash. And that's what the media industry has done in ever larger quantities.

In the past three national election cycles, we have seen record-shattering amounts of private, special-interest money pouring into the political process. All told, the mere 535 members of Congress, two major political parties, and two presidential candidates raised $2 billion in 1992. This same group of people raised $2.4 billion in 1996. And in the 2000 election cycle, this same small group raised more than $3 billion . . . and that's just the money that we know about. We certainly aren't talking about funds collected at backyard barbecues and neighborhood bake sales.[270]

At the same time that more than $3 billion poured into these campaign coffers, we saw the worst campaign-finance scandals since Watergate. Moreover, we have seen the worst voter disillusionment in more than half a century. As politicians have become so deeply engrossed in this never-ending pursuit of money and increasingly linked to large and powerful economic interests, the American people have turned away.

The public's belief in government has sunk to historic lows. In the 2000 election, for example, nearly half of the electorate—100 million eligible voters—simply decided not to participate. This turnout of 51 percent was only slightly better than the voter participation in 1996—which was the lowest in any presidential year since 1924 and the second lowest since 1824. In 1998, only 36 percent of eligible voters even bothered to go to the polls, the lowest turnout since 1942.[271]

The American public's antipathy toward the system seems pretty understandable and clearly reveals what this orgy of money has done to our political process. "The abuses of the campaign-finance system, as practiced by both parties in 1996 . . . destroyed what was left of this country's campaign-finance laws," the journalist Elizabeth Drew wrote in her 1999 book, *The Corruption of American Politics*. "There were now effectively no limits on how much money could be raised and spent on a campaign, and the limits on how it could be raised were rendered meaningless. Powerful people had undermined the law."

And who are these powerful people? Well, if you were Al Gore, it just might be the Walt Disney Company, eighth on the list of the top biggest donors to the Democratic Party. The same Walt Disney Company was ninth on the list of top ten career donors to his primary challenger, Bill Bradley. Third on the list of the Democratic Party's top twenty donors was Seagram's, which, led by Edgar Bronfman Jr., just happened to be the owner of MCA/Universal in the late 1990s. Also in the list of top twenty donors to the Democratic Party were the Communications Workers of America (#2), Loral Space and Communications (#7), AT&T Corporation/TCI (the cable giant at #12), and MCI WorldCom (#13).

For Al Gore personally, in addition to Disney, his "Top Ten Career Patron" list included BellSouth Corporation (#2), Viacom, (MTV, Nickelodeon, CBS, Paramount, etc . . . at #6), and the toy company Mattel (#7). The "Top Ten Career Patrons" of Bill Bradley also featured Time Warner (#5), which as we all know is now referred to as the even bigger media conglomerate AOL Time Warner.[272] I wonder if any of those contributions might have been made in the hope of gaining FCC approval of the merger?

The story of media and communications cash on the Republican side is equally revealing. George W. Bush's single biggest career patrons come from the oil business, including Enron, hardly a surprise given his own career in oil and his remarkably pro-oil industry energy policies as president. But number four on President Bush's "Top Ten Career Patron" list is the firm of Hicks, Muse, Tate and Furst. This firm specializes in leveraged buyouts, including a number in the media and communications arena. Hicks, Muse formerly owned AMFM, the nation's largest chain of radio stations (now owned by Clear Channel) and bought the Texas Rangers from then Governor Bush and his wealthy benefactors/partners in 1998.

Bush's top challenger in the 2000 primaries, John McCain, has also benefited handsomely from the extraordinary campaign donations of a number of media and communications companies. The list of McCain's "Top Ten Career Patrons" begins with US West (the huge, Denver-based communications company, which recently merged with Qwest Communications). McCain's A-list also includes AT&T/TCI (#3), Viacom, Inc. (#4), BellSouth Corporation (#6), and Motorola, Inc. (#9). Not coincidentally, Senator McCain has been heavily involved in the communications and media industries as chairman of the Senate Commerce Committee—although, to his credit, he has taken an independent position on a number of key media issues.

The Republican Party itself has also had enormous success raising vast sums of money from media and communications conglomerates. The GOP's list of "Top Twenty Patrons" is led by big tobacco (Philip Morris is #1, RJ Reynolds / Nabisco is #4, and U.S. Tobacco Corporation is #8). However, right behind them come such media and communications giants as AT&T/TCI (#5), Bell Atlantic Corporation/Nynex (#9), Seagram's (#10), MCI World-Com (#16), and News Corporation (Rupert Murdoch's company, which owns Fox and so many other media properties, at #17). And remember, these are just the media and communications companies in the top twenty!

This "bipartisan" strategy practiced by Jack Valenti is also employed by most media and communications giants. They don't hesitate to grease every palm. AT&T/TCI, which controls the nation's largest cable company as well as numerous other telecom businesses that affect our daily lives, is on just about every list. They are clearly an equal opportunity donor. So, too, is Seagram's, which owned MCA/Universal and all of its film, music, and television properties before selling them to Vivendi. AOL Time Warner has given huge sums of money to politicians on both sides of the aisle. Its new CEO, Dick Parsons, has long been known as a politically savvy, gifted corporate diplomat with particularly close ties to high-ranking Republicans, such as Secretary of State Colin Powell and his son Michael, the chairman of the FCC. Remember, Michael Powell's agency is supposed to regulate the media behemoth of which his family friend, Dick Parsons, is chief executive.[273] The list goes on and on, and the story is basically the same. Media and telecommunications interests spend hundreds of millions on campaign donations . . . and clearly expect to get something in return for their largesse.

Microsoft, for example, began showering millions of dollars on politicians of both major parties once it became clear that they could influence America's most prominent antitrust case. For Microsoft the stakes were huge, and they've already seen a big payoff. The Bush Justice Department dramatically altered the position of the Clinton administration and abandoned the government's plan to break up Microsoft for a raft of antitrust violations and monopolistic practices. As Thomas Reilly, attorney general of Massachusetts, said about the Bush administration's proposed settlement, "There's no question in my mind that Microsoft will use this agreement to crush competition, and they would have the imprimatur of the U.S. government to do it." Stanford professor Timothy Bresnahan, who was chief economist for the Justice Department's antitrust division in the Clinton administration, agreed, noting, "this settlement amounts to the government taking a dive."[274]

The current Justice Department's retrenchment and its much criticized settlement agreement in the Microsoft case seem to epitomize the Bush administration's belief that government should not play a decisive role in key business affairs. This conviction can also be seen in the administration's decision to relax or eliminate a host of decades-old regulations that have kept the nation's largest broadcasters, cable companies, and media conglomerates from growing bigger.[275] It also epitomizes how effective corporate contributions can be, since President Bush received more money from corporate donors than any candidate in history.

Overall, Microsoft and its employees were the country's fifth largest political donor in the 2000 election, contributing $4.7 million to politicians and their committees. Republicans received about 53 percent of that money, but Microsoft is nothing if not pragmatic. They gave money to Republican House Speaker Dennis Hastert and to his Democratic counterpart, Minority Leader Dick Gephardt. They gave money to both Republican Senator Mike DeWine and Democrat Senator Herb Kohl and many others. This should come as no surprise, but it's very different from the way the powerful software company used to behave. And what a payoff they've gotten on their investment.

Microsoft didn't always seek support in Washington, D.C. For years the software giant prided itself on steering clear of national politics and lobbying. But when its legal troubles started and it was threatened with a breakup, that attitude quickly changed. As Arizona Senator John McCain told the *San Francisco Chronicle* in 2001, "Microsoft, before their antitrust case, had almost no presence in Washington. Now, I almost don't know a lobbyist who is not on their payroll."[276]

But the story of media money and its influence on politics hardly stops there. Why did politicians raise the ungodly sum of $3 billion during the 2000 election cycle? To buy ads on television, of course. Get it? They raise huge sums of money from media companies in order to turn around and spend the great majority of that money on . . . the media companies' very own television stations. What a great system we have built. The money goes out one door and comes in through the other. And the television stations just love to charge those very same politicians huge bucks for airing their campaign advertisements.

In the 2000 election cycle, the cost of all political ads on television alone approached $2 billion. That's right. Nearly $2 out of every $3 raised in our corrupt campaign finance system was spent on TV ads, charged to desperate political campaigns by local and national television outlets owned by large media giants. It would clearly be far cheaper for us taxpayers to pay for those commercials directly. But that's too simple and far too common sense an approach.

We have created a campaign system of pay and payoff that essentially forces politicians to sell their influence and favors to large media interests . . . which ultimately diminishes the voice of the vast majority of American voters. The saddest irony of all is that the system most certainly doesn't have to be this way. Indeed, Congress and the FCC could easily demand that the networks provide free airtime to match every purchased minute, just as they have provided free airtime for antidrug campaigns and other public service announcements. Or even better, Congress could simply require that national networks and local TV stations redeem their debt for the free use of the publicly owned spectrum by giving candidates ample free time to present themselves and their views on key issues. That's *exactly* what a government-sponsored commission that studied the problem of fair campaigning recommended for the 2000 election cycle. And that's what any number of foreign democracies require as well. But not here. Not in a society where the current system is weighted toward a handful of very powerful interests, among the biggest of whom are huge media and telecommunications giants, who profit handsomely from the current way of doing business.

One of the most noticeable new trends in the desperate search for campaign cash is the growing influence of technology and new media companies in the political mix. Hollywood studios, not to mention the broadcast and cable industries, figured out how to play and win this campaign game a long time ago, but the technology companies and the Internet companies (whichever few dot-coms remain standing, that is) are aggressive new players in this arena.

It didn't take very long for the new media and technology barons to learn the ways of their "old media" competitors. Millions of dollars poured into campaigns from the newly enriched Internet and technology companies. Until the collapse of so many of the dot-coms, you couldn't go anywhere or read any political article in the Bay Area without hearing about how Silicon Valley was now the new power player in American politics. DOT-COM FIRMS LEARNING TO PLAY LOBBYING GAME: INDUSTRY SENDS PEOPLE, MONEY WASHINGTON'S WAY, headlines brayed.[277] SILICON VALLEY HELPING SHAPE NATIONAL POLITICS, read another.[278] "Think big money rules politics? Wait until the new dot-com lobby makes good on its plan to hand out stock options as campaign donations," declared a feature article in *The New York Times Magazine*.[279]

This effort has generally been led by TechNet, the bipartisan Silicon Valley lobbying group spearheaded by famed venture capitalists, bankers, and dot-com executives. Under TechNet's leadership, this high-tech version of the media world—"Hollywood North" or "Siliwood" as some came to call it—has become a huge player in the campaign cash game that dominates our political system. The lobbying groups, the donor parties, the fawning politicians—we've got plenty of that in the high-tech media world now. Fewer face-lifts and liposuctions perhaps, but loads of campaign cash. And although many of the Internet companies have faded from the scene, the big players such as Microsoft, AOL, and Yahoo! are here to stay.

SHAREHOLDER DEMOCRACY

I recently attended a high-level affair in San Francisco that epitomized the new media world's approach to campaign cash. The event was entitled "Silicon Valley Meets Washington, D.C.," and it was held in the Grand Ballroom at the Westin St. Francis Hotel in Union Square.

You can pretty much imagine the scene. A big ballroom with many chandeliers. Boring fund-raiser-type food (rubber chicken and gelatinized desserts). Lots of investment-banker types in suits. Ninety-five percent white audience. Mostly men. A few Asian-Americans and African-Americans sprinkled throughout the crowd. But this time, not a single politician trolling for cash.

Rather, this event was an occasion for Silicon Valley power brokers to talk about how they could get even more influence in Washington on key technology and media issues. A panel discussion featured Rick White (the new president of TechNet), Eric Schmidt (chairman of Novell), Eric Benhamou (chairman of the board of Palm), Kim Polese (cofounder of Marimba), and Floyd Kvamme (partner-emeritus of the venture firm Kleiner Perkins Caufield and Byers and President Bush's new chief technology adviser.)

What was really quite revealing about the event (other than the title) was the conversation. First you had Rick White, a former congressman with his wavy brown hair and those smooth, politician-type good looks, observing, "In Silicon Valley, there is 'Moore's Law' [the well-known Silicon chip formula of Intel founder, Gordon Moore] while in Washington, you have 'Moron's Law':

How much you can contribute to my campaign and then we'll talk about that legislation you want." After White we heard from Eric Schmidt, who said, "Do you wanna know what Washington is all about? It's pretty simple. Asking for favors and being expected to give money. Nothing has changed under George W. Bush."

Here was a very powerful group of new media and technology leaders decrying the very system they participate in, but still acknowledging how important it was to their business to play the campaign-cash game to the max. Floyd Kvamme, President Bush's chief technology adviser, actually said, "We live in a shareholder democracy." At that point, I almost lost my chicken and Jell-O lunch. "Shareholder democracy"? That's what our Founding Fathers envisioned? What happens to all of us who aren't big shareholders? What about our kids, who generally aren't shareholders in anything but baseball or Pokemon cards?

It was all too familiar and depressing. The rules about media and technology—the stuff we all see and hear, the devices we use to communicate and compute, the boxes we all have in our homes— are being set every day by a small group of people who traverse the corridors of that Hollywood, Washington, and Silicon Valley axis. And it's all driven—whether the players like it or not—by this steady stream of campaign cash. You and I are pretty much shut out, even though we and our kids fund much of this as the consumers of this media and technology.

Now, these guys at the "Silicon Valley meets Washington, D.C." event may be pretty powerful folks when it comes to the rules about what goes (or doesn't go) in the worlds of media and technology. But it may be a little hard to see how they and their companies affect our kids' lives every day. Not so for the two gentlemen I'd like to tell you about next: two men whose empires affected the lives of tens of millions of children in our country and around the globe. These two men, until very recently, were business partners, united in the pursuit of profit even though they support different political parties. They both became extremely wealthy selling media to kids over the past decade—media that many people find damaging and abhorrent. These men have become masters at playing the game of politics and campaign cash. I know them by their first names, Rupert and Haim. But kids around the world know them as the creators and former owners of Fox Kids and Fox Family Worldwide.

THE RUPERT MURDOCH–HAIM SABAN SAGA

It's instructive to look at the campaign expenditures and shrewd political behavior of the two men who built and recently sold Fox Family Worldwide to Disney for a hefty profit. This fifty-fifty joint venture between media barons Rupert Murdoch, founder and CEO of News Corporation, and Haim Saban, founder and CEO of Saban Entertainment, included the Fox Family cable channel, the Fox Kids Block on the Fox broadcast network, as well as numerous kids' media libraries and European cable interests. In the fall of 2001, the Walt Disney Company agreed to buy Fox Family Worldwide for the ultimate price of $5.2 billion, in yet another disturbing example of media industry consolidation.

Rupert Murdoch is one of the most powerful men in the media world. His News Corporation is a global media empire. It spans six continents and includes newspapers, books, broadcasting, satellite television networks, movie studios, and cable interests. New Yorkers know him for the *New York Post*. London residents know him for the *Sun* and *Times* as well as for BSkyB television. Here in the United States we all know him for Fox Broadcasting, Twentieth Century Fox Studios, and HarperCollins Publishers. Murdoch is a huge media player. His rival, Sumner Redstone, the CEO of Viacom, has said of him: "He basically wants to conquer the world. And he seems to be doing it."[280] He's also extremely conservative politically and is willing to use his media empire, including the Fox News Channel, to further his partisan views. And he has been a major player in kids' television since he first launched Fox as the fourth major U.S. network in the mid 1980s.

Murdoch began his career in the newspaper business in Australia, and early on he showed a preference for profit at the expense of taste. In 1969, he purchased the *Sun,* one of England's popular newspapers. Under his leadership, the *Sun* put the "Sun Lovely" (a topless model) on page three and expanded its tabloid nature with mountains of gossip posing as news. In 1976, Murdoch bought the *New York Post,* the oldest continuously published daily in America, and turned it into the classic standard bearer for tabloid journalism in the United States. Thomas Kiernan, who has written a biography of Murdoch, notes, "He's a complex personality, because if you read the editorials in his newspapers, they are very highly moralistic and they are very highly principled and so on, and yet they appear in papers that are almost without principle journalistically."[281] This sounds to me like the same kind of approach that he has taken toward the Fox Television Network and other properties he owns in the United States. In the words of Harold Evans, who resigned as editor of the two-hundred-year-old *Times* of London one year after Murdoch acquired it, "He's a good businessman and a lousy journalist, a lousy journalist in the sense that he doesn't believe in public interest journalism, and he doesn't keep his promises."[282]

In 1985, Murdoch acquired Fox Studios and began the process of launching Fox as the fourth major television network in the United States. According to Tom Shales, TV critic for The *Washington Post,*

> Fox was given every break throughout the eighties on the grounds that a new network should be encouraged. The FCC decided that we needed more networks, therefore a lot of hurdles that Fox should have had to jump over were just sort of quietly laid down, and Murdoch was allowed to just drive right on through. The irony is that Congress was complaining about violence and smuttiness on TV, and Rupert Murdoch has been the vanguard of that, at least his Fox network has. I mean it has established sort of new lows in taste on television. This argument about giving people what they want . . . it's probably what Nero said when he fed the Christians to the lions. As far as I know, the ratings on that were very high; it was

a big crowd pleaser. . . . A terrible accident on the highway causes people to slow down and stare at it, but that doesn't necessarily mean you want to put it on prime time.[283]

Much of the early success of the Fox network was driven by its daily afternoon and Saturday morning Fox Kids Block, under the artful programming eye of Margaret Loesch, as well as its early prime-time success with such teen-targeted shows as *Beverly Hills 90210* and *Melrose Place*. As most TV viewers know, the latter featured a heavy dose of sexually explicit themes; even Murdoch himself admitted, "I wouldn't let a thirteen-year-old watch *Melrose Place*," but that didn't stop Fox from airing it at 8:00 P.M., the traditional family hour.[284] So Rupert and his empire have had an enormous impact on media programs aimed at kids and teens, and he has profited handsomely from these often lowbrow efforts.

I should mention here that I have had a couple of conversations with Rupert Murdoch over the past few years and, on a personal level, have always found him very courteous. He's a white-haired, craggy-faced man of nearly seventy, with a soft voice and noticeable Australian accent. Despite his reputation as a ruthless and cunning media baron, he is by most accounts a devoted father to his four children and has involved three of them in various roles in his media empire. Obviously incredibly bright and ambitious, he can also be very gracious. He even offered me helpful suggestions on where to travel in Australia with my family. But his personal charm notwithstanding, his huge media empire has been one of the most negative forces in the kids' media world. I completely agree with Tom Shales's assessment that Fox has been *the* leader in targeting U.S. teens with frequently offensive programming. Ever since Murdoch and his then-partner Barry Diller launched the Fox network in the mid-1980s, it has been the network that most pushed the envelope with risqué programming, ranging from the early, irresponsible days of *Beverly Hills 90210* to *A Current Affair, Cops,* and the recent 2001 embarrassment *Temptation Island.*

In the kids' television arena, Fox is the network that introduced *Power Rangers* and its toy-driven, violent action figures to the Saturday morning lineup. In general, despite some respectable early efforts by Margaret Loesch, programming on Fox Kids has been epitomized by the aggressive action cartoons that make so many parents, like myself, profoundly uncomfortable. Indeed, when I think of Fox Kids, two basic concepts dominate: merchandise-driven cartoons and low-budget action adventures. Fox Kids is about the last place you'd look for quality edutainment for your children and probably the first place you'd want to go if you were a ten-year-old boy seeking aggressive action cartoons. As we've seen, Fox has now leased its Saturday morning block to the highest bidder (a toy and merchandising-driven company), with no serious commitment to the FCC requirements under the Children's Television Act.

Murdoch is also a master at influencing Washington officials through the frequent use of large campaign contributions and a very effective Washington lobbying presence, not to mention the unabashedly conservative Fox News channel, which he controls. And Murdoch has needed lots of influence in Washington because he's had his fair share of political problems and enemies. Over the past fifteen years, ever since he persuaded Congress and the FCC to approve the Fox network, Murdoch has made a practice of successfully cozying up to key Washington media power brokers like Representative Billy Tauzin of Louisiana, perhaps the most important Republican congressman on media issues. Murdoch has acted as a very generous underwriter of Tauzin's political career, in addition to handing out large contributions to such other key legislators as Republican Senate Commerce Committee leader Larry Pressler. In addition, Murdoch had a close relationship with longtime FCC commissioner James Quello, who opposed virtually all pro-child efforts at the FCC.

The reason for Murdoch's largesse to politicians is simple: he is an extremely bold and aggressive businessman, and he has needed many Washington favors. Whether trying to sidestep limits on foreign ownership of U.S. television stations (Murdoch and his News Corporation are Australian), opposing attempts to restrict alcohol advertising on television (beer and wine makers spend more than $600 million annually on radio and TV commercials), or trying to eliminate any positive requirements regarding kids' programming by the FCC, the efforts of Murdoch and News Corporation are shining examples of how big media companies can buy off the Washington politicians who are supposed to regulate them and protect the public interest.

HAIM SABAN

Murdoch's partner in Fox Family Worldwide was Haim Saban, the man who brought us *Power Rangers, BeetleBorgs,* and an assortment of other low-end, violent kids' television programs. Like his former business partner Murdoch, Saban is extremely intelligent, charming, and very wealthy. I enjoy him personally, and we have had many meetings in which he has been unfailingly gracious and witty. But he is also, in my opinion, one of the most negative forces in the kids' media world, largely because of the types of programs he chooses to make and distribute.

At first glance, Haim Saban may seem very different from Rupert Murdoch—different personality, different political views, and different career path. But in many ways, the two strike me as being very similar. It's no great accident that the two became partners in Fox Family Worldwide, since both of them seem to have an amazing ability to compartmentalize their lives. They appear charming and family-oriented in their personal lives, yet they produce and distribute media content that often seems inimical to the best interests of children and families. Moreover, they both have reputations for shrewd and often ruthless deal-making as well as ethics that have at times been questioned.

Haim Saban is an Egyptian-born Israeli who built his own kids' media empire virtually from scratch. Starting first in Paris with a partner, Shuki Levy, Saban tapped into two business markets that would one day make him very rich: cartoon theme music and obscure Japanese TV shows remade into European and American children's programs.

Saban set up shop in Los Angeles in the late 1970s and began selling cartoon soundtracks and Japanese cartoons. His big breakthrough came when he convinced Rupert Murdoch's Fox network to air *Mighty Morphin Power Rangers* in its 1993 kids' lineup. The show was widely and repeatedly criticized by educators and children's advocates for its violent content, but Saban defended it as a "fantasy show" and said that kids could tell the difference between fantasy and reality. Although few educators or kids' advocates agreed, Saban didn't seem to care too much. The *Power Rangers* became a global merchandizing phenomenon and formed the foundation of his media empire. As one of Saban's top cable TV competitors said of him, "He's all about transactions. It's a different mentality. It's all about money and toys. There's a formula behind everything he does."[285] In 1996, Saban merged his company, Saban Entertainment, with the kids' programming and distribution assets of his new partner, Rupert Murdoch. Together they purchased the Family Channel from Pat Robertson and launched Fox Family Worldwide.

One of the aspects of business success that Saban seems to have learned well from his partner is how to use money to protect himself from his many critics and to gain important influence in Washington, D.C. Saban has been extremely effective at courting Washington politicians, most notably leading Democrats. According to *The New York Times,* he has given over $10 million to the Democratic Party over the years. In addition, he has been one of the major donors to the Clinton Library project in Little Rock, and in a relatively short time he has established himself as one of the most influential Hollywood donors to the Democratic Party. This influence has enabled Saban to escape significant criticism of his programming content and gain smooth sailing for his media business transactions, as well as the ear of national leaders for his views on Israeli and Middle East politics.

Why is this so troubling? Because Saban, like Rupert Murdoch, has been a prime architect of some of the most damaging trends in kids' television programming. In its very successful pursuit of huge profits,

Saban's media empire has brought the world's children a steady diet of toy-driven, violent action figures, focusing on "the deal" to the exclusion of any commitment to positive values or children's needs.

Haim Saban has been quoted as saying that "children don't watch television to be educated and they never will." But *all* media educates. And what kids can learn from much of the media Saban produced and distributed over the Fox Kids network are lessons I'd prefer they did without. In fact, in our home, our kids are simply not allowed to watch any Fox shows.

As is now well documented, *Power Rangers* elicited worldwide protest from parents' and teachers' groups. Government agencies in Canada and elsewhere banned the series, and it came to symbolize the classic violent cartoon. For me, however, it's the show's focus on toys and merchandise that's most troubling. This type of media is created not out of a regard for kids or quality programming, but rather in an effort to spend as little money as possible on the content while selling as much licensed merchandise as possible.

Saban may be charming, and he remains someone I always enjoy chatting with on a personal level, but he has been a disaster for kids' television content. Like his partner Rupert Murdoch, he has made kids' media a world of profits rather than principle.

THE $70 BILLION SPECTRUM GIVEAWAY

Nowhere is the nexus between gobs of campaign cash and shamelessly pro-industry political behavior more clearly demonstrated than in our federal government's recent $70 billion "giveaway" of the digital spectrum to our nation's broadcasters. This is truly a story worth telling, because it represents the classic combination of media, money, and politics acting against the proper public interests of the nation. You couldn't make up a sadder tale if you tried.

In early 1996, media industry leaders from all key sectors—phone companies and cable to satellite and broadcasting—gathered alongside our government leaders to celebrate a revolutionary revision of America's communications law. This was indeed a big deal. It was the first major overhaul of America's telecommunications policy in more than sixty years (since 1934, to be exact). The politicians and their counterparts in the media spoke of millions of jobs, tremendous GNP growth, new choices for consumers, competition, new services we never dreamed of. You name it, they said it.

What the president and the congressional leaders did not mention, however, was that the true beneficiaries of the 1996 Telecommunications Act were the media giants themselves, who had lobbied long and hard for the legislation's passage. If you had attended this bipartisan lovefest of a press conference, you would have thought the *public* was the big winner. But the true picture was very different. As one leading advocate put it, "The Telecommunications Act of 1996 was like giving the broadcasters a blank check with television—do with it what you want."[286]

One provision of the bill that America's television broadcasters had long sought, and finally got, was the lifting of restrictions on the number of local TV stations that one company could own. That was clearly a win for big media companies and a loss for small local broadcasters and consumers. But it was something in another part of the bill—one that was never mentioned at the back-scratching press conference—that stood to make the broadcast industry giants many, many billions of dollars. It was something called the digital spectrum.

The average American family does not know what the digital spectrum is. Why should they? But in Washington, D.C., all the politicians and media barons do understand the subject, and the stakes, very well. The new legislation gave broadcasters an immensely valuable slice of the public airwaves—basically, a set of new channels (digital ones) over which it is possible to bring viewers a better, high-definition picture. But broadcasters saw something even more valuable in these new digital channels—huge marketing opportunities never before imaginable over our publicly owned broadcast spectrum.

As one of my colleagues said at the time, "Having a piece of the digital spectrum is like having the keys to Fort Knox." This was a gold mine for the broadcast giants. Digital technology and the new digital spectrum will allow broadcasters to take each analog channel that they own right now (courtesy of the public and our elected officials, mind you) and turn it into five or even ten new channels. This new technology and digital spectrum will allow broadcasters to create new, interactive channels that allow you to simply click on a commercial to buy a product, as well as new, niche channels on which to sell more commercials. In short, this digital spectrum will give broadcast giants lots of new channels as well as piles and piles of new money . . . all for free from the American public courtesy of our trusted political representatives.

Now, since we, the public, *own* the digital spectrum, you might wonder why we aren't charging the media giants for their use of this valuable American resource and spending the proceeds for all sorts of positive social things, like better media for kids, or free political time for candidates, or even better health and child care for American families. After all, it's our spectrum. We own it. It's worth approximately $70 billion. Why shouldn't American society and families get something for it from the media industry?

Imagine if we had given all of our public land away for free to giant corporations and big real estate developers. We wouldn't have Central Park in New York City. We wouldn't have Yellowstone or Yosemite National Park. We'd have more shopping malls and high-rise office buildings instead. Imagine if we had given away all our land in the 1800s to the railroad companies without requiring them to build land grant colleges and lots of other public works. It would have been highway robbery, and it would have been terrible for our nation.

In the mid-1990s, the Federal government auctioned off the digital wireless spectrum to wireless phone companies. These auctions raised something in the neighborhood of $16 billion for the United States Treasury. So if you have an AT&T digital phone or a Sprint PCS phone or a Verizon or a Nextel or whatever, all of these companies are using spectrum that they paid huge sums of money for. So why would we ever give away $70 billion worth of the digital spectrum to giant media broadcasters just a short time later?

Well, the broadcasting giants—the people who bring us our leading prime-time shows and many of our favorite sports events and soap operas—also bring us our local and national news programs. That is their dirty little secret and the reason they are so powerful—probably more powerful than any other lobbying group when they want to be. The fact is, broadcasters control more than mere millions in campaign contributions. Broadcasters often control the fate of America's politicians and shape our political issues.

Here's how Senator John McCain describes it:

> Let me tell you how they do that. There's an issue before the Congress, which affects their industry. Call in the station managers from the congressman's district or the senator's state. They all come to Washington. They sit down with the senator or representative. Now, there's never any threats made, there's never any statement that if you don't do this, we're going to say bad things about you in the newscast, but they are the messengers. They portray you and your work here in Washington to the people in your state or districts. That's incredibly powerful.[287]

John McCain was one of only two senators who actually opposed the giveaway of the digital spectrum to the broadcasters. Another was then-Senator and presidential candidate Bob Dole. They are both pro-business Republicans, who usually bend over backward to be generous to American industries. Neither has ever championed kids' media issues or the kind of legislation that can promote positive media for the broader public interest. But at least they knew a huge rip-off when they saw one. And as free-market capitalists, they thought that the broadcasting giants ought to pay.

As Senator McCain recalls:

> I heard and saw many other members of Congress who said, "This is good for America; all Americans are going to get a

much better picture on their TV set; things are going to be great," and I agree with that. But why should a profit-making corporation get that asset for free and not have to pay for it? . . . If we had said, "Look, we've got $10 billion worth of public land out there in the West, and we're going to give it to various corporations in America for them to use, and they're going to give us some other land which really isn't nearly as good in exchange for that," the American people would have never stood for such a thing, ever.[288]

Now, you'd think that a $70 billion giveaway would have had the makings of a major news story. Here we had huge, powerful corporations picking the pocket of American taxpayers. It's exactly the kind of scandal that TV news broadcasters love to investigate. You get major journalism awards and huge audiences for this kind of stuff. As we know by now, TV news loves a scandal. So what happened?

The Telecommunications Act of 1996 was introduced in the spring of 1995 and finally passed in February 1996. During that period of nearly a year, the three major network news programs—those of CBS, NBC, and ABC—aired a grand total of nineteen minutes of coverage.[289] Moreover, none of these nineteen minutes included a single mention of the debate over whether the broadcast media giants should pay for the use of the digital spectrum or whether they should incur major new public-interest obligations in return for the free ownership of this $70 billion publicly owned asset.

Not one single story in nearly a year! Even though this was the most important piece of communications law in sixty years. Even though a number of newspapers including the *New York Times* and the *Washington Post* and even Ann Landers editorialized against it. Even though the NAB itself—the broadcasters' lobbying arm—was worried enough about their chances that it launched a multimillion-dollar campaign in support of the act. The NAB ad campaign never mentioned the spectrum giveaway. Instead they claimed Congress was planning to tax viewers. So there was zero news coverage by the broadcasters of this scandal. Talk about the corruption of politics and media in our society. The broadcasters were using the publicly owned airwaves, which they had received for free, to ensure that there would be no coverage of an issue with enormous implications—both social and financial—for the American people . . . and for American kids in particular. From their point of view, it is understandable. As one of my colleagues in the advocacy world said, "It would be like a bank robber stopping a bank robbery and saying, 'look at what we're doing here. Let's have a press conference in front of the bank while we're doing it.' "[290]

The broadcast industry was dumping tens of millions of dollars into the hands of our elected officials at the time of this key legislation, and we had no public discussion about it. The public never got upset about this giveaway because they didn't know. The worst irony of all is that the same media giants claim to be guardians of "free speech." They are the protectors of our hallowed First Amendment. They are the first to cry censorship when we try to promote things like the Children's Television Act or a V-chip rating system for families. Doesn't it make you feel great to know that *these* are the guys—along with the politicians whom they so effectively control—who are protecting our constitutional rights to free speech and free press?

THE GORE COMMISSION

The FCC staffers and Chairman Reed Hundt, who had watched in outrage as the huge rip-off went down with nary a story, could not reverse the law. So they did what they always do in Washington, D.C., when they have no clue what to do and have basically run out of ideas or political courage: they formed a commission. They leaned on the president and vice president to create a commission charged with designing a public-interest agenda for the broadcasters who had just received this $70 billion gift from Congress. Since this was an intelligent and activist FCC staff under Chairman

Hundt, they knew that there were two obvious ways the media giants could contribute to the broader public interest—by making a major new commitment to air quality kids' television, and by making an equally significant commitment to provide free airtime for political candidates, a move that could help end the corruption that underlies our multibillion dollar electoral system.

Unfortunately, the Gore Commission turned out to be like most government commissions—all talk and no action. The commission had all the right intentions, and it included some of the most thoughtful and knowledgeable people in the media and public-interest arenas. But the vice president and his staff made a fundamental mistake. Trying to appear fair and open-minded, they included a number of representatives from the TV and media industry itself. They even agreed to have it cochaired by a huge player in the broadcast TV world—Les Moonves, the president of CBS Entertainment. In truth, Al Gore and his staff should have known better. As a result of their well-intentioned efforts to appear fair to all sides, they got basically nothing done. They had a divided commission, which came up with a set of watered-down recommendations, none of which actually pressured the broadcasters to do anything meaningful, and in the end the Gore Commission essentially faded away into the place where most Washington, D.C., commissions end up—oblivion

So, bottom line, what happened? The media industry giants— the broadcasters—won, and America's families lost. This was an unbelievable opportunity to raise $70 billion for American taxpayers or to require the broadcast industry to do far more for America's kids. We can still reopen the debate, and as I'll argue in chapter 11, we absolutely should. Leaders like former President Clinton and Senator McCain who now recognize the error in the giveaway might be recruited to lead the effort. But for now, money and politics won the game, and the public lost. It's that simple . . . and it's that sad.

Part Two

TAKING BACK CONTROL: STRATEGIES FOR CHANGE

Eight

IT ALL STARTS
AT HOME

Few things make me angrier than seeing media and political leaders lay all the blame on parents for exposing kids to overly violent or sexualized media. As the FTC recently proved, media companies frequently do everything in their power to peddle this material to children. Politicians, meanwhile, often turn a blind eye to these practices because they don't want to alienate big campaign donors. And instead of changing their products and marketing practices, it's much easier and safer for the media leaders to scapegoat parents, who, their argument assumes, are able to monitor their children's media use twenty-four hours a day.

Obviously, as any parent knows, that's not the case. Media messages and images so saturate our lives that it's not possible for parents to protect their kids from every potentially harmful media exposure. As a parent, I regularly feel overwhelmed and undermined by the media's influence on my own kids, and I know that millions of other parents feel just as alarmed that their children's media exposure is, to a great extent, out of their control. It often seems that no matter how vigilant you are, how much you pay attention, there is always some edgy new song, movie, video game, or TV show that makes you wonder what kinds of distorted perceptions and values your children are absorbing.

PARENTS: THE FIRST LINE OF DEFENSE

But the truth is, as parents, we *do* need to take whatever steps we can to control the media's impact on our children. There is not much we can do about the creative and marketing decisions of media companies, and we can't make up for the dearth of government leadership on these issues. But as parents, we are our children's first line of defense, and we have to take that responsibility seriously. We can't just shut our eyes to the problem and ignore the "other parent's" constant, cumulative influence. We have to be just as involved and aware of our kids' media use as we are of their friends, their schoolwork, and their physical and emotional well-being.

What does that mean in practical terms? Although it's impossible to shield our kids completely from the bombardment of media images and messages, we can give them basic tools and values to help them filter those messages successfully and make good judgments. Specifically, there are two key things that we can do:

1. We can limit our children's access and exposure to the media, especially when they are young.

2. We can help our kids process and understand media messages and, as a family, make the most of many positive media experiences.

In this chapter, I'm setting out my Top Ten Steps for Parents, reviewed by child-development experts such as Dr. T. Berry Brazelton. These are relatively simple steps that all parents can take to help create a safer media environment for their kids.

1. Establish Good Media Habits Early

It's almost axiomatic that your kids are never too young to start learning good habits and values. And when it comes to establishing good media habits, the earlier you start the better. In my experience, those habits should be set as early as the age of two or three.

In practical terms, this means setting clear limits on your child's media use and choosing the content of that media wisely. It is best to start when kids are toddlers, so that they'll grow up with a sense that media use is a privilege instead of a constant activity. Establish rules about when, where, and how your kids can use the media, and be very selective about what you let them play with, listen to, and watch. The younger your child is when you set those rules, and the more consistently you enforce them, the more successful you'll be in shaping your child's future expectations and behavior.

If you don't set and enforce those rules, media can easily consume more hours of your child's life than any other activity except sleeping.[291] The average American child, in fact, spends five-and-a-half hours per day—thirty-eight hours per week—consuming media and approximately 33,500 hours just watching television by the time he or she graduates from high school. That compares to the 13,000 or so hours the average child spends in school, from kindergarten through twelfth grade, and far outstrips the amount of time he or she spends with family, in creative play, and in other important, healthier activities.

At the same time, study after study shows that kids who spend more time engaged in learning and personal enrichment activities—including hobbies, sports, household chores, and community youth programs—are far more likely to be high achievers in school. The healthiest choice, without a doubt, is to start channeling our kids' time and attention when they are young away from the media and into active and creative alternatives.

I'm not suggesting that you get rid of your CD players, computers, TV sets, and other types of media in your home. I am, however, talking about balance—setting limits and paying attention, as parents, to what media content our children are consuming. It's easiest and best to start establishing good habits early, before children's behavior patterns are set and there's a risk of igniting a power struggle with your child. But it's never too late to start paying attention and using whatever strategies you can to influence the amount and content of your child's media consumption.

2. Location, Location, Location: No TV or Computer in Your Child's Room

One of the most important decisions is where to put those electronic boxes we call TVs and computers. Considering that two-thirds of all American youngsters who are eight years and older have a TV in their bedroom—along with a third of all two-to-seven-year-olds[292]—I can't think of a more fundamental issue.

Where you put a television or a computer sends an incredibly important message to your child and to yourself about whether media is a choice or a habit. That's why I propose this very clear and simple rule: Do not put a television in your child's bedroom. TVs should only be in common areas or family rooms where you can supervise what your kids are watching.

The same goes for computers, in my opinion, although I know that there are millions of teenagers who will kick and scream when they hear this. In fact, in an interview for this book, AOL chairman and Internet pioneer Steve Case discussed at length how crucial it is for parents to be involved in and able to control their child's access to the Internet—and he added that even his own children don't have computers in their rooms.

Basically, media usage should be more of a family affair, not a private act performed without guidelines or supervision. When TVs and computers are located in common areas, it makes it a whole lot easier for parents to be actively and positively involved in their kids' media consumption. As they say in the real estate business, it's all about "location, location, location."

Geraldine Laybourne—the innovator and teacher who built Nickelodeon into the powerhouse of the kids' television world—clearly understood the importance of the television's location in her own home. As she tells it:

I would never let the television set be in the same place. It would be in the front hallway for two months, and then I would move it to the back study, then I would move it to a closet. I just kept changing the place it was in. I didn't want my kids to get in the habit of thinking it was there. . . . I think parents should try to be as intrusive in the experience as they possibly can be, to get kids aware that they are spending valuable time. And if they're going to commit their time to it, what is it that they're watching? And why?[293]

Once you put the TV and computer in a place where you can supervise your children's access, it's time to think seriously about the amount and types of media that your family is consuming.

3. Set a Media Diet and Stick to It

Perhaps the simplest and most effective way for parents to approach their child's media use is to think of it in terms of a "media diet." This model has been suggested by many authorities, from the American Academy of Pediatrics to respected experts like Milton Chen, president of the George Lucas Educational Foundation and author of *The Smart Parent's Guide to Kids' TV.* Setting a media diet implies limits as well as balance. It does not mean banishing all media from your home and attempting to eliminate it from your kids' lives; that's about as practical as trying to outlaw every piece of junk food. It does, however, mean sending a clear message to children and teens about the need to control the quantity and quality of media exposure in their lives.

The junk food analogy is especially appropriate. Most concerned parents don't let their children eat whatever they want, whenever they want it. Instead, they recognize that what kids put into their bodies can affect their health, how they perform in school, and their state of mind. As a result, many parents actively encourage a diet that balances good nutrition with kids' natural desire for special treats. The same approach and philosophy can be applied to media.

To create a media diet for your child, start by asking yourself and family members these basic questions and keep track of the answers:

- How much TV do you watch?

- When do you watch it?

- What music do you listen to and when?

- How many movies do you go to a month?

- What video games do you play?

- Do you ever enjoy media together as a family?

- Do younger brothers and sisters watch the same TV programs as older siblings?

The questions and answers may surprise you, and they'll help you take stock of your family's current level of consumption.

The next step, as Milton Chen and others recommend, is to keep a media diary for yourself and other family members for a week or two. It's critical that, as a parent, you examine your own behavior and choices as part of this experiment, because you are the most important role model for your child. Keep track of all the media that each family member uses and post the results in a conspicuous place, like on the refrigerator door. Once the tracking period is over, add up the total number of hours that each family member spent using various types of media, listed by category—TV, music, computer, video games, books, magazines, movies, and so on. Then take a look at the specific content that each family member used— what kinds of music, TV programs, games, or Web sites they selected—and see what kinds of patterns emerge. What types of music did your son or daughter listen to? How many times did your child play the same video game? How many magazines or books did you read? Did you watch TV or movies with your kid? Trying this little experiment for a week or two can make your family members much more conscious of their media use.

Next, come up with a healthier media diet for your family. First, set clear limits on the total number of hours that each family member should spend using all forms of media each week. What those limits should be is your decision, but I personally would recommend a maximum of fifteen hours a week (about two hours a day) for all media, and I'd set a lower limit within that figure for TV (never more than two hours a day, with exceptions for special, agreed-upon events, such as election returns, the Super Bowl, New Year's Eve specials, and the like). There really is no magic number, however. The important thing is to set clear limits and stick to them.

You can start your media diet, like any diet, in different ways. For some families, a "Media Turn-Off Week" (or two) may be the best way to begin. Others find that the best way is to change media use patterns gradually, a few hours a week. However you start, keep in mind that it isn't easy to change habits. But when parents agree on media rules and enforce them, children's patterns of behavior can and will change. The fact is, kids often respond well to limits; once they know what they are, they learn to live with them.

In addition to limits on the quantity of media, set limits on the type and content of the media products that your child can use. One of the most important issues is age appropriateness. Although this can be a complex issue, general principles of age-based development hold true. In other words, if you're the parent of a four-year-old, and a movie rating indicates that the film is for children six and older, *pay attention to the rating*. Even if that child is exceptionally intelligent, it's usually wise for her not to watch the movie. Though she may be advanced in reading or math, developmentally she will still process story lines and characters like other four-year-olds. As family movie expert Nell Minow points out, "Children are less cynical than adolescents and adults about what they see, more prone to confuse important issues raised by what they view, less able to see actions in light of motives and consequences, more apt to confuse fantasy and reality, and more ready to accept screen characters as behavior models. As a result, children are more vulnerable to the potential negative messages in what they watch, including violence and other inappropriate behavior."[294]

There are other conscious choices that parents need to make. For kids under the age of nine or ten, I believe that for the most part you should shop for content that is consciously designed to be educational and choose media products that are "nutritional" instead of "junk food." Every once in a while, of course, you can choose a few "treats" that are pure entertainment. At our house, for example, we let our seven-year-old son, Kirk, watch *Pokemon* for half an hour most Saturday mornings and let him play with a Game Boy once in a while. Otherwise, though, we limit his use of media pretty strictly.

Parents need to do some homework, too, to help their kids make good media choices, learning more about the basic content, messages, and characters of the media their kids consume. Take time, for example, to watch a few shows from a TV series with your child. By co-viewing, you'll discover what your child is watching and make it clear that you care about the messages and images in those programs. Similarly, by listening to songs, playing computer games, or surfing the Internet with your child, you'll learn what content your son or daughter is exposed to and can begin to set knowledgeable limits.

Of course, since democracies work better than dictatorships, your family's media diet will be a whole lot more successful if you involve your child in the process of making media choices. As Dr. Brazelton points out, if parents are overly controlling with media, then kids will use the media behind their backs. "It's better to be open and listen to them," he advises, "instead of setting impractical rules."

4. Teach Your Child to Ask Permission to Use Media

If your kids want to watch TV, play a video game, or listen to music, teach them to ask for your permission first. This is a simple way to get children to think of media not as a constant presence but as an activity that they do "by appointment only." If they have to ask permission to use the media, they will understand that it's a privilege and not something to be taken for granted. Making kids ask permission gives you the chance to ask good questions, like, "Why do you want to play that particular computer game?" or "Do you really need to watch TV now?" It also gives you the opportunity to suggest alternative activities, like reading, playing outside, or doing something special together.

TV is, by far, the most pervasive of all forms of media. In millions of American homes, the tube is turned on as soon as some family member wakes up or comes into the house, and it stays on whether anyone is watching it or not—an average of sixty hours per week or eight and a half hours per day in the typical American home with children. People who watch the average amount of television—twenty-eight hours a week—spend thirteen years watching TV by the time they are seventy-five.[295]

One of the healthiest things we can do for our kids is to teach them to make TV and media use a choice, not a habit. It goes without saying, however, that they won't learn this lesson if we mindlessly plunk ourselves down in front of the tube all evening long. Since kids model their behavior on what they see, parents need to alter their approach to media too.

5. Watch and Listen with Your Kids—Then Tell Them What You Like, Don't Like, and Why

Most parents wouldn't think of just sending their kids off to school without being involved in the experience—asking their children how things are going, for example, and checking in with teachers or administrators. Since kids often spend *more* of their time with the media than they do at school, it's every bit as important to be involved and know what and how your kids are doing in the media world.

That may sound like a daunting task, but it's not that difficult. Pay attention to what media your children are consuming. Sit down and watch television or videos with them. Listen to the music that they like. Play their video games with them. You might be surprised at how enjoyable it is, and it can give you a whole new way to share important aspects of their lives. By exploring their media world with them, you are showing that you respect and are interested in their choices. It's an opportunity to build good, open communication and trust.

Moreover, if you watch or listen with your kids instead of ignorantly passing judgment on the media they like, you will have a far greater chance of influencing them. If you spend time with your kids' favorite media choices and don't feel comfortable with those products, say so and explain why. Your kids may roll their eyes and tell you that you "just don't get it," but they have heard you and absorbed your values, whether they admit it or not.

My friend Rebecca, for instance, uses that strategy with her two teenage daughters, ages fourteen and seventeen. Now that her girls are in high school, she's pretty realistic about her inability to control their exposure to music and other types of media. "I have no expectations," she says, "that I can keep my kids from listening to misogynistic or explicitly sexual music, because it's all around them. It's in their atmosphere, their world." But she does draw the line, as clearly as possible, when she can. "When we're in the car, for example," Rebecca says, "I let the kids pick the radio station we listen to. But if a violent, explicit, or misogynistic song comes on, I'll say to them, 'Not in my car. I don't want to listen to this song because it's offensive to women, or violent, or grossly sexual.' They respect that, and they'll flip to another station. They hear what I say, and they don't fight me on it. I'm not telling them they can never listen to that kind of stuff, but I am drawing a big red circle around that song and telling them *why* I don't approve of it."

Child development experts like Mike Cohen will tell you that parents drawing those kinds of lines and explaining to their children *why* they disapprove is incredibly powerful and effective. When Rebecca's daughter hears that same song at her friend's house, for instance, she'll remember that someone important in her life disapproves of it and has explained why, coloring her interpretation of the song forever. When you let your kids know how you feel and why, they may disagree with you, but they'll remember what you said. They may continue to listen to that misogynistic music or play that violent video game, but it will never be as much fun. They will never experience it in the same way again . . . even those hard-to-reach teenagers who always seem to be putting up brick walls.

There's another important reason to watch and listen to media with your kids—to keep them from feeling traumatized or over-whelmed by frightening messages and images. For our family and millions of others, the tragedy of September 11, 2001, was an unfor-gettable example. Children saw the horrendous pictures of the World Trade Center and victims in the rubble, and they needed parents to help them understand the tragedy. They had tough questions, and many had nightmares and ongoing fears. As parents, we all needed to be involved. By sharing and talking about difficult or frightening media experiences with our children—avoiding their repeated expo-sure to scary images, staying in control of our own emotions, and conveying information as well as our own feelings and values—we can help them process the experience and limit the anxiety they feel.

6. Set Clear Rules Regarding Your Child's Media Use in Other Homes

Even if you have a strict media diet and rules in your own home, it can be difficult to control what your child is exposed to in the homes of classmates, neighbors, relatives, and friends. Our own children have friends whose parents have either few or no rules regarding their kids' media consumption, and from talking to lots of other par-ents, I know how common this situation is. So what can you do?

The way I see it, your own children's media rules should be the same no matter whose home they're in. As always, honest commu-nication is the key. First, parents need to acknowledge that it's an issue and talk frankly with their own family about it. It's not neces-sary to badmouth other children or their parents. It's enough to say that you have certain media rules that your kids need to follow wherever they might be. It's also helpful to role-play a bit with your kids, so they'll know how to tell their friends about the rules. Most peers will respect that.

Second, it's important to let other parents know about your child's media limits. This may not be the easiest thing in the world to do, but who ever said parenting was easy? Actually, these conversations can lead to some frank and positive discussions about media, and that's an added plus. Most parents I've talked to say that they felt much better after they addressed the issue head-on, often with positive results.

7. Have Pediatricians Review Your Kids' Media Use as Part of Their Annual Checkup

For at least the past few decades, physicians have been raising concerns about the media's impact on children, and many have come to see it as a public health issue. When I was running Children Now and helping to spearhead national advocacy efforts around kids' media issues, doctors groups were often some of our best allies. Whether it was the American Medical Association, the American Academy of Pediatrics, or noted experts like Dr. T. Berry Brazelton, physicians saw control of kids' media consumption as an important part of their healthy development.

The American Academy of Pediatrics, which represents most of the pediatricians in the United States, has taken an increasingly outspoken stance on these issues, particularly where issues of violence and sexuality are concerned. Moreover, medical researchers have long recognized a negative correlation between kids' sedentary media habits and their physical health. As a result, the AAP now recommends that pediatricians should review media consumption as part of children's annual physical exams.

You can encourage this healthy practice. The next time you bring your kids in for a checkup, ask your pediatrician to talk with them about their media consumption, as well as their basic diet and nutrition. Both parents and kids will learn a lot from this annual exercise, and it's one more way to reinforce the importance to your kids of making conscious and intelligent choices about their media diets.

8. Teach Media Literacy in School and at Home

At the end of the day, it's clear that whether we like it or not, kids learn a great deal from media, beginning at the earliest stages of life. Most kids simply absorb these messages. However, if they learn how to think critically about the media—to analyze, evaluate, interpret, and deconstruct it, if you will—they can get more benefits from it and be protected from many negative effects.

That's where the concept of *media literacy* comes in.[296] In my opinion, it's one of the most important survival skills that kids can have. Most parents and schools, unfortunately, know very little about media literacy, and our society has invested very little in it, to our children's detriment.

Media literacy is a pretty simple concept. Researchers define it as the "ability to access, analyze, evaluate, and process media." The primary goals in teaching it are to help kids learn to use TV, music, and other media consciously and selectively and to help them think critically about the media messages and images they receive.[297] It's an important part of any child's education. Young kids, especially, can't easily tell the difference between fantasy and reality, and they often take literally what the media shows and tells them. The four-year-old son of a friend of mine, for example, thought that if he ate a certain kind of candy, he'd be able to fly, because he saw that happen on a TV commercial. Older kids, too, often tend to take at face value and internalize many of the commercially driven messages that the media sends—about body image, for example, or sexual behavior. Media literacy is designed to give kids the tools to see through the hype and filter the media that surrounds them.

The concept has been around since the 1960s and 1970s, when

educators in Great Britain and Australia recognized how much their students were learning from the media, especially television. Concerned primarily about the media's negative effects, these educators developed a media literacy curriculum that taught kids how to think critically about the information they received. The program was so successful that it was widely adopted in English and Australian schools.[298]

In the early 1980s, Canada followed England and Australia's lead in adopting a media literacy curriculum. Parents and educators in each of these countries have since seen substantial improvement in kids' critical awareness of media as well as a significant reduction in the amount of time that kids spend watching television in particular. Children in these countries now appear to be less easily influenced by what they are exposed to in the media and better able to analyze critically, and in certain cases reject, its content and messages. Today, media literacy is a core part of the national educational curriculum in more than half a dozen countries around the globe.

But here in the United States—the unquestioned media capital of the world—the media literacy concept is not very well known and has received little or no support from our government or the media industry. A couple of states such as New Mexico have started to adopt media education as part of their school curricula, but so far it's a limited effort, and few parents are even aware of media literacy's potential.[299]

You can help change this climate of ignorance and apathy about media literacy. First of all, you can start using its techniques in your own home. They're well documented in such books as Milton Chen's *The Smart Parent's Guide to Kids' TV* and Lauryn Axelrod's *TV-Proof Your Kids*. Equally important, you can ask your child's school to start teaching media literacy as a regular part of the curriculum, using simple materials that are widely available. I've already met with the principal and teachers at my own kids' school and suggested that they include media literacy in the standard curriculum as early as first grade.

Obviously, there are huge possible roles for our government

and the media industry itself in all of this, and I'll address those in subsequent chapters. But as we wait for a much broader and more comprehensive commitment to media literacy, parents can start leading the charge in their own homes, communities, and schools.

9. Read to Your Child and Share Positive Media Experiences

As most parents know, one of the most important and valuable family activities you can engage in is reading to and with your children. I propose taking that a step further. Listening to music, playing computer games, or watching a TV program with your kids can also be an important educational experience, strengthening family ties while giving you opportunities to link media messages to lessons about life and values. As child-development expert T. Berry Brazelton advises, "My bottom line is that you should share media experiences with your kids and be ready to talk with them about what they are experiencing. That's the best thing a parent can do."

Kids definitely benefit when parents take part with them in educational media experiences. Research has shown, for example, that children who co-view programs like *Sesame Street* with their parents show the greatest learning gains. And there's plenty of great educational media around. Preschool TV, for example, is a very fertile ground for positive media experiences. *Sesame Street*, of course, was created for educational purposes, and every year its preschool learning curriculum is refreshed by Sesame Workshop. Virtually all the preschool series you'll find on PBS or Nick Jr. are designed around educational goals and strong curricula. Many other shows like *Reading Rainbow, Blue's Clues, Between the Lions, Bear in the Big Blue House, Dragon Tales,* and even *Barney & Friends,* are also consciously and expensively designed to promote learning, and most deliver on that promise day in and day out.

In fact, let's take a closer look at *Barney* for a minute. Two noted child development experts from Yale University, Drs. Jerome and Dorothy Singer, conducted a lengthy study of *Barney & Friends* and revealed that he's actually a pretty deep dinosaur. Indeed the Singers' research concluded that this seemingly silly show was "nearly a model for what a preschool program should be." The program actually addresses six major areas that are important in preschool education.[300] So "The Big B," as my daughter Lily now cynically calls that purple dinosaur, is actually a highly developed preschool teacher.

There are also hundreds of computer software programs I could list, from *Reader Rabbit* to *Oregon Trail* and *Carmen Sandiego*, that were explicitly designed as educational tools. In the old days, before massive mergers led to the buyout and destruction of much of the educational software business, companies like Davidson and the original Learning Company and Broderbund were built to serve kids' educational needs. As a result, there's much to be proud of out there and tons more potential for good content that kids will enjoy and learn from.

But even media that is designed purely as entertainment—like sports or movies—can be a great opportunity to bond with your children—to share life lessons, to ask questions, to laugh and play together. I remember that when I was little, my father worked long hours. I didn't see much of him during the week, and sometimes not on weekends either. He worked very hard, and he was often tired. But when he came home, he would sometimes let me watch Marx Brothers or W. C. Fields movies with him. I must have seen *A Night at the Opera* twenty times. Those were family events—special times to share together—and brought my dad and me closer.

The point I'm making here is that when parents are thoughtful and selective about the media that their families consume, it can stop seeming like an oppressive "other parent." Instead, media can actually be used to create positive family experiences—to build knowledge, teach values, and bolster family ties.

10. Switch the Dial to "Off"

Need I say more?

Top Ten Steps for Parents

1. Establish good media habits early.
2. Location, location, location: no TV or computer in your child's room.
3. Set a media diet and stick to it.
4. Teach your child to ask permission to use media.
5. Watch and listen with your kids—then tell them what you like, don't like, and why.
6. Set clear rules regarding your child's media use in other homes.
7. Have pediatricians review your kids' media use as part of their annual checkup.
8. Teach media literacy in school and at home.
9. Read to your child and share positive media experiences.
10. Switch the dial to "off."

Nine

CALLING THE MEDIA INDUSTRY TO ACCOUNT

You would think that the most natural place to start looking for solutions would be at the root source—the media industry itself. Well, think again. It's certainly true that there are a large number of well-meaning, talented, and socially committed people within the media world, many of whom are devoted and concerned parents like you and me. And many of these people contribute time and money to important social issues. But the broader industry itself is another story. I'm deeply skeptical about how much positive change we can expect unless enormous public pressure is brought to bear in a sustained manner. Let's spend a little time looking at who some of these people and companies are—the shining examples as well as some who are among the worst offenders—to get a better sense of whether we can ever expect the media industry to do far better for our kids.

"SCHIZOPHRENIC/BIFURCATED LIVES"

Many of the people I know in the media industry are very intelligent and capable. Many are good parents. Many truly believe in their hearts that they're doing positive things for society with the products their companies produce and distribute. So how is it that so much of what our kids see, hear, and interact with can be such offensive crap?

At the end of the day, much of what the large media companies *do* is very different from much of what their leaders think and feel and actually say. Why? As always, it comes down to their fixation with quarterly profits and stock price. They can tell you all the good things they do and believe in. They can give you the most articulate examples of artistic freedom and unique creativity. But at the end of the day, the bottom line is the bottom line. It's all about money. That's what ultimately dictates their decisions, and the decisions of the individuals who work for them.

Media analyst Ken Auletta is arguably the most knowledgeable and incisive observer of today's media and communications world. His recent book, *The Highwaymen,* provides an extraordinary insider's view of the various media titans as they compete to control the global communications and entertainment industry. When I decided to write this book, I went to see Auletta, because he has the best grip of anyone I know on the psyches of the leaders of the media entertainment business. As we talked about how these industry giants approach the kids and family audience, Auletta kept saying to me, "They're basically schizophrenics. They lead bifurcated lives. They're in denial." I have to say that that has been my experience too.

Doing research for his book, Auletta asked of a number of America's most powerful media leaders a very revealing question, "What *won't* you do?"

What I found out is that Michael Eisner, or Rupert Murdoch or many other of these people would tell you, 'I would not let my kids watch certain shows on television,' and yet by night and by day they would go and make the very shows they wouldn't let their own kids watch. And they disassociate it. They didn't connect that they were making these shows. So then you have to ask the question, Why? And I think you get to a basic schizophrenia. I think these people bifurcate what they do for the shareholders to increase profitability. Just like the cigarette manufacturers advertise, "Don't smoke if you can help it," and the lotteries advertise, "Don't bet over your head." They *want* people to bet. They *want* people to smoke. They *want* kids to watch these shows. *Period.* Because that's how they make money. . . . And what you have to do is introduce the element of shame to get them to connect the two persons that reside within the same body.[301]

The person who perhaps more than any other individual shapes the minds of kids and families around the globe is Michael Eisner, the enormously successful chairman and CEO of the Walt Disney Company. According to Auletta, Eisner bristled when asked the question, "What won't you do?"

"I believe there is nothing you should not be allowed to do," Eisner replied. "I don't believe strongly that government has any right to be involved in anything, or almost anything"[302] in the entertainment world. When Auletta mentioned how then-President Clinton was urging Hollywood to tone down sex and violence and the thousands of studies showing how television affects the behavior and attitudes of young viewers, Eisner said, "There are studies that show the opposite too . . . that it's a release from built-in tension. I do not think the president of the United States has an obligation to encourage censorship. There's nothing wrong with him expressing his opinion. . . . I'll tell you what I am offended by. I'm offended by those who get on a platform and berate Hollywood for violence in the movies, on the one hand, and ignore the proliferation of handguns—something they could do something about—on the other." When asked about studios that make violent movies, Eisner responded, "It's not a moral issue. I'm glad they do it. It brings people to the movie theaters."[303]

Later in the interview, Auletta asked Eisner about a producer who said he'd never let his ten-year-old see any of the movies that he'd made. Eisner replied, "I would never make a movie that I would not allow my ten-year-old to go to. I find that disingenuous. Now, maybe ten is not the line. Maybe it should be twelve or thirteen." And what about Disney's rather violent and scary *The Hand That Rocks the Cradle?* Eisner responded: "To me, *The Hand That Rocks the Cradle* was a complete fantasy. It ended up being pro-social, in that there was a whole relook at the question of leaving your children with people who haven't given you decent references. That was a silly movie. A fun movie."[304]

Rupert Murdoch, the chairman and CEO of News Corporation, is somebody I've already discussed at length in this book. Let's hear what this white-haired mogul had to say to Auletta's question:

> You wouldn't do anything that you couldn't live with, that would be against your principles. It's a very difficult question if you're a man of conscience. If you thought that you were doing something that was having a malevolent effect, as you saw it, on society, you would not do it. . . . But is violence justified? To the violence of *Lethal Weapon.* Okay. I think so. If it involves personal cruelty, sadism—obviously you would never do that. The trouble is, of course, that you run a studio, and how free are you to make these rules? The creative people give you a script and are given last cut on a movie. The next thing, you have a thirty-million dollar movie in the can, which you may disapprove of.[305]

After noting that his London newspaper The *Sun's* daily page three photos of bare-breasted women was just harmless fun, Murdoch assailed Hollywood's knee-jerk reaction against "family values" and fellow conservative and former Vice President Dan Quayle. So how does he reconcile the two seemingly opposite Murdochs—the man who embraces "family values" and Dan Quayle versus the one whose various studios, networks, and newspapers distribute trashy content that undermines these values? "Well," he says, "without being specific or apologizing for anything—I'm sure I've made lots of mistakes in sixty-two years—I'm not going to spend my life looking back."[306]

Later in the interview, Murdoch strongly criticized AOL Time

Warner's then-CEO Gerald M. Levin for defending gangsta-rap recording artists under the First Amendment and acknowledged that he and other media leaders do, in fact, have the right and power to control the content that their companies produce and distribute. But when "Mr. Family Values" was asked about Fox's tabloid TV show *A Current Affair* and some recent segments entitled, "Hollywood Sex," "Topless Haircut," "Killer Doctor," "Sexy Calendars," "Super Bowl Hookers," "Felony Nannies," "Teacher Pervert," and "Sex Addiction," Murdoch replied, "If you want me to get up and defend every film, [or] every program, I won't do it." He added that he wanted *A Current Affair* to be seen as a popular edition of *Nightline*.[307]

Auletta also interviewed Jack Welch, the recently retired chairman and CEO of General Electric, owner of NBC. Welch has been revered, like Eisner and Murdoch, as one of the world's most successful business leaders. His recent biography will no doubt outsell this book, and he is considered a titan among titans, one of the most respected CEOs ever. But when Auletta mentioned that NBC was the first network to show a television movie about the Amy Fisher–Joey Buttafuoco scandal, and that *Dateline,* the NBC newsmagazine, was caught doctoring and sensationalizing the fiery crash of a GM truck, Welch said, "that wasn't a Jack Welch or a GE decision. That was an NBC decision to do that. . . . I'm not into programming like Eisner is and other people are. That's their business. It's not my business. It's Bob Wright's business [president of NBC]." When asked if there was perhaps a dichotomy between Jack Welch, citizen and father, and Jack Welch, the businessman whose network and stations air programs and promotions that he wouldn't want his own young kids to watch, Welch replied, "I delegate to Bob Wright the responsibility. Just like it's not my job to build appliances."[308] It's so easy to point the finger and shift the blame when there are so many corporate divisions and so many faceless executives with exalted, overinflated titles.

I could go on and on. Auletta asked Tom Freston, CEO of MTV Networks (owned by Viacom), about the MTV videos featuring young women who simulate oral sex and dance partners who grind and squeeze each other's buttocks. He replied carefully, "There's an inference of sex. You won't see any actual sex. In any case, we don't make the videos, so we don't control what's in them."[309]

WHEN PROFITS RULE ALL, VALUES SUFFER

Industry leaders rationalize their excesses in a variety of ways. There's the "artistic freedom" argument that you hear so frequently. There's the "no two people view the same TV show the same" line. There's even the "I can point to studies that show that media violence doesn't cause violence and is actually a healthy release of tension" train of thought that we just heard from Michael Eisner.

Interestingly, one sees a general distinction between the views of artists, producers, and directors and those of corporate executives. The creative types almost always defend their own artistic freedom and point the finger at the corporate executives who control the distribution of media. That's just cynically passing the buck. While corporate executives may dictate the maxim "profit above all else," the artists or producers are still responsible for the content that they create, from editing and language to visual images, over which they have control.

The corporate executives, on the other hand, usually hide behind the "censorship" defense. As we've seen, these First Amendment arguments are almost always a red herring. This is not about First Amendment freedoms or censorship. It's about responsibility.

Let's be very clear here. Distribution companies don't have to sell albums by Eminem. Television networks don't have to make *A Current Affair* or put *Temptation Island* in prime time, just as certain adult-movie distributors don't have to distribute snuff flicks. They don't have to market violent cartoons or gruesome video games. Just because you believe in an artist or a director's First Amendment right to create patently offensive messages doesn't mean you have a duty to manufacture or to sell it. That's what corporate responsibility is all about. Time Warner didn't have to sell rage-rock records by Nine Inch Nails or Ice-T's gangsta-rap. Artists have the right to free expression in their songs, but large corporate entities don't have to market and sell them. Disney has the right to overcommercialize its videos and other products aimed at three-to-five-year-old consumers, but no obligation to do so. My friends at Yahoo! have the right to distribute pornography (with certain restrictions on their global Web portal). Would declining to do so be censorship? No. It's their judgment call. But all of these media corporations and their top executives need to be held accountable for their decisions.

And the media industry's practice of repeatedly calling critics "censors" is a bogus and irresponsible defense. The conservative writer Michael Medved wrote a book called *Hollywood vs. America* that catalogued innumerable gruesome and disgusting scenes from mass-marketed records, movies, and videos—everything from people drinking urine to torturing women and ripping out toenails with pliers. He said Hollywood has "a bias for the bizarre."[310] Medved was widely criticized as a "censor" by many in Hollywood and attacked for his views. But why is it *censorship* if he (or I for that matter) criticize media content and call for industry leaders to think a whole lot more about the consequences of the products that the media create? I don't happen to agree with Medved's politics or many of his opinions. But I completely agree with his right to criticize the media industry for its offensive content. That's not censorship. That's free speech, and it's ironic to see such criticism slammed as "censorship" by those who always run for cover to the First Amendment.

Media leaders also try to avoid accountability by pointing fingers and blaming each other. When C. DeLores Tucker, the chairman of the National Political Congress of Black Women, joined with the conservative William Bennett in 1995 to criticize the gangsta-rap music produced by Time Warner's music division, then-CEO Gerald Levin actually responded, "Why don't you attack Rupert Murdoch? He's worse than us."[311] That's as lame as tobacco company executives pointing to their competitors and saying, "Blame the other guy—their cigarettes have more nicotine than ours."

Unfortunately, you see this dynamic all the time in the media industry: "Since Fox is putting on oversexed shows designed to titillate twelve-year-olds at 8:00 P.M., we need to do so as well or our ratings will go down." Or, "Time Warner has *Jenny Jones,* so we need to at least have *Jerry Springer* to compete in the talk show genre." Or, "Well, Warner Bros. is marketing violent movies to teens and making gobs of money, so what are we going to do, just sit there?"

A third defense—perhaps the most pernicious one that corporate media leaders offer—is, as we discussed in Chapter Eight, to blame parents (and sometimes kids and teens themselves). I have seen and heard this one more times than I can count. "It's not our fault. We're just media creators. It's the parents. Why don't you talk to them?" It's disingenuous at best and downright shameful at worst.

When all that the CEOs are held accountable for is "shareholder value," when their lives and those of the companies they lead are driven by the pursuit of mega-profits and mega-mergers, virtually all other values fall by the wayside. At the beginning and the end of the day, the Murdochs and Eisners and Sabans answer to one constituency—their shareholders and the Wall Street analysts. There are few mediating influences anymore and few situations where other values enter into the equation in any significant way. That's sad, because it doesn't have to be that way. One of the media industry's proudest moments in recent memory was in September 2001, when the major broadcast networks provided extensive, advertising-free coverage of the devastating terrorist attacks on the World Trade Center and the Pentagon. They lost many millions of dollars in advertising revenue, but they served the public interest. In the field of media, there are many other examples of people and companies that have done well by doing good, or by at least balancing pure profit motives with other equally important considerations.

THE NICKELODEON SUCCESS STORY

As most every kid and parent knows, the premier network for kids in the United States is Nickelodeon. It has the largest audience share, gets the largest amount of advertising revenues, and is the most profitable of all kids' TV networks. Indeed, it's the most successful network in all of cable television. Equally important, Nickelodeon is a veritable cash cow for its corporate parent, Viacom, and stands as a crown jewel among their many business holdings.

So Nickelodeon is a great business from the shareholder's standpoint. But it's also a network that's committed to kids and their well-being. And over the years it's been populated by dozens of talented executives and creative people who have shown the world that when its comes to children and media, you can do extremely well financially and still run an ethical, caring, pro-family business. Not every parent approves of every program that's ever run on Nickelodeon. Clearly shows like *Ren and Stimpy* have caused some consternation, and I've heard some pretty fair critiques of *Rugrats* and a few other shows too. But by and large, the programming on Nickelodeon is exceptional. It's nonviolent. It's creative. It's diverse. It gives kids a voice. It's bold and fresh. And kids happen to love it. As a parent, I trust Nickelodeon, and I entrust my children to its care, with certain limitations. The only other networks I feel that way about are PBS, and now, with a new infusion of talent led by ex-Nickelodeon veterans, the Disney Channel. Sure, I've got some quibbles about a few programs, but overall I have great respect for Nickelodeon, its values and success, and most of the people who have built it.

Nickelodeon started out as a sleepy little commercial-free cable station that no self-respecting kid would admit to watching. The year was 1979. During its first few years, Nickelodeon ran at a financial loss and served up entirely forgettable fare to an extremely small audience. At the beginning, Nickelodeon had no personality and no real driving force. Staffers actually referred to it as "the green vegetable network" because kids seemed to like it about as much as spinach. Virtually nobody watched. But the one smart thing the original Nickelodeon did was to hire Geraldine Laybourne, a former schoolteacher and producer of children's television from New Jersey.

When Gerry Laybourne took over Nickelodeon in 1984, her first step was to research children's attitudes and to ask them what they wanted. As Gerry tells it, "We had this really radical [idea] of 'Why not ask them? Why not bring kids themselves into the process?' So even when Nickelodeon was fledgling and we had no money to spend, we always had kids as part of the process. And we took them seriously, gave them a vote and included them."[312] That hardly seems a radical concept today, but Nickelodeon was the first kids' media channel to do it. So with children's help, Laybourne and her friends set out to refashion the image and programming of Nickelodeon.

That included the decision to take commercial advertising. As Laybourne sees it, it was a critical and correct choice. "For me," she said, "what was important was the fact that we had the money to spend to make great product and that we'd create something that could never be taken away from kids. . . . It was easy for me to make my peace with taking advertising, because I felt that if we could really improve the quality in our original productions, that would ensure Nickelodeon's future and make something great for kids."

At that time, the commercial broadcast networks and their Saturday morning cartoon lineup were saturated with cheap, toy-based TV shows like *GI Joe* and *Care Bears,* which completely dominated the kid's show syndication market. At the other end of the spectrum, PBS was committed to its long-standing educational approach, with old favorites like *Mr. Rogers* and the extraordinary preschool success *Sesame Street.* So you had the gold standard of preschool programming on PBS and a slew of unimaginative and exploitative toy-based properties on the commercial stations. There was little in between, which is where Nickelodeon saw and seized its opportunity. Under Laybourne, the network asked kids what they cared about and made its mark by putting children first. Looking at the world from a kid's point of view was a good and noble place to start. It also turned out to be a very good business idea.

Their research showed that kids wanted a place that was for them, not adults. Thus was born the "Nick Is Kids" philosophy, a positioning and core commitment that showed immediate results.

By the end of 1985, Nick was tied for second place in the cable rat-ings, and that same year, the network turned its first profit. Led by such inventive creations such as *You Can't Do That on Television* and *Double Dare,* a game show on which kids race through food and slime, Nickelodeon's success grew.

The network first concentrated on game shows and live action, then began experimenting with more animated properties—but not those toy-based cartoons that flooded the market in the 1980s. Laybourne and her team sought out and discovered a whole new set of creators—"original producers who had characters living inside of them," as she described it. Sure enough, these efforts bore fruit as well. Among the notable successes that marked the next stage of Nickelodeon's growth were such perennial favorites as *Doug* (about a ten-year-old who copes with issues that matter to a ten-year-old) and *Rugrats* (an animated show about life as seen through the eyes of toddlers). Creators like Jim Jinkins, Arlene Klasky, and Gabor Csupo gave life to this popular genre of kids' programming, and they brought huge new advertising revenues to Nickelodeon and its new corporate parent, Viacom. Suddenly kids' TV was great busi-ness, but Nickelodeon stayed true to its nonviolent mission and its core commitment to kids rather than products.

Gerry Laybourne and her original team had the good fortune to be supported by corporate chieftains who believed in their pro-gramming philosophy and creative new approach to kids. The pres-ident and CEO of Viacom during that time was Frank Biondi, a longtime industry leader. Committed to kids' issues, Frank was on the board of Children Now and is now a director of JP Kids. He and his then-colleagues Sumner Redstone (chairman of Viacom) and Robert Pittman (now chief operating officer of AOL Time Warner) gave Gerry the support she needed and scored a big economic win as a largely unexpected part of the bargain. Gerry Laybourne left Nickelodeon in 1996 to join the Walt Disney Company, then left Disney a couple of years later to become chairman and CEO of Oxygen Media, the new women's cable and Internet network. But her celebrated legacy and commitment to children lives on.

Today, the president and chief executive of Nickelodeon is Herb Scannell, who had been programming chief under Laybourne. Even though he's never bought a show from us (which shows poor taste, I think), Herb is a very good guy who is deeply committed to kids—his own two daughters, Caroline and Isabelle, and the millions of children who still make Nickelodeon the premier kids' network in the U.S. Scannell is a bit more self-effacing and unassuming than Laybourne, but he has proven himself to be every bit as savvy about and committed to the children's audience. Since taking over in 1996, Herb has built Nickelodeon into a multibillion-dollar multimedia powerhouse and has nearly doubled its revenue and profits.

With his boyish face and mild personality, Scannell is somebody you'd trust with your own children, like a good teacher or a camp counselor. But his likeable, low-key manner belies an intense competitive drive. Rather than being a caretaker of Laybourne's legacy, Scannell has built on it and taken Nickelodeon to new heights, while withstanding heavy competition from the likes of a revamped Disney Channel and Cartoon Network. Scannell has expanded Nickelodeon's movie offerings, launching such features as *Good Burger, Snow Day,* and *The Rugrats Movie,* and has increased the network's programming offerings, with responsible and popular new hits such as *SpongeBob SquarePants.* Perhaps more important, in tandem with the head of Nick Jr., Brown Johnson, Scannell placed new emphasis on Nickelodeon's preschool block, which features the megahit *Blues' Clues,* a breakthrough for both Nickelodeon and the early childhood TV genre.

As Scannell explains, *"Blues' Clues* is the first idea in preschool television that wasn't from the same well as *Sesame Street* and *The Muppets.* Every property in the preschool area had some derivative variation of people putting on puppets, whether it was *Barney* or *Sesame Street.* But here was something created by a new, computer-literate generation, using forms that were new to children's television in a way that was respectful of its audience: "As kids become more and more engaged in interactive media as their entertainment, here was television figuring out a way not to be passive media."[313] As a parent of three kids who have loved *Blues' Clues*—and having watched more episodes with them than I can count—I agree with Scannell's assessment. Under his leadership and that of Brown Johnson, Nick Jr. has given parents of preschool children a network they can trust, along with old reliable PBS. That is no mean feat.

Scannell is the son of social workers, and this is evident in his commitment to kids and diversity in programming. His father was a social worker in Harlem and later Suffolk County, Long Island. His mother was a Puerto Rico-born caseworker for Catholic Charities. Herb has continued their commitment to social activism for kids under the "The Big Help" format, first launched by Gerry Laybourne. In addition, he's repeatedly gone out of his way to find programming with strong female leads and role models and made this an overt part of Nickelodeon's programming agenda. He also recently green-lighted the first two kids' TV shows to feature Latino lead characters, *Taina* and *The Brothers Garcia*—investing serious money to back up this commitment—and has lectured Stanford students about how media can promote racial diversity and mutual understanding among kids of different ethnic and socioeconomic backgrounds.

Under Scannell's leadership, Nickelodeon also launched the first educational cable network in the United States, called Noggin. A joint venture with the best-known name in educational television, Sesame Workshop (formerly the Children's Television Workshop), Noggin is a commercial-free channel that airs primarily as a digital cable channel. It's not profitable yet, but under the steady hand of longtime Nickelodeon executive Tom Ascheim, Noggin appears to be at least headed toward breakeven. More important from my standpoint, it's the first openly and admittedly educational channel for kids on the air. That takes some real courage and vision. Several huge media giants, including both Disney and Viacom, previously considered launching an educational channel, but the Noggin folks are the first to take the plunge.

I'm not alone in my respect for Herb Scannell's ability to blend business success with a true commitment to kids and positive family values. As Peggy Charren, the much-respected child-advocacy pioneer and founder of Action for Children's Television, recalls, "When Gerry Laybourne left, I thought 'Who are they gonna find now?' Well, lo and behold, it may be the miracle of the television age that Herb has turned out to be just as creative as his predecessor, someone who found all kinds of programs that meet the needs of a diverse audience and understands that girls are people too."[314]

And how does Gerry Laybourne feel about her successor at Nickelodeon? "I am Herb's number one fan and am tremendously thrilled with his success," says Laybourne. "He's a guy with a whole lot of heart and brains and cares deeply about kids, so it doesn't get much better than that. I don't think there's any way I could have left Nickelodeon if he hadn't been there."

What lessons can we draw from the success of these two industry leaders? First and foremost, there's the example they set about personal leadership and commitment. Both Gerry Laybourne and Herb Scannell have proven themselves to be tough and successful businesspeople in the rough-and-tumble world of cable television. But they've achieved that success by focusing on the kids' audience first and foremost, by listening to kids, and by creating a safe and enjoyable environment in which children can have fun and learn. Nobody who knows them would dare underrate their business acumen, but there's so much more to their success than that. In fact, much of their business success results directly from their commitment to and high standards for kids. Both of them have taken risks and tried new, innovative approaches. Both have pushed the envelope—but not by adding more sex and violence or viewing kids mainly as consumers. Not surprisingly, both are devoted parents, who draw upon their own kids' lives and ideas in their daily work. And both came from backgrounds—education and social work—that sparked a lifelong commitment to children.

Both Laybourne and Scannell have been willing to finance programs like the Peabody Award–winning *Nick News* with Linda Ellerbee and the social action special *The Big Help*—shows that lose money for the network but expose kids to important values. In this regard, they repeatedly put their money where their mouth is and don't just pay attention to their quarterly profit margins or every program's bottom line. As Peggy Charren points out, Herb followed Gerry's tradition for diverse programming and characters, and they've both set a standard for the rest of the kids' media industry to follow. Turn on Nickelodeon today, and you'll see brown, white, Asian, and black faces, and just as many girls as boys. It truly is a network for kids, and kids of all shapes, sizes, and colors.

Neither Gerry Laybourne nor Herb Scannell exemplifies the "schizophrenic," bifurcated lives that Ken Auletta referred to earlier in this chapter and which I see in so many media and entertainment executives. They don't live one world at home and another at work or ignore the social consequences and implications of the media they produce and distribute. There are others like them, too, in the media world—people who are willing to put kids and families first and to balance profit motives with more meaningful values.

LEVERAGING THE POWER OF ADVERTISING

Bob Wehling is one of them. He's not exactly the kind of guy you'd expect to see on a roster of leading advocates for better-quality media for kids. He's a gray-haired, ruddy-faced grandfather in his mid-sixties, and he spent his life designing advertising and marketing campaigns for products like Clairol hair products, Pampers disposable diapers, and Crest toothpaste. In fact, Bob Wehling is the recently retired chief marketing officer for Procter & Gamble, the Cincinnati-based consumer products giant that is the largest television advertiser in the United States. But he has another passion besides selling shampoo, toothpaste, and diapers. It's encouraging quality media content for families and kids. And like Gerry Laybourne and Herb Scannell, he is willing to put his money where his mouth is . . . over and over again.

I first met Wehling when he supported Children Now in launching our "Talking with Kids" public service advertising campaign with the Ad Council. Then, a couple of years ago, he called me with an idea for launching a new initiative among American advertisers regarding positive family media—something called the Family Friendly Programming Forum. The reason was simple. When leading television executives are criticized for their low-quality or sex-and-violence-laden prime-time programming, they often point fingers at their advertisers. The standard line is, "If the advertisers would only support more family-oriented programs, then we would make them and put them on the air. *They're* the ones with the real power." There may be some truth to that claim, and clearly both parties share a lot of responsibility. But until recently, little has been done to improve the dialogue between advertisers and TV executives. A few years ago, Children Now had brought leading advertising and media executives together at a conference to examine issues and solutions related to kids' and family media. It was like pulling teeth to get the conversation going, and there were few concrete results.

But Bob Wehling and his colleague Andrea Alstrup, senior vice president of advertising at Johnson and Johnson, set out to do something about this issue. Through their Family Friendly Programming Forum, they encouraged leading American advertisers to sponsor TV programs that parents and children could enjoy together. "As marketers," they explained, "we are concerned about the dwindling availability of family-friendly television programs during prime-time viewing hours—the environment in which we want to advertise. As members of American society, we are concerned about the TV imagery, role models, themes and language to which our young people are exposed." Under the aegis of the Association of National Advertisers (ANA), they enlisted more than forty of America's largest advertisers, including Coca-Cola, FedEx, AT&T, PepsiCo, McDonald's, and Kraft Nabisco. Together, these companies spend a total of more than $11 billion on television commercials each year. That certainly gets your phone calls returned in the media world.

The Forum's goal was to provide more family-friendly television during the old "family hour" time period. First, they established a fund to finance the development of new family-friendly TV scripts.

CBS, ABC, NBC, and the WB network have already agreed to participate in the Script Development Initiative, and in its first year, one series funded by the forum—WB's *Gilmore Girls*—made it on the air and won considerable critical acclaim.

The forum has also been a presence at industry conferences and meetings with network and studio executives, sharing concerns about the lack of family-friendly material in prime-time television. The group is also underwriting scholarships at university television-studies departments to encourage young writers' interest in family-friendly programming, and it is putting considerable PR behind the initiative. For the first time since I've been involved in the kids' and family media cause, advertisers are actually taking the initiative and proactively encouraging giant media companies to do better. It's not a huge effort yet, and there's certainly a long way to go to improve the prime-time programming landscape. But Bob Wehling and Andrea Alstrup have already shown that leadership and commitment from a few good people with clout can make a difference.

OTHERS WHO SET THE STANDARD

Over the past decade, I've come across other media leaders who are willing to stand up and be counted for kids. People like Norman Lear, who created *All in the Family* and *The Jeffersons,* and who has long seen media as a means for promoting positive messages and progressive social issues; Gary David Goldberg, the creator of *Family Ties* and *Spin City,* who is a longtime champion of kids and family causes; and Grant Tinker, former chairman of NBC, who was a longtime advocate for responsible TV programming. They and some of their colleagues in Hollywood have set examples for others to follow and remind us all that "good guys" can indeed blend social responsibility and successful business practices within the strictures of the entertainment industry.

In the new media and Internet arena, I've also gotten to know a number of good and committed people, whose positions of leadership hopefully bode well for the future of this interactive and potentially rich medium for kids. The initial team who built Yahoo!—led by Jerry Yang, Tim Koogle, and Jeff Mallett—are all socially committed and responsible people. They have always been willing to consider, head-on, the social consequences of their work and have fostered an internal culture and a variety of projects, including Yahooligans! and Camp Yahoo!, that promote education and social activism. They give time and financial resources to kids and families, and they live those values at work.

So too, Steve Case, the chairman of AOL Time Warner, seems genuinely committed to using the new medium he has helped to popularize as a vehicle for greater educational opportunity and positive social change. Steve's older brother, Dan, who recently stepped down as chairman and CEO of the investment bank Hambrecht and Quist, is a good friend as well as an investor (through H&Q) in JP Kids. And both brothers followed the memorable line about risk-taking and foresight in media and technology: "As Wayne Gretzky says, go where the puck will be, not where it's currently at." Both of the Case brothers have shown a long-standing commitment to kids and education, and more and more of Steve's recent speeches have come to focus on education and the opportunity to use the Internet to make a positive difference. When I interviewed Steve Case, in fact, he strongly urged media companies to recognize and act upon their role as public trustees—acknowledging that the industry had become "much too focused on what the stock price is tomorrow."[315]

Only time will tell whether these words will be matched by a similarly deep and ongoing commitment of resources from these new media companies, but I'm optimistic. These Internet pioneers seem cut from a somewhat different cloth than many of their traditional media colleagues. And since they are creating a medium with such extraordinary global potential for education and children in the twenty-first century, I hope that their "good guy" instincts and value systems will translate directly into a truly pro-social and pro-family future for this groundbreaking new platform—not to mention for the vast landscape of other media that AOL Time Warner controls.

THE TOP TEN STEPS FOR MEDIA INDUSTRY ACCOUNTABILITY

The people and stories mentioned above should give you a sense that there are some "good guys" and some positive potential in the media industry. But there's so much more that the industry should do to make the "other parent" more of a positive force in children's lives. Here's my Top Ten list for the media industry, a blueprint that would begin to make them more accountable to America's kids and families.

1. Embrace Public-Interest Responsibilities

Significant change will occur from within the media world only when owners and senior executives recognize that shareholder value is *not* the only value that matters. Put differently, if media executives would recognize that all media educates—for better or worse—they would more clearly recognize the public-service aspect of their work. This is particularly true for the broadcasting arena, where the owners of large media entities should serve as trustees of the public interest in exchange for the public use of the publicly owned airwaves. This model of public trusteeship is hardly far-fetched. Indeed, it was supposed to be the operating principle for the entire broadcasting world, and it was, up through the 1960s. Leaders like William Paley and Frank Stanton at CBS; Donald McGannon at Westinghouse Broadcasting; Robert Kintner and Grant Tinker at NBC; and Elmer Lower, Elton Rule, Dan Burke, and Tom Murphy at ABC recognized their unique public-service obligations, not to mention their role as public trustees. They and other broadcasters, publishers, and media leaders spoke often and convincingly of their responsibility to the public.[316]

Many of today's broadcasters and media leaders, unlike the pioneers of the business, do not view broadcasting or other forms of media as carrying public interest responsibilities. They see it as a business, period. When the merger of Viacom and CBS was announced, the two CEOs held a press conference to talk about all the advantages of the merger. Not a single sentence—*not a single word*—was devoted to whether the merger would benefit the public interest. Here was one of the original broadcasting empires, CBS—once known for its long-standing tradition of public service—and yet the leaders of this combined media giant addressed not a word to this tradition and ongoing responsibility. It's time for media leaders to return to their roots and acknowledge that public trusteeship, a tradition that they recently recalled with their extensive broadcast coverage of the terrorist attacks in September 2001.

2. Stop Crying Censorship

It's completely legitimate for parents, politicians, critics, and industry figures themselves to openly criticize much of what's in the media today. I've devoted chapters to the excess of violence, sexuality, and commercialism and to its consequences for kids, families, and our society. But industry figures repeatedly attack their critics as "censors" instead of addressing the legitimate substance of their critiques. This is tragic and dishonest. Media leaders should stop, once and for all, their false claims of censorship. Similarly, they should stop characterizing public interest-focused, legislative enhancements of speech, like the Children's Television Act or new government funds for digital media education, as a form of "censorship." That's a cynical attempt to use First Amendment freedoms to protect maximum profits.

3. Think About Your Own Kids: Responsible Self-Regulation

We've looked at media leaders who bifurcate their lives and live by one set of rules at work and a different one at home. If they would keep the needs and concerns of their own children front and center (and I don't just mean their kid's need for a new sports car), many would surely approach the content they produce and distribute in a very different way. I remember speaking with one of the top producers of *Good Morning America* at a Children Now conference a few years back. He told me that he had a simple rule while using the edit room or preparing questions for his guests—he had to produce something that he would feel comfortable having his ten-year-old daughter see or hear, since he knew that there would always be a number of children in the audience across America.

Responsible self-regulation is at the heart of what individuals and companies in the media industry should do. The First Amendment gives creators and distributors of media content tremendous freedom, but along with that should come even greater responsibility, particularly for those who control distribution. Individuals from both the executive and creative ranks of the media world have simply got to stand up more often and say, "No, I won't do that," and consider the youngsters who may be in the audience.

Self-regulation can have a significant impact. I've watched TV writers, music producers, and magazine publishers attend workshops on child development or sexuality, then change what they write or the context in which they raise issues in the media. But let me be clear: self-regulation alone is not enough, because only some, not all, will act responsibly.

4. Fund Quality Media for Kids and Families at Breakeven

It's a basic fact. Some of the best and most important content for kids will never make as much money as X-rated or sports media. So the huge companies that dominate the industry need to rethink their profit-centered approach to much of their kids' and family offerings.

Look at Nickelodeon, where executives choose to fund excellent programs like *Nick News* or *The Big Help* at breakeven or a loss. Why can't other media companies do the same? Must they squeeze every last drop of profit out of every single piece of media they produce and distribute? What's wrong with balancing profits with your public-interest obligations? How much money is enough?

5. Fund Nationwide Media-Literacy Efforts

Take a portion of the profits that the huge media companies make (say 1 percent) and use that to support and distribute a nationwide media-literacy program for all kids in elementary school. Use the distribution platforms of TV, the Internet, radio, film, and video to make this media-literacy curriculum available to all families everywhere, not just in school. Just as the Partnership for a Drug-Free America or the Ad Council's public service campaigns are industry supported, so too should the media world help create and distribute a massive media-literacy campaign for kids and families over the next decade. In their drive for maximum profits, the industry may view media-literacy efforts as counterproductive to their business objectives. But like anti-drunk-driving and anti-smoking campaigns funded by industry, they're consistent with the best interests of our society and responsible business practices.

6. Lobby Government for Greater Public Funding for Kids' Media

The industry should use some of its smooth, highly paid lobbyists, as well as their powerful trade associations like the National Association of Broadcasters (NAB), the Recording Industry

Association of America (RIAA) and TechNet, to lobby government to increase funding for top-quality kids' content.

Industry leaders should also lobby on behalf of selected tax credits and other government tax incentives along the lines of the Canadian and European model, which I'll outline in the next chapter. At the very least, and if nothing else, the leaders of the media and communications giants should stop opposing government efforts on behalf of quality kids' offerings.

7. Create and Fund Educational Uses of the Internet

Enlightened leaders of the Internet boom—including Jerry Yang, Steve Case, and eBay CEO Meg Whitman—recognize the educational and public-interest power of the Internet. It's time to start realizing that potential, while bridging the digital divide by ensuring quality access and content for kids of all socioeconomic and ethnic backgrounds. By devoting a small fraction of their enormous profits (1 percent annually) to this effort, they will help ensure future generations of educated users.

8. Fund Regular Workshops and Conferences for Industry Professionals

Workshops sponsored by child development groups such as the UCLA Center for Communications Policy, the Kaiser Family Foundation, and Children Now provide vital child-development information and dialogue for media professionals from both the creative and executive ranks. The media industry itself should take a far more active role in planning and financing these efforts.

I recommend that an industry-based group contract with an outstanding media institution, such as the UCLA Center for

Communications Policy or the Annenberg Schools at the University of Southern California and the University of Pennsylvania, to run a decade-long series of workshops and conferences for media professionals. This would be a joint, public-private partnership, but its *primary* funders and ultimate beneficiaries would be the media industry itself. This ten-year effort would focus on educating both creative and executive people *across* various media industries about child and family development and media issues.

9. Use Advertisers' Clout

As the story of Bob Wehling and the Family Friendly Programming Forum makes clear, advertisers have enormous clout in media—tens of billions of dollars of clout—particularly in television, radio, the Internet, and other ad-driven businesses. Following the forum's lead, the advertising industry should greatly expand the reach and funding of this effort. Money talks to the media companies, and if advertisers are increasingly willing to fund pro-family and pro-kid content, whether on prime-time TV or on the Internet, the distribution networks that depend on them as their lifeblood will follow suit. So I propose a major expansion of the forum's effort, as well as a joint, decade-long commitment by advertisers and media companies to further its early progress.

Advertisers should also start openly criticizing or refusing to sponsor a lot of the tasteless garbage we see and hear in the mediascape today. This is hitting large media companies where it hurts—their wallets. As right-wing Christian boycotts led by the Reverend Donald Wildmon and others have proven, pressure works. If the same advertisers who are spearheading the forum also started speaking out against and refusing to support offensive content on TV, radio, and elsewhere, I can assure you that the tremors would be felt up and down Madison Avenue and Hollywood.

10. Develop New Leadership and Responsibility at the Top

Ultimately, the leaders of the giant, consolidated media companies have the greatest power to reshape their industry. At the end of the day, we're talking about a relatively small number of people. You know some of the names: Murdoch, Eisner, Case, Parsons, Redstone, Karmazin, Diller, Malone, Pittman. These are the leaders. They bear the greatest responsibility. They profit the most personally. They need to be accountable for the actions of their megacorporations and their numerous subsidiaries. And their accountability must not be just to Wall Street and a handful of large investment concerns—"the shareholder value" crowd— but to the society and world that their companies shape so profoundly.

It's time to see an end to what Ken Auletta refers to as their schizophrenia and bifurcated lives. It's time to see some balance between pure profit motives and a far greater sense of public interest and accountability. The history of American business is replete with examples of successful leaders whose vision included far more than the bottom line and the insatiable pursuit of growth, including Bill Hewlett, David Packard, Sam Walton, and Andrew Carnegie. The early days of the broadcasting industry saw its share of principled, enlightened leadership from the Paleys, the Sarnoffs, and others—people who understood the unique public-service component of their work and the extraordinary role they had in shaping the lives of future generations.

Where are the similar individuals of vision and leadership at the top today? People like Steve Case and Jerry Yang give me some cause for optimism, but it's time for others, new leaders, to step up to the plate. Ultimately, the true measure of their accomplishments will not be how many billions of dollars that they make, the number of competitors they outlast or acquire, or the amount of profits they return to a few large shareholders. Their legacy will be how they shape our society and world—for better or worse.

Ten Steps for the Media Industry

1. Embrace public-interest responsibilities.
2. Stop crying censorship.
3. Think about your own kids: responsible self-regulation.
4. Fund quality media for kids and families at breakeven.
5. Fund nationwide media-literacy efforts.
6. Lobby government for greater public funding for kids' media.
7. Create and fund educational uses of the Internet.
8. Fund regular workshops and conferences for industry professionals.
9. Use advertisers' clout.
10. Develop new leadership and responsibility at the top.

PROTECTING THE PUBLIC INTEREST

"This instrument can teach, it can illuminate; yes, and it can even inspire. But it can do so only to the extent that humans are determined to use it to those ends. Otherwise it is merely lights and wires in a box."
                                              —Edward R. Murrow, famed broadcast journalist

Today, we stand at a crossroads in terms of government support for quality media and regulation of the industry's most pernicious excesses. Although much of the 1990s was spent undoing the damage of the mindless, "anything goes" ideology of the 1980s, we also witnessed in the last decade an alarming, unprecedented rise in massive media consolidations. Nonetheless, in the past ten years, we saw some notable improvements in the areas of children and family media, largely under the leadership of the two activist FCC chairmen, Reed Hundt and Bill Kennard. It's worth taking a brief look back at those accomplishments before outlining a twenty-first-century agenda. In addition to the bipartisan passage in 1990 (over George Bush's veto) of the Children's Television Act—and the enforcement teeth added during FCC rule-making proceedings—the bipartisan passage of V-Chip legislation in the mid-1990s marked another step forward for families and the public interest.

The 1990s also saw a well-coordinated public and government outcry against the surge of violent images that had proliferated across so many media platforms. That effort brought concrete results, particularly in the area of media violence. When the Fox network and Haim Saban are forced to defend *Power Rangers* on a regular basis, and Time Warner's top management succumbs to pressure and sells the company's stake in the gangsta-rap business, you are seeing progress.

Similarly, FCC Chairman Kennard, joined by advocacy groups such as the NAACP and Children Now, forced the media industry at least to acknowledge its sorry record of minority ownership, characters, and themes in prime-time programming. With an increasing drumbeat of government pressure, we saw most American schools wired for the Internet, with the strong involvement of a number of leading technology firms such as Sun Microsystems and Hewlett Packard. We also saw limits on the number of commercials in kids' TV, and politicians on both sides of the aisle at least made children's safety and privacy concerns an important if poorly legislated issue in the early regulation of the Internet.

Finally, we saw the Federal government and various states sue Microsoft on antitrust grounds. This represented virtually the first major antitrust action against the huge oligopoly forces that have come to dominate the media and technology spheres in recent years, an important victory for consumers and industry competition. In sum, the 1990s showed that the government's balancing hand can protect the public interest in a media environment ruled by the marketplace.

PUTTING PROGRESS IN JEOPARDY

Unfortunately, the current Bush administration is already unwisely abandoning these safeguards. In fact, not since the Reagan administration's wholesale reversals of regulatory policies have the scales tipped so dramatically in favor of big business, according to lobbyists on both sides of these issues. Which leads, of course, to the FCC and its approach under President Bush and its new chairman, Michael Powell.

I've met Mike Powell. He seems like a pleasant guy. But parents and families in America should be downright scared by Mike Powell's agenda at the FCC. One of the first things he did as the commission's chairman was to change the rules so that America's largest broadcasters, cable companies, and megacorporations could grow even bigger and dominate new markets. As reported in *The Wall Street Journal* and The *New York Times,* Powell departed radically from more than sixty years of policy and began relaxing long-standing restrictions on media companies that want to own multiple distribution outlets in major population markets. He justified his deregulation scheme by talking at length about the important free speech rights of corporations. "In a marked departure from decades of Supreme Court opinions on the subject," the *Times* reported in a front page story, "the agency (FCC) has become significantly more sympathetic to the free speech rights of corporations and more skeptical of the role of government in promoting diversity in mass media. Consumer groups say the regulations that are being rolled back have been crucial instruments for promoting a diversity of viewpoints in the news and entertainment business."[317]

Why does this matter? First, government is the only protection that children and consumers have against big business. The ownership restrictions have been vital to ensuring that the American public has access to news, programming, and information reflecting many different tastes and different viewpoints. That's what free speech is all about. But now, thanks to Chairman Powell and others, we have a cartel-like group—similar to OPEC—dominated by just a handful of owners with increasingly common interests, even as American society is growing ever more diverse. This is deeply troubling in terms of kids and media and the diversity of viewpoints and programming choices.

But just as disturbing are Powell's early pronouncements about the glories of deregulation:

I do not believe deregulation is like dessert you serve after people have fed on their vegetables and is a reward for the creation of competition. I believe that deregulation is instead a critical ingredient to facilitating competition, not something to be handed out after there is a substantial number of players in the market.[318]

Why should American parents be scared when they hear such statements from the chairman of the FCC? Because the last time the FCC had such a deregulatory ideology running its efforts was during the *disastrous* 1980s under Mark Fowler and the Reagan administration. What did kids and families get from them? A vast proliferation of sex, violence, and unchecked commercialism in all forms of media. Thirty-minute toy-based commercials masquerading as TV cartoons. The worst kids' programming ever, with virtually no redeeming qualities—exactly what an unchecked, deregulated free-market ideology always offers children. If that's the kind of "leadership" we can expect from Chairman Powell and his colleagues, all of us have great cause for concern.

TEN STEPS THAT GOVERNMENT SHOULD TAKE

Since the new Bush administration and the Mike Powell–led FCC seem bent on further deregulating the media, Congress and respected leaders like Senators Joseph Lieberman, John McCain, and Ernest Hollings need to stand firm to protect the interests of American children and families. Massive consolidation has returned us to an environment in which only a handful of giant corporations dominate the media. As a result, our government needs to play a far more activist, regulatory role, as it did in the 1950s, 1960s, and 1970s when only three major networks controlled the television landscape. Here are ten proposals that, if enacted by our national government, would go a long way to making the media a far more positive force in our society. Some of these ideas are controversial, and some may seem politically unfeasible. But all are eminently achievable over time—provided we have the public will and political leadership that all meaningful progress in this area requires.

1. Break up the Big Media Companies

You heard it right. It's the single best step our society could take, and only government has the power to do it. I'm by no means alone in this opinion. Recently, one of the most powerful and influential figures in the global children's media world said to me, "If you truly care about kids, the number one solution is to break up the huge vertically integrated corporations that control virtually all media that children see or hear, including the corporation I work for."

Now, remember, this person (who understandably declined to be quoted by name) is someone who has profited very handsomely from media mergers. But his answer was unflinching and dead-on. These behemoths care only about building the next generation of consumers, not the next generation of minds. Only by breaking them down into smaller pieces can we restore some scmblance of public interest and direct public accountability to the media environment.

The fact is, the biggest problems with the media today are rooted in the current structure of the marketplace. And the only institution in our society that has the power to change this structure fundamentally is government. The federal government and, in certain cases, state governments have the power and responsibility to regulate commerce. You may think that I've really lost my marbles, but we need to start a national conversation about this. Change won't happen overnight—it may take twenty years—but in terms of positive social goals, it's sort of like the moon landing. We have to start aiming for it now. And some courageous and visionary public figures have to start telling it like it is, even if they are terrified of its impact on their media-funded political campaigns.

We could start, perhaps, by asking media conglomerates to divest those business units that directly distribute and create content for kids and teens. We should also set up marketplace rules that balance pure profit objectives with those of the public interest. If this country truly cares about kids, we need to start envisioning a media landscape in which it's not just five or six companies controlling everything. This is the number one solution to this long-term challenge, whose importance will loom ever larger in the media/information environment of this new century.

2. Establish a Major Public Fund for Quality Kids' Media Content

As chairman of one of the only serious, independent kids' educational media companies in the United States, I can tell you firsthand: high-quality, educational content is expensive to produce. In TV terms alone, one half-hour episode can cost between $250,000 and $500,000. The subsidiaries of the huge vertically integrated media companies, with their obsessive focus on profits, will not foot the bill for budgets like that. But if you can bring these companies thirteen or twenty-six episodes that are at least half funded or more from other sources, they would much more likely be interested. Where would that kind of funding for high-quality content come from? Why, the same place that virtually every other Western industrialized nation goes to when it wants to encourage the production of good programming for kids—the government.

In fact, most other countries support and subsidize various forms of quality content for kids, particularly television, because they believe it's in society's interest to make children's media better. What does the United States—the media capital of the world—do in its infinite, free-market wisdom? Virtually nothing. We do have PBS and the Corporation for Public Broadcasting, but unfortunately, they're overstretched and underfunded, and PBS recently leased its

Saturday morning lineup to a Canadian company (which, of course, uses Canadian government subsidies to create program-ming—and profits). We also have the National Endowment for Children's Educational Television, funded by Congress in the early nineties to the minuscule tune of $2–3 million. What a joke! If spent wisely, that money might fund a grand total of five or six episodes of one series, one time. Our government spends more on one hog farm in Iowa than we do on the entire national budget for kids' educational media.

So here's what to do. Commit at least $500 million *per year* for ten years to fund educational media for kids and families. That's $5 billion over ten years—less than the Bush administration's antici-pated tax-cut benefits for Bill Gates and Paul Allen alone. Take most of that money and use it to fund high-quality kids' content for TV, the Internet, computer games, and other media. The greatest need, by far, is for funding of content and production. But reserve 5 percent a year ($25 million) for research and training to help grow a new generation of media professionals committed to creat-ing high-quality educational content across all media platforms. Once again, this idea just requires a little political will, a little lead-ership, and, by current standards, a relatively small amount of funds.

3. Just "DO IT" for the Internet and Digital Age

While we're on the subject of money, let's get serious about the Internet and the emerging digital age. As I've said throughout the book, the Internet and other interactive media and technology have the potential to reshape our entire educational system and the way our kids learn and grow. With such unique potential for kids and learning, it would be a shame if we screw them up the way we did TV. The Internet should not be developed with a singular focus on the highest profit margins and lowest-common-denominator con-tent. And much as I respect the new media leaders, like the guys at

Yahoo! and AOL's Steve Case, this should be led at the highest governmental levels.

Recently, a group of leading media experts—including such luminaries as the former president of NBC News and PBS, Lawrence Grossman, and former FCC Chairman Newt Minow—proposed the creation of the Digital Opportunity Investment Trust (DO IT). This nonprofit, nongovernmental agency would be charged with transforming our educational system for the digital age, unlocking the potential of the Internet and other new informational technologies for education in the broadest sense. Like the National Institutes of Health and the National Science Foundation, DO IT would disperse funds to stimulate research, learning, and national progress in this critical area.

This new digital initiative would

- fund new models and techniques to train teachers in the best uses of new information technologies in the classroom

- digitize America's collected memory stored in our nation's universities, libraries, and museums, making these materials available for use at school, home, or work

- create new voice-sensitive computer programs to teach language skills to fourth graders and new immigrants

- develop computer programs to measure the learning progress of individual students so teachers can adjust their methods to the specific needs and abilities of each child

DO IT would be financed by revenues earned from investing the $18 billion of anticipated revenues received from the recently mandated FCC auctions of unused radio spectrum.[319] This parallels the historic use of revenues from the sale of public lands—the Morrill Act—which helped finance public education in every new state and created the great system of land-grant colleges in the 1860s. Instead of just giving the spectrum away for free to corporations—our historic blunder in the digital spectrum gift to TV broadcasters—DO

IT would put those auction funds to use for all Americans, especially kids. Congress should ensure its passage.

4. Adopt the Canadian Model for Funding Quality Kids' TV

While America leaves kids' TV to the profit-obsessed ethos of the marketplace, other countries, from Canada to Australia and many of those in Europe, subsidize the creation of high-quality content with enormously successful results. Indeed, these government efforts have worked so well that Canadian and European production companies now dominate the world when it comes to quality kids' TV. Americans lead only in toy- and merchandising-based products. As I've mentioned, PBS, our nation's public broadcaster, recently leased its entire Saturday morning kids' block to a Toronto-based company, Nelvana. As a result, much of what your kids see on your U.S.-taxpayer-funded national public broadcasting system (not to mention on Nickelodeon, Disney, Fox, and other networks) was created and produced in other countries. It's an absurd situation, but it would easily be corrected if the United States would adopt the vastly superior Canadian model.

Here's how it works: the Canadian government, led by its version of the FCC (the CRTC), invests in the creation of high-quality kids' programming through simple tax credits and tax subsidies. As a result, it costs nearly 30 percent less to create the same quality TV show for kids in Canada than in the United States. Producers there receive tax credits and other targeted, market-based incentives for developing quality kids' content.

The U.S. government provides billions of dollars in tax credits, subsidies, and other incentives to everybody from hog farmers to oil producers, but we do nothing for kids' media. After September 11, 2001, our government bailed out the airline industry. It's time to recognize that our children are worth an investment too—a relatively tiny one at that, compared to other taxpayer-funded efforts.

The model is right there in plain view. Congress and the president should adopt the Canadian system and help make far more high-quality children's programming possible.

5. Support PBS with Adequate Funding and Leadership

America does have a public broadcasting system. It's called PBS, and though it's chronically underfunded and overly complex (consisting of a national network as well as hundreds of independent local stations), it delivers by far the best educational, arts, and cultural fare on American television. Much of the best content for kids is available only on your PBS station, shows such as *Sesame Street, Reading Rainbow, Arthur, Dragon Tales,* even *Barney*. Most parents know that they can trust their kids to PBS. It also funds a terrific kids' Internet site—PBSKids.org—and provides numerous educational and cultural benefits to communities and families across the nation.

So why don't we fund and support PBS more consistently and generously? Because it doesn't have any of the lobbying power of the huge, commercially driven broadcasters and media companies, and because PBS is often used as a political football by self-serving Washington politicians. Congress should set its partisan point-scoring aside when it comes to quality kids' programming. When you look at other countries, you realize how pathetic our national support for PBS truly is. In recent years, federal spending for public broadcasting has been about $1 a year per person in the U.S., while Japan spent about $17 per person, Canada $32 per person, and Great Britain $38 per person. In Britain, in fact, every household pays an annual "broadcast license fee" (recently, about $122) to support the BBC's excellent assortment of kids', cultural, and educational programming. Similarly, in recent years, households in Japan and Sweden paid at least $294 and $185 respectively.[320]

Even though Britain has about one-fifth of our population, it commits almost forty times the amount we do to public broadcasting. Why not, for example, impose an excise fee (say, $10) on the purchase of every TV set, which would go into a trust fund for non-commercial broadcasting? It's way past time for our government to step up to the plate and deliver some real results and decent funding for PBS.

6. Adopt Media-Literacy Curricula in All Schools

Since our children are growing up in a media-saturated environment, they need critical-thinking skills to better process all those images and messages they receive. So let's make media literacy part of the American school curriculum now. The models are already there. The know-how, skill set, and tools already exist. All we need is the public will and the leadership of our educational establishment.

And we need to start teaching media literacy early. By the time children are in second or third grade, they've already been bombarded with inappropriately violent, sexualized, and commercial images and messages. Media literacy, in effect, is a vital complement to parental guidance and judgment.

In the previous chapter, I recommended that the media industry, on a voluntary basis, should set up a major fund or a tax to finance media-literacy programs in schools and homes nationwide. But if the companies are slow to move, our government and Department of Education should step in, appropriate the funds, and levy a tax on the media conglomerates. We shouldn't wait any longer. Our children are already being "educated" by the "other parent" for five or six hours every day. Let's teach them how to make the best sense of those messages.

7. The FCC Should Assert Its Enforcement Powers and Revoke Some Licenses

Congress, the FCC, and the Federal Trade Commission (FTC) have significant constitutional and statutory authority when it comes to regulating media. As Senator Joe Lieberman said in an interview for this book, "The critically important place to start is with the FCC. They have so much power to make media better for children, and they have the proper statutory authority." The problem is they rarely use it, and it's about time that changed. Remember, a broadcast license is a privilege, not a right, and broadcasters go through a license renewal process every few years. These are publicly owned airwaves, and the FCC has the power to grant and renew licenses at its discretion. Unfortunately, as part of the 1996 Telecommunications Act, Congress "defanged" the FCC's license renewal process. Bowing to the broadcast lobby again, they made it virtually impossible for citizens' groups to challenge licenses during the renewal process and gave broadcasters a ludicrous safe haven from public accountability.

Congress should reverse this error, and the FCC should refuse to renew the licenses of the worst abusers. The commission should clearly spell out in advance the criteria for getting and keeping a television and radio broadcast license and tell those who protest it, "Take it or leave it. There are ten thousand other businesses that want this license." If the FCC used its statutory enforcement power, defined clear public-interest criteria for all licensees, and pulled a couple of licenses in a well-publicized manner, I can assure you that you'd see much better compliance with the Children's Television Act and other public-interest obligations. The impact would be incalculable in the long term.

Similarly, the Federal Trade Commission recently came out with an exhaustive study documenting how movie studios intentionally market inappropriate content to underage kids. This is a violation of the law, and the FTC has the power to enforce that law by means including fines. I urge the FTC to hit the violators where it hurts with huge fines—say $100 million and upward—for major, repeat violations. I promise you that the entire movie industry would sit up, take notice, and reflect a whole lot more on its public-interest responsibilities and the law.

8. Provide Incentives for a Positive Family-Viewing Period

Back in the 1970s, the "family hour" was a voluntary agreement by the broadcast networks not to show content that was "inappropriate" for family viewing during the first two hours of prime time. There are certain First Amendment limits on what the government can mandate in this regard, but it certainly can take steps to encourage broadcasters to return to that voluntary standard.

I urge that Congress and the FCC develop an incentive system that would provide tax and other monetary incentives to broadcast and nonpay cable networks to use the first two hours of prime time, at least five nights a week, to provide programming that is enriching and educational for kids and families. The sticky issue, of course, is defining the words "enriching" and "educational" and deciding who should define them, but we faced the same challenge fairly successfully with the Children's Television Act. Following the CTA's model, I recommend that the FCC be charged with responsibility for defining those terms and setting some clear guidelines for their enforcement.

9. Enact Major Campaign-Finance Reform

As former Democratic senator and presidential candidate Bill Bradley put it, "Today's political campaigns function as collection agencies for broadcasters. You simply transfer money from contributors to television stations." We need to change that corrupt system, and we can.

I propose that we follow the British model for political campaign advertising, which prohibits the sale of broadcast time for political commercials. Each candidate and each party is allocated a certain amount of free airtime, and they figure out how to use it. Our government has the power to enact similar rules, and we, the public, own the airwaves. The problem, as usual, is finding the political will.

An important first step was the passage of the McCain-Feingold campaign finance reform bill, but the real solution is to use the publicly owned airwaves to provide free airtime to all candidates and parties.

10. Use the Bully Pulpit to Shame, Threaten, and Cajole

Our political leaders have enormous power to use the bully pulpit to influence behavior in our society, and President Clinton used it particularly well. Even though he was at times criticized for cozying up to Hollywood and the media industry, he effectively used the power of his office to shame and cajole the media bigwigs on a number of important issues. And he was very effective at times. Without his leadership, we would never have had the Children's Television Act or the V-Chip or a number of other voluntary industry efforts to curb some of the worst excesses. For example, President Clinton held meetings with top Hollywood and media executives to urge more responsible programming and a toning down of violence. He held a much-publicized "Prime-Time Summit" in 1996, which brought broadcast and cable TV executives to the White House to discuss sex and violence; it was there that the industry leaders announced their plans to develop the new television ratings system.

The fact is, shame works very well with media leaders, as does jawboning. Praise for good efforts also makes a huge difference because it rewards positive behavior. And it's not just the president who has this power. Senators, representatives, the FCC chairman, and the other commissioners have it too, and they should use it a lot more than they do.

IT'S TIME FOR NEW LEADERSHIP

If our government officials, both elected and appointed, fail to act as our representatives—to respond to the needs of our kids and families—then they fail in the most fundamental way. We have seen the abandonment of children's media concerns before, with disastrous results. So what do we do if the free-market ideologues take over the reins of power and bow low at the altars of big business and "shareholder values"? We get angry, and we hold them accountable. Most important, we get off our behinds and do something about it. Social change often starts from below, when people have the vision and the motivation to take action and to demand accountability. That's what the next chapter is all about.

Ten Steps That Government Should Take

1. Break up the big media companies.
2. Establish a major public fund for quality kids' media content.
3. Just "DO IT" for the Internet and digital age.
4. Adopt the Canadian model for funding quality kids' TV.
5. Support PBS with adequate funding and leadership.
6. Adopt media-literacy curricula in all schools.
7. The FCC should assert its enforcement powers and revoke some licenses.
8. Provide incentives for a positive family-viewing period.
9. Enact major campaign-finance reform.
10. Use the bully pulpit to shame, threaten, and cajole.

Eleven

THE CHALLENGE OF CITIZEN ACTION

There seems to be nearly one pro-business lobbyist per square inch in the nation's capital these days, and they all seem to be calling for deregulation or some kind of favorable tax break for their business clients. In this environment, advocacy groups, citizen activists, and parents who speak up are all the more critical. Actually, given the enormous impact of the media on our lives, you'd expect to see innumerable, well-organized advocacy groups with big budgets and experienced leaders targeting various aspects of the media industry for reform. You would think the scale of citizen activism on this issue would be comparable to what you see on the environment, tobacco, or the gun control debate.

Unfortunately, despite the diligent efforts of groups like the Washington-based Center for Media Education, as well as the thoughtful contributions of policy groups like the Children's Partnership and Children Now, there is as yet no widely known, organized force advocating on behalf of kids and families in the media arena. It's time for concerned parents and other new and articulate voices to step in and fill this void, speaking out on kids' behalf. If they're organized, those voices will be heard.

I've had the good fortune to spend much of my professional life as a public-interest lawyer, teacher, and child advocate. And I've learned a few lessons along the way. First, I've learned that individuals can make an extraordinary difference for positive social change. Like Candy Lightner, who turned her incalculable and unimaginable grief at the loss of her child at the hands of a drunk driver into the driving force behind MADD (Mothers Against Drunk Driving) and changed American laws, consciousness, and driving habits in the process. Like the teachers at E. Morris Cox Elementary School in the heart of impoverished East Oakland, where I volunteered for ten years, who go to work with such enormous energy and commitment day after day, bringing enrichment, learning, and love to the lives of the thirty-five children squeezed into each run-down classroom. Like my friend Lisa, a social worker, who helps homeless and abused children negotiate the Byzantine corridors of the child-custody system and finds them homes and foster parents who care for them. Like the countless New York heroes who rallied the city's spirit in the wake of the September 11 tragedy. We are indeed a democracy of ideas, but we are also a democracy of extraordinary people, many of whom take on challenges that most would find insurmountable—and conquer them anyway.

I have seen enormous contributions by individuals in the arena of children's media as well. As founder of Action for Children's Television, Peggy Charren was perhaps the leading voice in the 1970s, 1980s, and 1990s for greater responsibility in kids' TV. A few well-chosen words from Peggy Charren put many resistant media and political leaders in their place. She was the driving force behind the Children's Television Act and numerous other pieces of powerful legislation and litigation. She well deserves the Presidential Medal of Freedom she received.

And let's not forget Tipper Gore. As a mom and wife of a political figure, she put her neck on the line when she took on the recording industry and called for a labeling system for all music. She was excoriated for this, but she stuck to her guns and showed what individuals can do when they get mad and they get organized.

THE CARROT AND THE STICK

I've also learned that shame and well-targeted pressure campaigns work. Boycotts, especially, can be effective. Sometimes hitting companies in the pocketbook is the *only* way to get their attention. We need far more of these confrontational campaigns to influence media conglomerates that are increasingly becoming larger and less responsive. We also need a new bipartisan coalition to speak out on behalf of kids and parents. Both liberals and conservatives need to put political and personal differences aside and work as partners to find common ground, because these issues affect all Americans.

Finally, I've learned that the carrot can work as well as the stick to promote change. Praise for media companies that do the right thing, such as toning down levels of violence in the wake of September 11, is also important. Awards programs, too, can encourage writers, directors, and producers to create positive messages and content in all media. In addition, they nurture closer cooperation between social advocates and the media industry. Regular workshops and conferences, too, can provide a welcome venue for collaboration between the creative community and child development experts and foster continuing improvements in family and kids' media.

TEN STEPS FOR NEW VOICES AND LEADERS

Each one of us can work effectively to increase the pressure for change. By adding our voices to those of millions of other parents and citizens who are fed up with an industry that at best shortchanges and at worst exploits our children, we can make sure that we're heard. Together, we must demand that the FCC and our elected representatives stand up for the interests of families, not just the free market and large corporations. Here are ten citizen-action steps that each of us can take to help reshape the media landscape to safeguard and benefit our kids.

1. Support Advocacy Groups and Get Others in Your Community Involved

Whether you choose to support advocacy organizations like Children Now or the Center for Media Education, or work to convince national groups like the PTA, the Junior League, and Girls Inc. to focus more on kids' media issues, you can help bring more pressure and attention on the media. If local members of PTAs, for example, started demanding media-literacy curricula in local schools, progress would be much swifter. There are dozens of other areas where increased citizen involvement and support for targeted advocacy can produce significant, long-term results.

2. Create New Advocacy Groups to Focus on Kids' Media Issues

New voices are much needed in the area of children's and family media. Senator Joe Lieberman, in an interview for this book, repeatedly called for strong new advocacy groups and leaders to help him and his colleagues in the Senate promote media policies for children and families. In fact, echoing former President Bill Clinton, he noted that this was truly a bipartisan issue on which conservatives and liberals could join together in a powerful new coalition for change.

I'm not suggesting that it's easy to build a new public advocacy group, nor am I minimizing the hard work and commitment of those organizations that are already in the trenches. But new leadership is needed to balance the far more powerful lobbying voices arrayed on the side of the corporate and deregulation interests.

3. Gain Foundation Support for New Media Policies and Advocacy Efforts

I spent the better part of seven years building Children Now into a respected national advocacy group for kids and families. It would *never* have been possible without the prescient and sustained support of a relatively small number of committed foundations and their outstanding executives, as well as the incredible generosity of a handful of wealthy individuals and business leaders. Similarly, *Sesame Street* would never have gotten on the air had it not been for the vision and financial support of a handful of foundation executives from the Carnegie Corporation and the Markle Foundation.

The good news is that the foundation world is growing by leaps and bounds. The roaring economy of the past decade has brought untold wealth into some of the grand old foundations, such as Rockefeller, Carnegie, Ford, and Hewlett. In addition, there are huge new foundations like the Bill and Melinda Gates Foundation, The Gordon and Betty Moore Foundation, and funds created by dot-com entrepreneurs who cashed in early (like Pierre Omidyar of eBay) adding billions of new dollars to the foundation pie. Indeed, in the year 2000, total U.S. foundation giving was an estimated $27.6 billion, up 18.4 percent over 1999, according to the Foundation Center. The good news is that there's a whole lot of dough that foundations want to invest in positive causes.

The bad news, however, is that the foundation world has generally been pretty ignorant or afraid of media policy and advocacy. With notable exceptions like the Markle Foundation in New York, the Kaiser Family Foundation in California, the Benton Foundation in Washington, D.C., and certain initiatives from the Pew Charitable Trusts, Carnegie Corporation, and other major funding institutions, the foundation world hasn't invested in media issues as much as they have in the environment, education, or issues like population control. That's a major reason that there are so few policy and advocacy groups in this arena.

It's time that changed. The foundation community should take some of its newfound wealth—much of which is directly attributable to the media and communications revolution of the past decade—and put it back to work in one of the areas where it's needed most—in media policies that improve the lives of children and families.

4. Get Religious Groups and Congregations Involved

Although fundamentalist Christian groups have gotten most of the headlines—and notoriety—for speaking up about the media and families, we need all concerned religious organizations of every faith to make their voices heard about these issues. Religious groups are an obvious arena for sustained community and citizen response. This is a bipartisan issue on which Americans of all faiths and political perspectives can find common ground.

5. Use the Internet as an Organizing and Advocacy Tool

We've only just scratched the surface of the Internet's enormous potential for organizing citizen-action efforts. As groups like MoveOn.org have shown, this new medium has amazing possibilities for grass-roots political action, from membership alerts to petitions and legislative e-mail campaigns. So here's a clarion call to Jerry Yang, Meg Whitman, tech guru Esther Dyson, and all the other high-tech pioneers who care about social change—help harness the amazing organizing power of the Internet to help connect people and make better media policy for kids.

6. Support Targeted Consumer Boycotts of Media Companies

As I mentioned earlier, boycotts, or even the credible threat of boycotts, hit big media conglomerates in the only place it truly seems to hurt—the wallet. They are also excellent vehicles for shaming companies into modifying their behavior and messages. Advertisers, too, are a notoriously cautious group and take the threat of boycotts very seriously. Conservative Christian activists have long demonstrated the power and impact of media boycotts, though I disagree with many of their targets and viewpoints. On the liberal side, both the NAACP and leading environmental groups have also effectively used boycotts to change the policies of large corporations. Today, it's time for activists of all convictions and political persuasions to use these tools to target media companies that, time after time, put profits before the best interests of kids and families.

7. Challenge FCC Licenses

Traditionally, one of the most effective means for checking broadcasters' abuse of the airwaves was to mount citizen-based challenges to their licensing or renewal hearings. Public-interest advocates should pressure Congress to restore that vital check and balance on the broadcast industry—one that was unconscionably eliminated by the 1996 Telecommunications Act. It's time to hold the FCC's feet to the fire again. With legislative support from Congress, parents and other citizen advocates need to demand that the FCC restore public challenges to broadcast licenses.

Similarly, parents, citizens, and advocacy groups need to be more aware of billion-dollar spectrum giveaways and the negative effects of unchecked media mergers, speaking out—loudly—to protect the forgotten interests of children and the American public. The FCC must represent the public interest in this regard, and its commissioners should be held publicly accountable.

8. Write the FCC and Media Leaders to Air Your Concerns

Just try it. See what happens when you take the time to write a thoughtful e-mail or letter to the general manager of your local television station. You'll be amazed at how effective such a simple act can be, especially if you can get a few other friends or colleagues to write as well. Former FCC Chairman Bill Kennard has lots of stories about how reasonable e-mails from American parents affected his thinking, and I know many local and national TV and radio executives who respond the same way to letters or phone calls from thoughtful members of their broadcast audience. FCC Chairman Powell should be hearing from many American parents right now.

Advertisers, too, care a lot about what consumers think, and they respond. Recently, for example, JCPenney ran a TV ad featuring a mother who urged her daughter to wear her pants slung lower on her hips. The department store chain got so many complaints from parents that it took the commercial off the air.[321] So send a letter or an e-mail or pick up the telephone and start making your opinions heard.

9. Sponsor a "Turn-Off-the-TV Week" in Your Local Community

It may sound corny, but it works. I've given a number of talks recently that were tied to the annual "Turn-Off-the-TV Week" campaign, held across the country every April, and I'm a convert. At the very least, these community-wide events draw our attention to the issues. They spark awareness. They can change behavior, at least for a short period of time. And most of all, they can make us think about the huge role that the media plays in children's lives.

So join in your local community "TV Turnoff Week" event. If there isn't one, take the plunge; organize one with your friends, colleagues, or fellow parents, using simple kits that are available on the Internet (at tvturnoff.org). And here's another thought—maybe we should schedule a nationwide "TV Turnoff Week" event during network "sweeps week" to really get our point across.

10. Organize a Media-Literacy Program in Your School or Community

As I've stated, I strongly believe that media literacy ought to be a required part of every student's curriculum, from grade school on up, and that government and the media industry should support a comprehensive program nationwide. But until that day comes, and until we make it a national priority, parents and citizens groups can at least bring media literacy to their own communities. Talk to the principal at your child's school about including media literacy in the curriculum, or organize an after-school media-literacy program. You will be making a real, tangible difference in children's lives, and there are many resources out there to help you get started.

Ten Steps for Citizen Activists

1. Support advocacy groups and get others in your community involved.
2. Create new advocacy groups to focus on kids' media issues.
3. Gain foundation support for new media policies and advocacy efforts.
4. Get religious groups and congregations involved.
5. Use the Internet as an organizing and advocacy tool.
6. Support targeted consumer boycotts of media companies.
7. Challenge FCC licenses.
8. Write the FCC and media leaders to air your concerns.
9. Sponsor a "Turn-Off-the-TV Week" in your local community.
10. Organize a media-literacy program in your school or community.

SAFEGUARDING THE MEDIA ENVIRONMENT

The fact is, we do not have to let the "other parent" raise our children. We don't have to let media—and giant media corporations—make all the rules. The sole concern and bottom line of many media companies and their top executives may be money. And the bottom line for many of our elected representatives may be staying in office, no matter how much this may mean compromising the public interest. But the bottom line for most parents and many others is ensuring a safe and healthy environment for children. In the post–September 11 world, it is more important than ever to root out the destructive forces in our media landscape. We must use the awesome power of media and technology to help us make our children stronger, wiser, and more aware of their social responsibilities.

So many of us have tuned out for so long. That has to change. We need to take charge of the media in our own homes, and speak out loudly to build public pressure for social change. Today, the media has phenomenal global reach and extraordinary new potential to enrich or harm our children's lives. We need to take back control. As media visionary Marshall McLuhan pointed out, the age of technology is also the "age of 'do-it-yourself.' " Everyone has a meaningful contribution to make.

What are we waiting for?

Afterword

When I was a little girl, my parents let me watch one television show a night and unlimited amounts of TV on Saturday morning. Lots of movies filled my weekends, and as I got older, music filled my days and nights, at home and with friends. My parents, at least one of them, tried to watch as much of the TV I did with me (maybe less often during Saturday morning cartoon binges), and certainly I rarely saw a movie without my parents or a friend's parent until I was ten or eleven. Media consumption was always a family event when I was young. As I got older, particularly in high school and beyond, my parents and I watched less TV and fewer movies together, and my parents' and my music tastes diverged significantly. Still, my parents were curious about what I was watching, reading, seeing, and listening to and always wondering what I thought about what I had experienced. Even while I was in high school, media consumption remained a collective event.

My sophomore spring at Stanford, I took a class taught by Jim Steyer and Martin Carnoy on the intersection of race, education, and the media in the United States. I loved the class and I loved the professors. Toward the end of the class, I got to know Professor Steyer better and was excited when he asked me to help him research a book he was preparing to write on kids and the media. My acceptance of his offer led to one of my most important academic and personal experiences at Stanford. Over the next year, I worked on compiling information about studies spanning everything from the way race is portrayed in the media, to the digital divide, to the ways in which violence in different media affects kids differently, to the ways in which commercialism affects both what media kids consume and how. The last topic interested me most, and it was to it that I devoted most of my time. Throughout this survey work for Jim, as I at some point started calling him, I realized a great deal about not only the pervasive nature of the media in kids' lives and developing consciousness, but also about how the media had affected me as I had developed. I realized that it was not the constraints my parents had placed on my media consumption that enabled me to understand that what I was watching was not real and not reality, but the fact that they often watched with me and talked to me about it. I came to see that my parents had practiced parental media literacy with me.

I hope that this book will serve families, parents, kids, teenagers, and people my age, those of us no longer children but not yet parents. I hope that parents and kids start talking about their media experiences more and more, both those that they share and those they don't. I hope this book is one of the pieces of media that they can share together, in conversations about what the media is. I hope that people my age will realize that we, too, are in some part media products and will read this book both to understand ourselves and to better understand how to be better parents, whenever that may be. As Jim helped reveal to me, media is everything and everywhere. I expect people of all ages who read this to do so critically, to look at it as media about media.

I am at Oxford now, further from my family than I have ever been. I miss my parents all the time. We try to talk as often as we can, but like many families, we are each busy living our own lives and it's hard to find meeting points for real conversations in three hectic schedules. We do find the time though, and when we talk, my parents still ask what I am reading and what I have seen recently. Media is a part of our lives as it is a part of almost all lives anywhere in the world. Talking about media's role in each of our lives is probably not as important as it was when I was little, but those conversations are still a valued and important facet of understanding what we each are doing, thinking and feeling, and even, for me, who I am always becoming.

I hope everyone who reads this book enjoys it as much as I enjoyed working on it and watching it take shape.

Chelsea Clinton
2002

Acknowledgments

Writing a book is no simple undertaking, particularly when you have a growing family and a day job. For me, it definitely falls into that special category of life experiences that starts with, "If I'd only known what I was getting myself into . . . "

Fortunately I had a terrific colleague, who collaborated with me on this book from the outset. Susan Wels, who has been my friend since our freshman year in college, is a bestselling author in her own right and a first-rate editor to boot. Susan worked with me on the book from proposal stage to final editing. Quite simply, I couldn't have asked for a better partner. This book has benefited immeasurably from her fine writing skills and excellent judgment every step of the way. I can never thank Susan enough for that collaboration and her innumerable contributions to the final product. It was truly a team effort.

Chelsea Clinton, too, provided invaluable research help. Chelsea was my student in several courses at Stanford, and she coupled her excellent research and writing skills with great energy and enthusiasm while actively participating in a number of the key interviews for the book. Chelsea made valuable contributions to the chapters on commercialism and violence and is a remarkable young woman, who, time and time again, has done her parents, her country, and her professor proud.

As always, I also relied on a wide assortment of friends, family members, and experts who helped me get my arms around this complex subject. Two people, especially, played key roles in urging me to undertake this effort. One is my brother Tom, my oldest and most trusted friend, as well as my partner in virtually every enterprise I've undertaken. He's been telling me to write a book for years, possibly to get me to talk a bit less, and my appreciation for his encouragement, love, and frank advice cannot be overstated. In addition, my friend and JP Kids' colleague Ann Dilworth, a publishing star in her own right, also deserves credit for convincing me that the time was right to put my thoughts and experiences in the kids' educational media world down on paper.

Countless others were also generous to me with their time and insights. My first interview was with Ken Auletta, whose extraordinary access and insights into the world of media have been so valuable to my own thinking. My old friend and esteemed colleague Newt Minow, the former FCC chairman, was also a key inspiration for this book. Newt has provided wise counsel to me since the early days of Children Now, and he, too, encouraged me at all stages of the process. I deeply appreciate his ongoing wisdom and support, not to mention the fact that, in his words, he "ruined his summer vacation" in order to read a first draft of this book.

Geoff Cowan, the dean of the Annenberg School at USC, also deserves my sincerest thanks. A founding board member of Children Now, he helped me conceive and launch the organization's Children and the Media Program in the early 1990s. A noted author, scholar, and social entrepreneur, Geoff has inspired and provided excellent advice to me for many years and read and critiqued the book's first draft. I'm grateful, too, for the assistance of Bill Baker, president of WNET in New York City, whose insights into the decline of the television industry are so ably chronicled in his fine book *Down the Tube*. My friend Herb Scannell, president of Nickelodeon, was unfailingly helpful and generous, sitting through two interviews and lecturing to one of my classes at Stanford. His former colleague, Gerry Laybourne, CEO of Oxygen Media, has long been a friend and inspiration to my work, and she provided very helpful comments and advice. My college classmate and friend Bill Kennard, the former chairman of the FCC, also offered valuable insights and candid assessments of the inner workings of the FCC, as well as the current state of the media world. Julius Genachowski, counsel to former FCC chairman Reed Hundt and now general counsel to Barry Diller at USA Networks, also provided a remarkable inside perspective on the FCC during Hundt's tenure and patiently described the digital spectrum "giveaway" among other key events.

My old college friend Mike Tollin, who has achieved much-deserved success in the worlds of film and television, was exceptionally helpful. Mike has been a committed kids' advocate since the days when he first helped me to found Children Now, and his candid insights as a director/producer of popular films and television shows were of enormous value to the book. The famed pediatrician T. Berry Brazelton, whom I first met during the early days of Children Now, was also very helpful with his insights, as was Steve Case, the visionary Internet pioneer and AOL Time Warner chairman, who spent nearly two hours with me in an interview for the book.

Milton Chen provided his always valuable perspective on the role of parents and television, and Danny Goldberg, one of the music industry's finest leaders and another original board member of Children Now, offered candid and thoughtful commentary. My colleagues Mike Cohen of ARC Consulting and Don Roberts of Stanford University provided years of academic experience as well as many practical insights. Matt James, Vicky Rideout, and Ulla Foehr of the Kaiser Family Foundation were generous in sharing their studies and perspectives. Scott Nash of Big Blue Dot, David Kleeman of the American Center for Children's Media and kids' advertising guru, Jon Mandel provided their unique perspectives as longtime leaders in the kids' media field. Michael Hudes and Janice Nakano Spivak provided helpful insights on the Internet and its impact on children, as did Jerry Yang, Jeff Mallett, Karen Edwards and John Place at Yahoo!, and John Yost at Black Rocket. My pal Mickey Drexler of the Gap shared his valuable marketing perspective, and Senator Joe Lieberman offered his keen assessments of what Congress and the Senate should do to reshape kids' media policy. Finally, President Bill Clinton was enormously generous with his time and insights into strategies for improving the situation in the future, and the entire Steyer family will forever appreciate his personal kindness over the past few years.

Don Kennedy, president emeritus at Stanford University and editor of *Science* magazine, has been a mentor and dear friend for nearly two decades, ever since he threatened to have me arrested for my role in a student protest. I can never thank Don enough for his wisdom and guidance over the past twenty years, and for reading the first draft and offering his usual valuable critique. Two other friends and colleagues, Lawrence Wilkinson, vice chairman of Oxygen Media, and Jack Boger of UNC Law School, also provided significant feedback on the first draft of the book. I'd also like to thank my friend and running partner, Larry Baer, as well as author Tom Wolfe and publisher extraordinaire Gerry Byrne, for their ongoing encouragement and support.

At JP Kids, Jeff Pinsker and Miranda Barry read the entire first draft and offered very helpful edits and comments. Other JP Kids' colleagues, including Angie Allen, Danielle Sorrenti-Gunthner, Liz Nealon, Cece Reyes, Kim Hatamiya, and Fionnuala McAdam, all provided assistance on this project. I'm also grateful to the Board Members of JP Kids— Bob Miller, Frank Biondi, Tench Coxe, and Leo Hindery—all of whom have supported me and the company steadfastly these past few years. I'd also like to acknowledge some key investors and friends—Warren Hellman, George Roberts, Mike Klein, and Ed Cohen—whose long-term support for both Children Now and JP Kids has meant so much to me.

My agent Kris Dahl of ICM has been a rock-solid ally and superb adviser from day one, and I'm proud to call her my friend as well. At Atria Books/Simon & Schuster, I had three editors, all of whom deserve my heartfelt thanks. Nancy Miller purchased the book and gave me initial advice and encouragement. Tracy Bernstein did much of the editing on the book and did an excellent and thorough job. Luke Dempsey came on for the final phases and added just the right mix of support and editorial judgment. Not surprisingly, all three are parents of young children who live in this media culture. I'd also like to thank Judith Curr, publisher of Atria Books, for her support when it counted most. Camille McDuffie, whose husband Bobby is one of my closest friends and who also read and critiqued the first draft, was also an invaluable adviser and confidante on virtually every aspect of the book. Liz Perle, my old friend from San Francisco, regularly provided the wisdom and guidance that she's famous for in the publishing world. And Charlotte Sheedy was helpful and candid from the outset, for which I am also grateful. So there you see, it was quite a team effort.

But all team efforts start at home, and my family has been wonderful in its support. My amazing mother, Marnie, has been unfailing in her love, encouragement, and wisdom. My late father, Roy, taught me how to write and edited my early work, just as he did for so many young litigators at Sullivan & Cromwell, so I'm sure he's smiling at this one from heaven. My brothers Hume and Tom encouraged me every step of the way. But it's my own family—Liz, Lily, Kirk, and Carly—who had to live through this adventure and without whom this book would never have been possible. My gratitude and love for them knows no bounds.

James P. Steyer
San Francisco, California

NOTES

1   T. Berry Brazelton, MD, interview by the author, October 2001.

2   Ted Turner, speech to Western Cable Show, as quoted in Cynthia Littleton, "Turner Sees 'Endgame' on Horizon for Cable Biz," *The Hollywood Reporter,* November 29, 2001, p. 1.

3   Robert McChesney (author of *Rich Media, Poor Democracy),* interview, "The Merchants of Cool," *Frontline,* Public Broadcasting System, 2001.

4   James Sterngold, "Censorship in the Age of Anything Goes," *New York Times,* September 20, 1998.

5   Herb Scannell, interview by author, New York, NY, January 22, 2000.

6   Steve Case, interview by author, AOL headquarters, Dulles, Va., September 26, 2001.

7   Joseph Lieberman, interview by author, Washington, DC, September 26, 2001.

8   Newton N. Minow and Craig L. LaMay, *Abandoned in the Wasteland,* New York: Hill and Wang, 1995.

9   Bill Baker, interview by author, New York City, November 16, 1999.

10   For an in-depth look at media consolidation, read the latest edition of Ben H. Bagdikian, *The Media Monopoly,* 6th ed. (Boston: Beacon Press, 2001).

11   Most of this data comes from public records and the PBS *Frontline* Web site on media giants, as well as an article on AOL Time Warner by Ken Auletta, "Leviathan," *The New Yorker,* October 29, 2001.

12   Aurora Wallace, interview by Auletta, "Leviathan," p. 53.

13   Ted Turner, quoted in "All Together Now," *Electronic Media,* December 15, 1997, p. 14.

14   Peter Chernin, quoted in "The Rules According to Rupert," *Fortune,* October 26, 1998, p. 104.

15   "Size Does Matter," *Economist,* May 21, 1998, p. 57.

16   Neil Strauss, "A Culture of Reruns and Pollsters at the Mall," *New York Times,* September 14, 1998, p. B1.

17   Mark Crispin Miller, interview in "The Merchants of Cool," *Frontline,* Public Broadcasting System, 2001.

18   Peter Bart, quoted in "Big Media," *Brill's Content,* January 2000, p. 97.

19   John F. Kennedy, quoted in Erick Barnorow, *The Image Empire* (New York: Oxford University Press, 1970), p. 196.

20   For an in-depth look at the impact of media consolidation on society, see Dean Alger, *Megamedia* (Rowman & Littlefield, 1998). Lanham, Md.

21   Ted Turner, interview by Mike Wallace, "Media Mogul," *60 Minutes,* CBS, Quoted in Alger, *Megamedia,* January 1997, p. 2.

22   Burt Neuborne (Director, the Brennan Center for Justice), quoted from "Free Speech for Sale," Bill Moyers Special, Public Broadcasting System.

23   Dan Rather as quoted by Ken Auletta, "Battle Stations," *The New Yorker,* December 10, 2001, pp. 61 and 66.

24   Lawrie Mifflin, "An ABC News Reporter Tests the Boundaries of Investigating Disney and Finds Them," *New York Times,* October 19, 1998, p. C8.

25   R. W. Apple, Joe Alex Morris Lecture at the Kennedy School of Government, Harvard University, April 18, 1993, as cited in Alger, *Megamedia,* p. 153.

26   Harold A. LaFount, quoted in William F. Baker and George Dessart, *Down the Tube* (New York: Basic Books, 1998), p. 14.

27   Mary Ann Watson, *The Expanding Vista* (New York: Oxford University Press, 1990), p. 154.

28   John Condry, "Thief of Time, Unfaithful Servant: Television and the American Child," *Daedalus* 122 no. 1 (winter 1993), p. 259.

29   Louis Chunovic, *One Foot on the Floor* (New York: TV Books, 2000), p. 15.

30   Ibid., p. 19.

31   Ibid., p. 24.

32   Ibid., p. 27.

33   Ibid., p. 26.

34   Alfred R. Schneider, *The Gatekeeper* (Syracuse, NY: Syracuse University Press, 2001), p. 34.

35   Jason Roberts, "Public Access: Fortifying the Electronic Soapbox." *Federal Communications Law Journal,* vol. 47, no. 1, October 1994, <http://www.law.indiana.edu/fclj/pubs/v47/no1/roberts.html>

36   Schneider, *The Gatekeeper,* p. 35.

37   Rick Shefchik (Knight-Tribune News Service), "Censorship Issue Both Divides and Unites: Groups Agree on Problem, Not on Solution," *The Florida Times-Union,* January 8, 2001.

38   Robert Thompson, quoted in Jim Rutenberg, "Hurt by Cable, Networks Spout Expletives," *New York Times,* September 2, 2001, p. 19.

39   Bradley S. Greenberg, Jane D. Brown, and Nancy L. Buerkel Rothfull, *Media, Sex and the Adolescent* (Cresskill, NJ: Hampton Press, Inc., 1993), pp. 12–13.

40   Kaiser Family Foundation, "Sex on TV(2)"(2001): Menlo Park: Kaiser Family Foundation.

41   Douglas Rushkoff, "Media: It's the Real Thing," *New Perspectives Quarterly* 11, no. 3 (summer 1994), p. 4.

42   Keenen Ivory Wayans, quoted in Robert W. Welkos, "Gross Opportunities," *San Francisco Chronicle,* Sunday, July 2, 2000, p. 48.

43   Neil Postman, *The Disappearance of Childhood* (New York: Vintage Books, 1994), pp. xi–49.

44   Joshua Meyrowitz, quoted in Richard Zoglin, "Is TV Ruining Our Children?" *Time,* October 15, 1990, p. 75.

45   Greenberg et al., *Media, Sex and the Adolescent,* p. 226.

46   Kaiser Family Foundation/Children Now, "Talking with Kids About Tough Issues: A National Survey of Parents and Kids," (Menlo Park: Kaiser Family Foundation, 1999).

47   Kaiser Family Foundation, "Sex on TV," (Menlo Park: Kaiser Family Foundation, 1999) p. 1.

48   L. Monique Ward, "Talking About Sex: Common Themes about Sexuality in the Prime-Time Television Programs Children and Adolescents View Most," *Journal of Youth and Adolescence,* vol. 24, no. 5 (1995), pp. 595–615.

49   Janelle Brown, "Trash Maps with Training Wheels," *Salon,* September 10, 2001, <http://www.salon.com/mwt/style/2001/09/10/teen_mags/index.html>

50   "The Naked Truth," *Newsweek,* May 8, 2000.

51   Lynn Ponton, MD, *The Sex Lives of Teenagers* (New York: Dutton, 2000), p. 5.

52   Drew Pinsky, MD, quoted in James B. Meigs, "The Trouble with Movies," *FamilyLife Magazine,* May 2000.

53   Larry C. Jensen, Jacqueline F. de Gaston, and Stan E. Weed, "Societal and Parental Influences on Adolescent Sexual Behavior," *Psychological Reports,* vol. 75 (1994), pp. 1504–06.

54   Department of Health and Human Services, *Healthy People 2000: National Health Promotion and Disease Prevention Objectives,* DHHS publication no. 91–50212 (Washington, DC: US Government Printing Office, 1990).

55   Kaiser Family Foundation, "Sex on TV(2)" (2001): Kaiser Family Foundation.

56   Ibid.

57   Jane E. Brody, "Teen-Agers and Sex: Younger and More at Risk," *New York Times,* September 15, 1998, p. F7.

58   Lynn Ponton, MD, *The Sex Lives of Teenagers* (New York: Dutton, 2000), p. 1.

59   Ibid., p. 3.

60   Ibid., p. 3.

61   Ibid., p. 7.

62   Condry, "Thief of Time."

63   "Hollywood Censored: The Production Code," *Culture Shock: The TV Series and Beyond,* PBS, 2000 <http://www.pbs.org./wgbh/cultureshock/beyond/hollywood.html>

64   "Hollywood Censored," PBS.

65   Meigs, "The Trouble with Movies."

66   Roger Ebert, "It's Time for a Commonsense System of Rating Movies," *Star Tribune,* Newspaper of the Twin Cities, October 30, 2000, p. 1E.

67   Greenberg et al., *Media, Sex and the Adolescent,* p. 56–8.

68   Ebert, "It's Time," p. 1E.

69   Greenberg et al., *Media, Sex and the Adolescent,* p. 56–8.

70   Bedsole, Melissa, "Misleading 'R' rating confusing to parents, a poor standard," *The Battalion* (Texas A&M Univ.) December 5, 2000.

71   Meigs, "The Trouble With Movies."
72   Peter G. Christenson and Donald F. Roberts, *It's Not Only Rock & Roll* (Cresskill, NJ: Hampton Press, Inc., 1998), p. 16.
73   Wendy Wilson, "Government to Keep Pressing Ratings Enforcement in 2001," *Video Business,* January 1, 2001, p. 59.
74   Christopher Stern, "Theater Owners Promise Controls on 'R' Previews," *Seattle Times,* November 13, 2000, p. D6.
75   Alan Horn, quoted in Faye Fiore, "FTC Says It Cannot Shield Children from Hollywood Regulation," *Los Angeles Times,* November 22, 2000, p. A1.
76   Kurt Hall, quoted in Christopher Stern, "Theater Owners Promise," p. D6.
77   Elaine Jarvik, "Another Clampdown on R Movies," *Deseret News,* November 15, 2000, p. AD1.
78   Christopher Stern, "Slowly, Studios Take On Ratings Reform," *Washington Post,* November 28, 2000, p. D6.
79   Elaine Jarvik, "Another Clampdown on R Movies," *Deseret News,* November 15, 2000, p. AO1.
80   Bob Bernick Jr., "Utah House Receives Bill Targeting R Films, Youths," *Deseret News,* February 22, 2001, p. AO1.
81   Ebert, "It's Time," p. 1E.
82   Lynn Elber (Associated Press), "Television Sex Is Getting Hotter, Sex Study Finds," February 6, 2001, *SF Gate News* <http:www.sfgate.com>
83   Parents Television Council, "The Sour Family Hour" (Parents Television Council Special Report, 2001), <http://www.parentstv.org/publications/reports/sour2001/sr20010801es.html>
84   Parents Television Council, "Unintended Consequences: With Ratings System in Place, TV More Offensive Than Ever" (Parents Television Council: Special Report, 1999) <http://www.mediaresearch.org/specialreports/ent/sr0526699.html>
85   Rula Razek, "Mom to TV: Delete All Sex and Violence," *USA Weekend,* December 17, 2000, p. 22.
86   Greenberg et al., *Media, Sex and the Adolescent,* p. 56–8.
87   (Cox News Service), "Parents Out of the Loop on Kids' Multimedia Activities," *San Francisco Chronicle,* June 26, 2000.
88   Razek, "Mom to TV," p. 22.
89   Kaiser Family Foundation, "Parents and the V-Chip 2001" (Menlo Park: Kaiser Family Foundation, 2001).
90   "Media Frenzy Consumes Americans' Leisure Time." *San Francisco Chronicle,* June 29, 2000.
91   Christenson and Roberts, *It's Not Only,* p. 64.
92   Laura Holson, "U.S. Is Said to Criticize Music Industry on Marketing," *New York Times,* December 4, 2001, p. A17.
93   Christenson and Roberts, *It's Not Only,* p. 63.
94   Ibid., p. 223.
95   Rod Nordland and Jeffrey Bartholer, "The Darkest Corner of the Internet," *Newsweek,* March 19, 2001, p. 49.

96   Carrie Kirby, " 'Startling' Number of Kids Solicited for Sex on Internet," *San Francisco Chronicle*, June 9, 2000, p. A1.

97   Judith Krug, quoted in Karen Thomas, "Inconsistency Plagues Net Filters," *USA Today*, February 15, 2001, p. 3D.

98   Kirby, " 'Startling' Number," p. A1.

99   Nordland and Bartholer, "Darkest Corner," p. 49.

100   Kirby, " 'Startling' Number," p. A1.

101   Bill Bond, quoted in Rick Bragg, "Past Victims Relive Pain As Tragedy Is Repeated," *New York Times*, May 25, 1998, p. A8.

102   John Leo, "Gunning for Hollywood," *U.S. News & World Report*, May 10, 1999, p. 16.

103   Timothy Egan, "Where Rampages Begin," *New York Times*, June 14, 1998, p. 1.

104   Ibid.

105   Ibid.

106   Amanda Bower, "Young Voices from the Cell," *Time*, May 28, 2001.

107   Ulysses Torassa, "Kids Less Violent after Cutting Back on TV," *San Francisco Chronicle*, May 15, 2001, p. A1.

108   Joanne Cantor, *Mommy, I'm Scared*, San Diego: Harcourt Brace & Company, 1998, pp. 14–15.

109   Joanne Cantor, "Confronting Children's Fright Responses to Mass Media," *Media, Children and the Family*, ed. Dolf Zillmann, Jennings Bryant and Aletha C. Huston, Hillsdale, NJ: Lawrence Erlbaum Assoc., Publishers, 1994, p. 147.

110   Fumie Yokota, MS, and Kimberly M. Thompson, ScD, "Violence in G-Rated Animated Films," *JAMA*, vol. 283 (20), May 24, 2000, pp. 2716–20.

111   Barbara F. Meltz, "Children's Movies May Scare the Little Ones," *San Diego Union–Tribune*, December 16, 2000, p. E-6.

112   Ibid.

113   Bruno Bettelheim, *The Uses of Enchantment*, New York: Alfred A. Knopf, 1976, p. 179.

114   Andre P. Derdeyn, MD, and Jeffrey M. Turley, MD, "Television, Films and the Emotional Life of Children," *Media, Children*, p. 137.

115   "Sesame Workshop Study: Unexpected Levels of Anxiety Found in Children Ages 6–11," *PR Newswire*, May 30, 2001.

116   Carl M. Cannon, "Honey, I Warped the Kids," *Mother Jones*, January 1993.

117   M. M. Lefkowitz, L. D. Eron, L. D. Walder, and L. R. Huesmann, *Growing Up to Be Violent*, New York: Pergamon, 1977.

118   Cannon, "Honey, I Warped."

119   Torassa, "Kids Less Violent," p. A1.

120   George Gerbner, quoted in Scott Stossel, "The Man Who Counts the Killings," *Atlantic Monthly*, May 1997.

121   Nancy Carlsson-Paige and Diane E. Levin, "Stop Marketing Violence to Tots," <http://www.youngmedia.org.au/yma/Subpages/violence.htm>

122   Ibid.

123   Kent Dulian, quoted in Gib Twyman, "Filmmakers Decry Violence, Censors," *Deseret News*, May 26, 2001, p. B1.

124   "Powerful Influences," Online News Hour, May 10, 1999, <http://www. pbs.org/newshour/bb/media/jan-june99/violence_5-10.html>

125   Bryan Brown, quoted in Twyman, "Filmmakers Decry," p. B1.

126   Les Moonves, quoted in Michael Krasny, "Passing the Buck in Tinseltown," *Mother Jones,* January 1993.

127   Cannon, "Honey, I Warped."

128   Ibid.

129   Elizabeth Thomas, "Making Connections: Media's Role in the Culture of Violence," Center for Media Literacy, Winter 1993, <http://www.medialit. org/Violence/articles/make_conn.htm>

130   Kalpana Srinvasan (Associated Press), "Hollywood Execs Admit Lapses in Judgment in Marketing R-Rated Films," September 27, 2000.

131   Doreen Carvajal, "Word for Word, Test-Marketing R-Rated Films," *New York Times,* October 1, 2000, Section 4, p. 7.

132   Bernard Weintraub, "Scratching Violence for Family Fare and Patriotism," *New York Times,* September 16, 2001, p. 7.

133   Mike Rubin, "The Sins and Sorrows of Marshall Mathers," *Spin,* August 2000, pp. 91–98.

134   Sharon Waxman, "Did 'Death Metal' Music Incite Murder?" *Washington Post,* January 23, 2001, p. E1.

135   Christenson and Roberts, *It's Not Only,* p. 115.

136   R. J. Smith, "Among the Mooks," *New York Times,* August 6, 2000.

137   Ibid.

138   Douglas Rushkoff, "The Merchants of Cool," *Frontline.*

139   Jimmy Iovine, "The Merchants of Cool," *Frontline.*

140   FTC Office of Public Affairs, "FTC Releases Report on the Marketing of Violent Entertainment to Children," September 11, 2000.

141   Amy Reiter, "Not the Real Slim Shady," *Salon,* March 13, 2001, <http:// www.salon.com/people/col/reit/2001/03/13/nptves>

142   Todd Cunningham, interview in "The Merchants of Cool," *Frontline.*

143   Brian Graden, interview in "The Merchants of Cool," *Frontline.*

144   Gerard Jones, "Violent Media Is Good for Kids," *Mother Jones,* June 28, 2000.

145   Timothy Egan, "Where Rampages Begin," *New York Times,* June 14, 1998, p. 1.

146   "Study Finds Significant Amounts of Violence in Video Games Rated as Suitable for All Ages," Harvard School of Public Health, July 21, 2001.

147   Gayle Hanson, "The Violent World of Video Games," *Insight,* June 28, 1999.

148   Paul Keegan, "Culture Quake," *Mother Jones,* November/December 1999.

149   Ibid.

150   Art Golab, "Officer Organizes Video Game Turn-In," *Chicago Sun-Times,* December 14, 2000, p. 8.

151   Andy Proffet (Associated Press), "Judge Rules on Video Game Ordinance," October 12, 2000.

152   Robert Stacy McCarn, "Television's Bloody Hands," *Insight on the News,* December 21, 1998, p. 14; "Are Video Games Really So Bad?" *Time,* May 10, 1999, p. 50.

153 Nicholas Lemann, "Crash Practice," *The New Yorker,* December 17, 2001, p. 36.

154 Keegan, "Culture Quake."

155 Bernard Cesarone, "Video Games and Children," *ERIC/EECE Digest,* January 1994.

156 Ibid.

157 Cheri W. Sparks and Glenn G. Sparks, "Why Do Hollywood and TV Keep Showing Us Violence?" *USA Today,* January 1, 2001, pp. 56–58.

158 McCarn, "Television's Bloody Hands."

159 Keegan, "Culture Quake."

160 George Lang, "Industrial Ratings System to Guide Parents in Video Games," *Daily Oklahoman,* November 10, 2000, p. 1B.

161 "Are Video Games Really So Bad?" *Time,* May 10, 1999, p. 50.

162 Katherine M. Skiba, "Senators Urge Parents to Scrutinize Video Games," *Milwaukee Journal Sentinel,* January 26, 2001, p. 8A.

163 Ibid.

164 Mike Snider, "Violent Video Games Within Kids' Reach," *USA Today,* November 24, 1999.

165 Mary Lou Dickerson, "Parents Can Take Control over Violent Video Games," *Seattle Times,* November 21, 2000, p. B9.

166 "Makers of M-Rated Games under Fire for Marketing to Kids," *Dallas Morning News,* December 14, 2000, p. 1F.

167 "FTC Releases Report."

168 Bob Dart (Cox News Service), "Retailers Ignore Rules on Games," *Chicago Tribune,* February 11, 2001, p. 8.

169 Keegan, "Culture Quake."

170 "Makers of M-Rated Games."

171 Keegan, "Culture Quake."

172 V. B. Cline, R. G. Croft, S. Courier, "Desensitization of Children to Television Violence," *Journal of Personality and Social Psychology,* 1973.

173 Executive Summary, "Youth Violence: A Report of the Surgeon General," Dept. of Health and Human Services, January 2000, <http://www.surgeongeneral.gov/library/youthviolence>

174 Maureen Dowd, "In the DC Matrix," *New York Times,* April 28, 1999, p. A29.

175 Stossel, "The Man Who Counts."

176 Bragg, "Past Victims Relive," p. A8.

177 James V. McNeal, *The Kids Market,* Ithaca: Paramount Market Publishing, 1999, p. 10.

178 Ibid., pp. 204–5.

179 Laurie Mifflin, "Critics Assail PBS over Plan for Toys Aimed at Toddlers," *New York Times,* April 20, 1998, p. A1.

180 Norma Odom Pecora, *The Business of Children's Entertainment,* New York: The Guilford Press, 1998, pp. 102–5.

181 Dan McGraw, "Is PBS Too Commercial?" *US News & World Report,* June 15, 1998, p. 42.

182 *Business of Children's Entertainment,* pp. 34–5.

183 Ibid., p. 38.

184   Ibid., p. 52.

185   Peggy O'Crowley, "To Market, to Market," *Star-Ledger,* Newark, NJ, February 20, 2000, p. 1.

186   Gary Ruskin, "Why They Whine," *Mothering,* November 1, 1999, p. 40.

187   Marilyn Elias, "Selling to Kids Blurs Ethical Picture," *USA Today,* March 20, 2000, p. 7D.

188   Lynn Spigle, "Seducing the Innocent," *The Children's Culture Reader,* ed. Henry Jenkins, New York: New York University Press, 1998, p. 126.

189   "How the Power Rangers Stole Xmas," *Ladies Home Journal,* December 1995, p. 126.

190   Laura Outerbridge, "TV's Lesson, Kick First, Talk Later," *Insight on the News,* March 25, 1996, p. 40.

191   George Will, "Consumers in the Cradle," May 7, 2001.

192   Victor Greto, "Ad Nauseum," *The Gazette,* August 19, 1997, p. Life 1.

193   *Kids Market,* p. 27.

194   Ibid., pp. 35–6.

195   Nancy Gibbs, "Do Kids Have Too Much Power?" *Time,* August 6, 2001.

196   James V. McNeal, *Kids as Consumers,* New York: Lexington Books, 1992, p. 136.

197   Janet Maslin, "Storytellers vs. Toy Sellers: We All Lose," *New York Times,* May 2, 1999, p. 30.

198   Rick Lyman and Julian E. Barnes, "The Toy War for Holiday Movies Is a Battle Among 3 Heavyweights," *New York Times,* November 12, 2001, p. C1.

199   Robert McChesney, *Rich Media, Poor Democracy,* Chicago: University of Illinois Press, 1999, p. 24.

200   Rick Lyman, "Coming Soon: Harry Potter and Hollywood's Cash Cow," *New York Times,* November 4, 2001, p. A1.

201   Jay Teitel, "The Kidnapping of Play," *Saturday Night,* April 1999, p. 54.

202   Hickey, "How the Power Rangers Stole Christmas," *Ladies Home Journal,* December 1995, p. 126.

203   Greto, "Ad Nauseum," p. Life 1.

204   *Kids Market,* p. 80.

205   "Merchants of Cool," *Frontline,* February 27, 2001, <www.pbs.org/wgbh/pages/frontline/shows/cool/etc/script.html>

206   Dan S. Acuff, *What Kids Buy and Why,* New York: The Free Press, 1997, p. 182.

207   T. Berry Brazelton, interview by author.

208   Todd Lewan (Associated Press), "When the Tube Reached the Tundra," May 20, 1999.

209   Kathryn Montgomery and Shelley Provik, "Web of Deception," Washington, DC: Center for Media Education, 1996.

210   "Kids for Sale," Media Awareness Network, <http://www.mediaawareness.ca/eng/issues/pnv/topics/kids4sale.htm>

211   "Web of Deception."

212   "COPPA—The First Year," Washington, DC, Center for Media Education, 2001.

213 Ellen Lee, "Coming of Age in a Material World," *San Francisco Chronicle*, March 7, 1999, p. W-1.

214 "Merchants of Cool," *Frontline*, <http://www.pbs.org./wgbh/pages/frontline/shows/cool/interviews/mcchesney.html>

215 Dee Dee Gordon and Sharon Lee interview, "Merchants of Cool," *Frontline*, <http://www.pbs.org/wgbh/pages/frontline/shows/cool/interviews/gordonandlee.html>

216 Robert Berner, "Just How Deep Are Those Teen Pockets?" *Business Week*, July 30, 2001.

217 Renee Stovsky, "The Gimmes," *St. Louis Post-Dispatch*, December 12, 1999, p. E1.

218 Charles McGrath, "Being 13," *New York Times*, May 17, 1998, Section 6, p. 29.

219 "Merchants of Cool," *Frontline*.

220 "Merchants of Cool," *Frontline*, McChesney interview.

221 *Rock 'N Roll Generation*, Alexandria, VA: Time-Life Books, 1998 p. 27.

222 Ibid., p. 104.

223 Ibid., p. 100.

224 "Merchants of Cool," *Frontline*, Gordon and Lee interview.

225 Josh Walk, "Pop Goes the Teen Boom?" *Entertainment Weekly*, June 8, 2001, pp. 27–36.

226 McChesney, *Rich Media, Poor Democracy*, p. 41.

227 "Merchants of Cool," *Frontline*.

228 "MTV Faces the Music," *Brill's Content*, June 2001.

229 "Merchants of Cool," *Frontline*.

230 Todd Cunningham interview, "Merchants of Cool," *Frontline*, <http://www.pbs.org./wgbh/pages/frontline/shows/cool/interviews/cunningham.html>

231 Ibid.

232 Ibid.

233 Billie Stanton, "Are Ad-Splashed Schools Selling Out Our Kids?" *Denver Post*, November 28, 1999, p. G1.

234 Andy Suppa, "Alvin Schools to Offer Channel One in Fall," *Houston Chronicle*, May 27, 2001, p. 13.

235 Alex Molna, "Colonizing Our Future," *Social Education*, November 1, 2000, p. 428.

236 Suppa, "Alvin Schools," p. 13.

237 Steven Manning, "Students for Sale," *The Nation*, September 27, 1999, p. 11.

238 Anna White, Gary Ruskin, Russell Mokhiber, Robert Weissman, "The Cola-ized Classroom," *Multinational Monitor*, January 1, 1999.

239 Constance L. Hays, "Math Textbook Salted with Brand Names Raises New Alarm," *New York Times*, March 21, 1999, p. 1.

240 Greg Lucas, "Complaints Grow over Brand Names in Texts," *San Francisco Chronicle*, June 26, 1999, p. A1.

241 Ibid.

242   Michael Bazeley, "Zap Me! School Role Debated," *Silicon Valley News*, March 21, 1999.

243   Dana Hawkins, "News You Can Use," *U.S. News & World Report*, April 17, 2000.

244   Mike Kennedy, "Public Schools, Private Profit," *American School & University*, February 28, 2000.

245   Bazeley, "Zap Me! School Role Debated."

246   Mark Walsh, "Internet-Access Provider to Schools Getting Out of Education Business," *Education Week*, November 1, 2000.

247   Minow, *Abandoned in the Wasteland*, p. 6.

248   Ibid., pp. 40–43.

249   Ibid., p. 41.

250   Ibid., pp. 41–42.

251   Ibid., p. 42.

252   Ibid., pp. 98–99, 20–21.

253   Ibid., p. 99.

254   Ibid., p. 7.

255   Ibid., pp. 217–218, for full explanation of the Fairness Doctrine.

256   Ibid., p. 218.

257   *Red Lion Broadcasting Co., Inc., et al. v. Federal Communications Commission et al.*, 395 U.S. 367 at p. 389 (1969).

258   *FCC v. Pacifica Foundation*, 438 US 726 (1978).

259   In the "Filthy Words" monlogue, George Carlin repeatedly used the words "shit," "piss," "fuck," "cunt" "cocksucker," "motherfucker," and "tits."

260   Minow, *Abandoned in the Wasteland*, pp. 46–49.

261   Ibid., p. 99.

262   Mark Fowler, *Texas Law Review* 60 (1982): pp. 209–210, quoted in Minow, *Abandoned in the Wasteland*, p. 103.

263   Minow, *Abandoned in the Wasteland*, p. 103.

264   Ibid., p. 103.

265   Ibid., pp. 51–52.

266   Ibid., pp. 53–56.

267   Dissenting statement of Henry M. Rivera, in re: *Children's Television Programming Practices Report ad Order in docket no. 19142*, 96 FCC 2d 658, 1983, quoted in Minow, *Abandoned in the Wasteland*, p. 104.

268   Bill Baker, interview by author, New York City, December 1999.

269   Yochi Dreazen, "FCC Plans to Ease Ownership Rules for TV Networks," *Wall Street Journal*, April 19, 2001, p. B11.

270   Charles Lewis, *The Buying of the President 2000*, Avon Books, New York, 2000, pp. 8–10.

271   Ibid., p. 9.

272   Ibid., p. 10.

273   Jim Rutenberg, "AOL's Future Chief to Bring Washington Connections," *New York Times*, December 8, 2001, p. C2.

274   Stephen Labaton and Steve Lohr, "U.S. and Some States Split on Microsoft, Risking New Delay." *New York Times*, November 6, 2001, Business section, p. 1.

275 Stephen Labaton, "U.S. vs. Microsoft: Going Back to Square One," *New York Times,* September 9, 2001, Week in Review, p. 3.

276 John Wildermuth, "Will Political Donations Keep Microsoft Intact?" *San Francisco Chronicle,* July 1, 2001, p. A1.

277 *San Francisco Chronicle,* March 13, 2000, p. A3.

278 "Silicon Valley Helping Shape National Politics," *San Francisco Chronicle,* February 14, 2000, p. E2.

279 Sara Miles, "The Nasdaq-ing of Capitol Hill," *New York Times Magazine,* August 13, 2000.

280 Ken Auletta, *The Highwaymen,* Harcourt Brace and Co., New York, 1997, p. 260.

281 Kiernan, *Citizen Murdoch,* quoted from *Frontline,* "Who's Afraid of Rupert Murdoch?" transcript, Public Broadcasting System, 1995.

282 Harold Evans, quoted from *Frontline,* "Who's Afraid of Rupert Murdoch?"

283 Tom Shales, quoted from *Frontline,* "Who's Afraid of Rupert Murdoch?"

284 Auletta, *The Highwaymen,* p. 279.

285 Leading cable TV executive who asked to go unnamed, interview by author, January 2000.

286 Jeff Chester (Executive Director, Center for Media Education), quoted from *Free Speech for Sale,* Bill Moyers Special, 1999 Public Broadcasting System.

287 John McCain, quoted from *Free Speech for Sale.*

288 Ibid.

289 *Free Speech for Sale.*

290 Charles Lewis (Director, Center for Public Integrity), quoted from *Free Speech For Sale.*

291 "Kids and Media at the New Millennium," Kaiser Family Foundation Study, Kaiser Family Foundation, November 17, 1999, introduction, Kaiser Family Foundation, Menlo Park, CA, 1999.

292 Ibid., p. 13.

293 Geraldine Laybourne, interview by author (New York City phone interview), May 2000.

294 Nell Minow, *The Movie Mom's Guide to Family Movies,* Avon Books, New York, 1999, p. 8.

295 Milton Chen, *The Smart Parent's Guide to Kids' TV,* KQED Books, San Francisco, 1994, pp. 90–91.

296 For an excellent analysis of media literacy, see Lauryn Axelrod, *TV-Proof Your Kids* (Secaucus, NJ: Citadel Press, 1997), pp. 14–22.

297 Axelrod, *TV-Proof Your Kids,* pp. 16–17.

298 Media literacy can be broken down into eight key concepts. I'll summarize them for you as follows:

   1. All media are constructions.

   2. The media construct reality.

   3. Audiences negotiate meaning in media.

   4. Media have commercial implications.

   5. Media contain ideological and value messages.

6. Media have social and political implications.
7. Form and content are closely related in the media.
8. Each medium has a unique aesthetic form.

299   Axelrod, *TV-Proof Your Kids,* pp. 16–17.
300   Chen, p. 144.

1. *Cognitive skills*—such as new vocabulary, letters, numbers, and colors.
2. *Emotional awareness*—such as expressing joy, surprise, anger, and approval.
3. *Social skills*—such as sharing, helping others, taking turns, and exercising self-control.
4. *Physical skills*—such as motor skills, coordination, and nutrition.
5. *Music and entertainment*—such as dancing, singing, and playing.
6. *Multicultural exposure*—such as introducing new people, ethnic groups, languages, and diverse cultures.

301   Ken Auletta interview by author, New York City, December 1999.
302   Auletta, *The Highwaymen,* p. 77.
303   Ibid., p. 78.
304   Ibid., p. 78.
305   Ibid., p. 71.
306   Ibid., p. 72.
307   Ibid., p. 73.
308   Ibid., pp. 93–94.
309   Ibid.
310   Ibid., p. 81.
311   Ibid., p. 295.
312   Geraldine Laybourne, interview with author.
313   Herb Scannell interview with author.
314   Verne Gay, "A Nurturing Hand at Nickelodeon," *Newsday,* February 18, 2001, p. D17.
315   Steve Case interview with author, September 26, 2001, AOL headquarters.
316   *Down the Tube,* p. 134.
317   *New York Times,* April 16, 2001, page A1.
318   *Ibid.*
319    $18 billion has already been bid for part of this spectrum, and the Congressional Budget Office has already estimated $28 billion total.
320   Chen, pp. 74–77.
321   Kate Zernike, "School Dress Codes vs. a Sea of Bare Flesh," *New York Times,* September 11, 2001.

INDEX

A&E, 30
ABC, 7, 30, 41, 103, 177, 216, 218
  -Disney merger, 29, 30, 34, 42, 103,
    146
ABC.com, 30
ABC Entertainment Television Group,
    34
ABC Family, 30, 34, 103
ABC News, 42
Action for Children's Television (ACT),
    134–36, 142, 213, 242
Activism, 24–25, 135–38, 143, 241–50
  advocacy groups, 5, 128, 135–38,
    143, 157, 227, 241, 244–46
  boycotts, 246–47
  citizen, 24–25, 241–50
  FCC and, 247–48
  foundation support, 244–45
  Internet, 246
  religious groups, 246
  ten steps for, 243–50
  "TV Turnoff Week," 248
Acuff, Dan, 106
Adolescence, 52
  sexualized, 52–68
Advertising, 8, 36, 44, 96–118, 121, 127,
    139, 170, 207, 208, 209, 210,
    214–16, 246, 248
  licensed products, 96–118
  sexualized, 53, 248
  using the power of, 214–16, 223
  See also Marketing
Advocacy groups, 5, 128, 135–38, 143,
    157, 227, 241, 244–46
AIDS, 54, 116
Allen, Paul, 232
All in the Family, 6, 45, 136, 216
Alstrup, Andrea, 215, 216

Altman, Drew, 54
American Academy of Child and Adoles-
    cent Psychiatry, 88
American Academy of Pedatrics, 7, 16,
    96, 187, 194
American Pie, 113
American Psychological Association, 16,
    100
AMFM, 160
Antitrust cases, 39, 162–63, 227
AOL, 31, 66–67, 165, 186
AOL Time Warner, 20, 29, 30–31, 32,
    121, 160, 161, 203–4, 210, 217–18
Apple, R. W., 42
Arthur, 235
Ascheim, Tom, 212
Association of National Advertisers
    (ANA), 215
AT&T/TCI, 30, 160, 161
Atlantic, 31
Auletta, Ken, 10, 11, 201, 214, 224
    The Highwaymen, 201–4
Awful Truth, The, 83
Axelrod, Lauryn, TV-Proof Your Kids, 196

Bagdikian, Ben, The Media Monopoly, 29
Baker, Bill, 27, 28, 141
    Down the Tube, 141
Baker, Susan, 64
Barksdale, Jim, 154
Barney & Friends, 3, 98, 103, 197–98,
    211, 235
Barry, Jack, 101
Bart, Peter, 38
Basketball Diaries, The, 70
Batman, 6
Batman Forever Web site, 109
BBC, 235

Beatles, 6, 48
Bennett, William, 24, 206
Berg, Jeff, 152
Bertelsmann, 30
Bettleheim, Bruno, *The Uses of Enchant-ment*, 75
Beverly Hills 90210, 169
Big Help, The, 213, 221
Biondi, Frank, 210
Birth of a Nation, 157
Blockbuster, 31
Bloodworth-Thomason, Linda, 157
Blue's Clues, 146, 197, 211–12
Bond, Bill, 69
Boston Public, 46, 47, 61–62
Boycotts, media, 246–47
Bozell, Brent, 61
Bradley, Bill, 160, 238
Brand names, 96–118
Brazelton, Dr. T. Berry, 4, 106, 184, 190, 194
Bresnahan, Timothy, 162
Bronfman, Edgar, Jr., 160
Brothers Garcia, The, 212
Brown, Bryan, 80
Buffy the Vampire Slayer, 61, 83
Burger King, 105, 115
Burke, Dan, 218
Bush, George, 132, 226
Bush, George W., 12, 140, 147–49, 157, 160, 162, 165, 166, 227–29, 232

Cable television, 6, 7, 16, 20, 30, 31, 33, 34, 44, 45, 83, 144, 148, 164, 173, 238, 239
    Nickelodeon values and profits, 207–14
    regulation, 121, 148
    sex, 45–47
Cahn, Alice, 97
Campaign finances, 150–79
    media and, 150–79, 238–39
    reform, 238–39
Canada, 77, 102, 173, 196, 222
    kids' TV funding, 232, 234–35
Cantor, Joanne, *Mommy, I'm Scared*, 73, 74
CapnCrunch.com, 110
Captain Kangaroo, 126, 139
Care Bears, 99, 209
    products, 99–100
Carlin, George, 133
Carlsson-Paige, Nancy, 78
Carmageddon, 88
Carmen Sandiego, 198
Carneal, Michael, 69, 70, 71
Carnegie Corporation, 245
Cartoon Network, 31, 211

Case, Dan, 217
Case, Steve, 20, 186, 217, 222, 224, 233
Castle Rock Entertainment, 31
CBS, 7, 11, 19, 20, 30, 31, 41, 42, 83, 121, 123, 139, 145, 160, 177, 216, 218
    -Viacom merger, 121, 145, 146, 148, 219
CBS Entertainment, 80, 179
CDs, 4, 5, 47, 48, 63–66
    warning labels, 64–66, 86
    See also Music
Cell phones, 121
Censorship, 22, 48, 56, 128–35, 202, 205–6, 219
    stop crying, 219
Center for Media Education, 101, 108, 142, 143, 241, 244
Center for Research on the Effects of Television, 45
Channel One, 116
Character World, 97
Charren, Peggy, 135, 143, 212–14, 242
Chen, Milton, 187, 188
    The Smart Parent's Guide to Kids' TV, 187, 196
Chernin, Peter, 33
Child Online Protection Act (1999), 67
Children Now, 5, 8, 9, 10, 26, 36, 79, 123, 143, 157, 194, 210, 214, 215, 222, 227, 241, 244
Children's Online Privacy Protection Act (COPPA), 109–10
Children's Partnership, 241
Children's Television Act (CTA), 9, 36, 130, 132, 142, 143–47, 170, 219, 226, 237–39, 242
Chunovic, Louis, 45
Cinemax, 31
Citizen action, *see* Activism
Clinton, Bill, 24, 67, 143, 145, 157, 162, 172, 179, 202, 239, 244, 251, 252
Clinton, Chelsea, 251–52
Clueless, 113
CNN, 31
Coca-Cola, 115, 215
Cohen, Mike, 98–99, 102, 106, 192
Columbia House, 31
Columbia Records, 84, 86
Columbia TriStar, 82
Columbine school shooting, 69–71, 82–84, 87, 89, 93, 94
Comedy Central, 31
Commercialism, 5, 7, 11–13, 14, 17, 26–44, 96–118, 119, 229
Communcations Act (1934), 120, 122–24
CompuServe, 31
Computer games, 3, 4, 5, 7, 12, 21, 47, 232
    limited use, 188, 190

location of computer, 186–87
rating system, 91–93
sharing with kids, 198
violent, 17, 69, 70, 77, 79, 88–94
Condry, John, 45, 55
Conglomerates, media, 12–13, 18–20, 22, 29–43, 145, 146, 148, 167, 207, 219, 229–31
breaking up, 230–31
Congress, 16, 19, 23, 24, 36, 41, 46, 67, 78, 97, 109, 120–24, 130–34, 139, 142, 145, 148, 159, 163, 168, 170, 176, 177, 178, 229, 232, 234, 235, 237, 238, 247; *See also* Government; *specific legislation*
Consumerism, 17–18, 25, 96–118
culture of, 101–2
licensed products, 34–35, 86, 96–118, 172–73, 234
Consumer Reports, 66
Corporation for Public Broadcasting, 231
Court TV, 31
Csupo, Gabor, 210
Cunningham, Todd, 114
Current Affair, A, 204, 205
Curse words, 48, 49, 56–57, 82

Dalian, Kent, 79
Dateline, 204
Dawson's Creek, 54, 113
DC Comics, 31
Democracy, and mega media, 38–42
Democratic Party, 122, 151, 155, 157, 158–60, 172
Department of Education, 236
Derdeyn, Andre, 76
Deregulation, 147–49, 155, 227–29, 244
Bush-era, 147–49, 227–29
Reagan-era, 6–7, 19, 46, 78, 94, 99, 101, 103, 136–41, 227, 228
Diablo, 88
Diet, media, 187–90
Digital technology, 7, 22, 23, 41, 173–78, 212, 232–34
DO IT, 233–34
spectrum giveaway by government, 173–78, 233, 247
Diller, Barry, 169, 224
Directors Guild of America, 60
Discover magazine, 30
Discovery Channel, 146
Disney Channel, 9, 30, 34, 103, 208, 211
Disney.com, 30
Disneyland, 126
Disney Publishing, 30
Disney (Walt) Company, 30, 33, 34, 42, 99, 103, 126, 146, 159–60, 167, 202, 206, 210, 212, 234

-ABC merger, 29, 30, 34, 42, 103, 146
merchandising, 99, 103–4
Disney (Walt) Pictures, 30
Disney (Walt) Television Animation, 30, 34
Disturbing Behavior, 82
Doerr, John, 154
DO IT, 233–34
Dole, Bob, 41, 176
Doom, 17, 70, 88, 89
Dot.coms, 109–10, 153, 164, 245
crash, 153, 164
Double Dare, 210
Doug, 210
Dragon Tales, 3, 197, 235
Drew, Elizabeth, *The Corruption of American Politics,* 159
Duke Nukem, 89, 92
Durst, Fred, 86
Dyson, Esther, 246

E!, 30, 34
Ebert, Roger, 57
Eccles, Dr. Jacqueline, 52
Eisner, Michael, 42, 104, 201–4, 205, 207, 224
Elektra, 31
Eminem, 48, 64, 65, 83–84, 86, 205–6
Enron, 160
Entertainment, 8, 32, 40, 53, 73, 79, 149, 150–52, 198, 202
Entertainment Software Ratings Board (ESRB), 91–92
Entertainment Weekly, 31
ESPN, 30, 34, 103
ESPN.com, 30
Evans, Harold, 168

Fairness Doctrine, 130–31
Fairy tales, 75–76
Falwell, Jerry, 46
Family.com, 30
Family Friendly Programming Forum, 215–16, 223
"Family hour" policy, 136, 238
Famous Jett Jackson, The, 9
Fantasy and reality, kids' distinctions between, 75–76, 81, 82, 95, 189
Federal Communications Commission (FCC), 15, 19, 20, 23, 30, 35, 46, 108, 119, 120–25, 128–49, 160, 163, 168, 170, 171, 178, 226, 227–29, 234, 236–38, 243, 247–48
deregulation, 136–41
inside story on, 121–25
licensing challenges, 236–37, 247
"three-hour rule," 144–46

Federal Trade Commission (FTC), 59, 65,
    82, 86, 92, 93, 118, 183, 236–37
Felicity, 113
Fifth Element, The, 82
Fiorella, Joseph, 84
First Amendment protections, 22, 23, 39,
    40, 59, 65, 79, 93, 119, 128–35,
    137, 178, 204–7, 219, 220, 238
Flintstones, The, 104, 142
Fortune, 31
Foundation support, 244–45
Fowler, Mark, 19, 137–40
Fox Broadcasting Company (FBC),
    35–36, 37, 61
Fox Children's Network, 6, 102
Fox Family Worldwide, 167, 171–73
Fox Kids, 12, 27, 37, 146, 167–71
Fox Kids Block, 167, 169
Fox News, 167, 170
Fox Television Network, 6, 101–2, 161,
    167–73, 227, 234
Freston, Tom, 204–5
Friday the 13ᵗʰ movies, 73, 80–81
Friends, 46
Fritts, Eddie, 126
Frontline, 85
Funding, children's media, 23, 97, 220–23
    Canadian model, 232, 234–35
    educational uses of Internet, 222
    foundation, 244–45
    nationwide media-literacy efforts, 221
    public, 97–98, 221–22, 231–36
    quality kids' media at breakeven,
        220–21
    workshops for industry professionals,
        222–23

Game Boy, 190
Gates, Bill, 232
Gates (Bill and Melinda) Foundation, 245
Gelbart, Larry, 14
Geller, Henry, 142
General Electric, 20, 30, 204
Generation Y, 111–14
Gephardt, Dick, 162
Gerbner, George, 72–73, 77–78, 95
Gilmore Girls, 216
Gingrich, Newt, 133
Gladwell, Malcolm, 112
Goldberg, Gary David, 216
Goldstein, Al, 45
Gore, Al, 159, 160, 179
Gore, Tipper, 64–65, 242
Gore Commission, 178–79
Government, 18–21, 41, 71, 97–98, 117–18,
    119–49, 196–97, 226–40, 250
    campaign finances and, 150–79,
        238–39

censorship, 128–35, 205–6, 219
deregulation, 136–41, 227–29
digital spectrum giveaway, 173–78,
    233, 247
FCC role, 121–25, 128–49, 227–29,
    236–38
funding for kids' media, 97–98,
    221–22, 231–36
Gore Commission, 178–79
gun lobbies and, 71
Hollywood and, 150–52, 156–60,
    164, 239
Internet regulation, 121, 227, 232–34
Murdoch-Saban saga and, 167–73
new leadership, 239–40
protecting the public interest,
    226–40
role of, with media, 23–24, 119–49,
    150–79, 221–22, 226–40, 243
Silicon Valley and, 152–56, 161–67
ten steps to take by, 229–40
Graden, Brian, 87, 112
Great Britain, 97, 167–68, 196, 235
Grossman, Lt. Colonel Dave, 89
Grossman, Lawrence, 33, 233
GT Interactive Software, 93
Gwich'in Indian tribe, 107–8

Habits, good media, 184–86
Halberstam, David, 33
Hall, Kurt, 59
Hand That Rocks the Cradle, The, 203
Hanks, Tom, 157
Hanna, Mark, 150
Hanna-Barbera Productions, 31
HarperCollins Publishers, 167
Harris, Eric, 69, 70, 87, 93
Harris, Mel, 82
Harry Potter movies, 104
Hastert, Dennis, 162
Haug, Ada, 97
Hays Office, 56
HBO, 31, 135
HBO Productions, 31
Hicks, Muse, 160
Histeria, 146
History Channel, 34
Hogue, David, 60
Hollings, Ernest, 148, 229
Hollywood, 56, 104, 203, 206, 216
    media politics and, 150–52, 156–60,
        164, 239
Horn, Alan, 59
Howdy Doody, 126
How the Grinch Stole Christmas, 74
Hundt, Reed, 15, 143, 144, 145, 147,
    178–79, 226
Hyperion, 30

Id Software, 93
I Know What You Did Last Summer, 82, 113
Innocence, loss of, 15–16
Interactive Digital Software Association, 92
Internet, 4, 7, 12, 21, 23, 28, 30–31, 36, 47, 122, 129, 164–65, 186, 223, 232
    as advocacy tool, 246
    funding educational uses of, 222
    government role, 121, 122, 227, 232–34
    limited use, 188, 190
    marketing, 198–10
    positive leaders, 216–18
    privacy issues, 108–10
    sexual content, 66–67, 206
    Silicon Valley and, 153–56
    violence, 70
Interscope Records, 83, 85, 86
In the News, 139
Iovine, Jimmy, 85, 86

Jackass, 37, 141
Japan, 171, 172, 235
Jetsons, The, 142, 145
Jinkins, Jim, 210
Johnson, Brown, 146, 211, 212
Johnson, Lyndon, 158
Johnson, Mitchell, 70
Jones, Gerard, 87
Journal of Personality and Social Psychology, 89–90
Journal of the American Medical Association, 74
JP Kids, 9–10, 11, 26, 27, 29, 36, 103, 123, 154, 210, 217
Justice Department, 162

Kaiser Family Foundation, 16, 47, 51, 54, 63, 222, 245
Katzenberg, Jeffrey, 152
Kennard, Bill, 145, 147, 226, 227, 248
Kennedy, John F., 39, 123, 157
KidsCom, 110
Kids WB, 146
Kinkel, Kip, 69
Kintner, Robert, 218
Klasky, Arlene, 210
Klebold, Dylan, 69, 70, 87, 93
Klein, Calvin, 53
Kohl, Herb, 92, 162
Koogle, Tim, 217
Kramer, Timothy, 100
Krug, Judith, 67
Kvamme, Floyd, 165, 166

LaFount, Harold A., 44
Lansing, Sherry, 83
Laybourne, Geraldine, 143, 186–87, 208–14
Lear, Norman, 216
Learning Company, 198
Leave It to Beaver, 142, 145
Lethal Weapon, 203
Levin, Diane, 78–79
Levin, Gerald M., 204, 206
Lewan, Todd, 107–8
Liberty Media Corporation, 30
Licensed products, 34–35, 86, 96–118, 172–73, 234
Lieberman, Joseph, 23, 148, 229, 237, 244
Liebling, A. J., 39
Life, 112
Lifetime, 30, 34
Limp Bizkit, 84–86
Lion King, The, 104
Little Vampire, The, 74
Location of TV or computer in the home, 186–87
Loesch, Margaret, 102, 169, 170
Look Who's Talking, 50
Loral Science and Communications, 160
Lorimar Studios, 80
Loukaitis, Barry, 70
Loveline, 53
Lowenstein, Carol, 97
Lowenstein, Douglas, 92, 93
Lower, Elmer, 218
Lucas, George, 104, 187

MADD, 242
Madonna, 65
Mallett, Jeff, 217
MapQuest, 31
Marketing, 37–38, 44, 96–118, 127
    demographic dream and kids, 102–8
    digital spectrum, 173–78
    Internet, 108–10
    licensed products, 34–35, 86, 96–118, 172–73, 234
    movie, 38, 103–5, 113
    music, 37–38, 112–14
    in schools, 114–17
    sex, 44–68
    teenage, 37–38, 110–17
    television, 96–108, 113, 214–16, 223
    using the power of, 214–16, 223
    violence, 69–95
Markle Foundation, 245
Married . . . with Children, 46
Marx Brothers, 198
Maslin, Janet, 58, 104
Matrix, The, 81, 94
Mattel, 160

MCA/Universal, 160, 161
McCain, John, 160–61, 163, 176–77, 179, 229, 239
McChesney, Robert, 111, 112
McDonald's, 103, 104–5, 116, 215
McGannon, Donald, 218
McGraw-Hill, 116
MCI WorldCom, 160, 161
McLuhan, Marshall, 250
McNeal, James, 96, 103, 105
"Mean-world" syndrome, 72–75
Media:
    as babysitter, 3–5
    campaign finances and, 150–79
    conglomeration, 12–13, 18–20, 22, 29–43, 145, 146, 148, 167, 207, 219, 229–31
    democracy and, 38–42
    deregulation, 6–7, 19, 46, 78, 94, 99, 101, 103, 136–41, 227–29
    developing new leadership and responsibility, 224
    FCC role, 121–25, 128–49, 227–29, 236–38
    First Amendment protections, 128–35
    government role, 23–24, 119–49, 150–79, 221–22, 226–40, 243
    industry accountability, 22–23, 35, 220–225
    industry schizophrenia, 200–205, 214
    new landscape of, 5–8
    of 1950s–1960s, 4, 6, 44, 45, 48, 101, 112, 125–28, 131, 136, 139, 195–96, 229
    parental control of, 183–99
    politics of, 119–49, 150–79, 230, 238–39, 243, 250
    profit motives, 11–15, 17–21, 26–43, 80–82, 94, 143, 144, 201–7, 220–21, 250
    public-interest responsibilities, 19–23, 35, 121–25, 128, 130, 139, 141, 177, 218–19, 226–40
    research studies on, 8–9, 17–18, 47, 51, 66, 67, 77, 90, 108, 197, 198
    sex, 44–68
    strategies for change, 181–250
    structure today, 28–33
    top ten steps for industry accountability, 218–27
    violence, 69–95
    See also Computer games; Internet; Movies; Music; Publishing; Radio; Television; Video games
Media literacy, 23, 195–97, 221, 236, 249
    funding nationwide efforts, 221
    at home, 195–97
    in school, 195–97, 236, 249

"Media Turn-Off Week," 189, 248
Medved, Michael, Hollywood vs. America, 206
Meigs, James, 57, 58
Melrose Place, 169
Merchandise, media-linked, 34–35, 86, 96–118, 172–73, 234
Mergers, see Conglomerates, media
Meyrowitz, Joshua, 51
Mickey Mouse Club, 126
Microsoft, 30, 161–63, 165
    antitrust case, 162–63, 227
Microsoft Flight Simulator, 90
Mighty Morphin Power Rangers, 101–2, 144, 169, 171–73, 227
Miller, Mark Crispin, 38
Minow, Newton, 25, 119, 123, 124, 143, 189, 233
    Abandoned in the Wasteland, 123
Miramax, 30
Mister Rogers' Neighborhood, 143, 209
Money, 31
Monroe, Marilyn, 157
Montgomery, Kathryn, 101
Moonves, Les, 80, 179
Moore (Gordon and Betty) Foundation, 245
Motion Picture Association of America (MPAA), 56, 91, 158
Motorola, Inc., 160
Movies, 4, 6, 12, 13, 29, 30, 31, 183, 211
    horror, 8, 73–74, 80–82, 113
    limited use, 188, 189
    marketing, 38, 103–5, 113
    of 1950s–1970s, 4
    1980s deregulation, 6–7, 19, 46, 94, 99, 227, 228
    preview trailers, 60, 74, 75
    rating system, 56–60, 74–75, 83, 189
    sexual content, 48, 50, 54, 56–60
    violent, 17, 60, 69, 70, 73–75, 78–83, 202–3, 205, 207
    watching with kids, 198
Moynihan, Daniel Patrick, 17
MTV, 31, 37, 53, 63, 86–88, 112–14, 160, 204–5
Mummy Returns, The, 60
Muppets, The, 211
Murdoch, Rupert, 33, 37, 40, 161, 167–73, 201, 203–7, 224
Murphy, Tom, 218
Murray, John, 90, 91
Murrow, Edward R., 226
Music, 3, 7–8, 12, 13, 21, 29, 30, 31, 37, 45, 47, 48, 63–66, 183
    limited use, 188, 190
    marketing, 37–38, 112–14
    parents listening with kids, 192

rap, 24, 64, 70, 83–86, 204, 205–6,
    227
sexual content, 47, 48, 50, 63–66,
    204–5
violent, 17, 64, 70, 79, 83–88, 204,
    205–6
warning labels, 64–66, 86
My Dog Skip, 74

NAACP, 227, 247
Nader, Ralph, 117
Nash, Scott, 49
National Association of Broadcasters
    (NAB), 126–27, 132, 135, 177, 221
National Association of Television Pro-
    gram Executives (NATPE), 27
National Association of Theatre Owners
    (NATO), 59, 60
National Institute on Media and the Fam-
    ily, 92
National Institutes of Health, 16, 72, 233
National Public Radio, 42
National Rifle Association (NRA), 71, 128
Natural Born Killers, 70, 81
NBC, 7, 19, 30, 41, 61, 146, 177, 204,
    216, 218
NBC News, 33
Nelvana, 234
Netscape, 31, 154
Neuborne, Burt, 40
New Line Cinema, 31
News, 6, 8, 32, 39, 41–42, 73, 76, 116,
    149
    false reporting, 41–42
News Corporation, 30, 31, 33, 40, 161,
    167, 170, 171, 203
Newspapers, 37
Newsweek, 69
New Yorker, The, 112
New York Post, 167, 168
New York Times, 14, 37, 42, 94, 164, 172,
    177, 228
Nickelodeon, 3, 12, 14, 31, 143, 144–46,
    160, 186, 207–14, 221
    values and profits, 207–14
Nick Jr., 3, 145–46, 197, 211–12
Nick News, 213, 221
Nightline, 204
Nightmare on Elm Street, 81
Nintendo, 93, 105, 107
Nixon, Richard, 136
Noggin, 212
Norway, 97, 117

Omidyar, Pierre, 245
Oregon Trail, 198
Other houses, media use in, 193–94
Ovitz, Mike, 152

Pacifica case, 133–34
Pahler, Eric, 84
Paley, William, 42, 218
Paramount Motion Picture Group, 83,
    160
Paramount Studios, 31, 160
Parenting, 31
Parents, 4–5, 183–99
    activism, 24–25, 241–50
    control of kids' media by, 21, 183–99,
        207, 220, 251–52
    media used as babysitter by, 3–5
    sharing media with kids, 191–93,
        197–98
    time spent with kids, 4, 106, 191–93,
        197–98
    top ten steps for, 184–99
Parents Music Resource Center (PMRC),
    65
Parents Television Council (PTC), 47, 61
Parsons, Dick, 161, 224
PBS, 3, 4, 7, 9, 27, 33, 85, 97–98, 132–33,
    143, 197, 208, 209, 231–32,
    234–36
    marketing, 97–98
    support with funding and leadership,
        235–36
PBSKids.org, 235
Pecora, Norma Odom, 99–100
Pediatricians, kids' media use reviewed by,
    194–95
Penney, JC, 248
People, 31
Permission to use media, 190–91
Perry, Reverend Chris, 88
"Pester power," 105–6
Pew Charitable Trusts, 245
Philip Morris, 161
Pinsky, Drew, 53
Pittman, Robert, 210, 224
Pokemon, 190
Politics, media, 119–49, 150–79, 230,
    238–39, 243, 250
    campaign finances and, 150–79,
        238–39
    censorship issues, 128–35, 205–6,
        219
    digital spectrum giveaway, 173–78,
        233, 247
    FCC role, 121–25, 128–49, 227–29,
        236–38
    Gore Commission, 178–79
    Hollywood and, 150–52, 156–60,
        164, 239
    Murdoch-Saban saga and, 167–73
    origin of, 120
    Silicon Valley and, 152–56, 161–67
    See also Government

Ponton, Lynn, MD, 54, 55
Pornography, 45–46, 47, 48, 61, 65, 66,
     129–30, 135, 206
Postman, Neil, 15, 49–50
Powell, Colin, 147, 161
Powell, Mike, 140, 147–48, 161, 228–29,
     248
Premiere magazine, 57
Primedia, 116
"Prime-Time Summit" (1996), 239
Procter & Gamble, 214
Profit motives, 11–15, 17–21, 26–43,
     80–82, 143, 144, 201–7, 220–21,
     250
     campaign finances and, 150–79
     conglomeration and, 29–42
     funding quality kids' media at
        breakeven, 220–21
     values suffering from, 205–7
     violence and, 80–82, 94, 205–7
Promised Land, 83
Prothrow-Stith, Deborah, MD, 81
Provenzo, Eugene, 93
PTAs, 244
Public-interest responsibilities of media,
     19–23, 35, 121–25, 128, 130, 139,
     141, 177, 218–19, 226–50
Publishing, 9, 12, 29, 30, 31, 36, 167, 168

Quake, 88, 89, 92
Quayle, Dan, 203
Quello, James, 170

Racial diversity, 212, 214
Radio, 4, 29, 30, 31, 37, 47, 63, 122, 124,
     160, 170, 223
     censorship issues, 128–35
Radio and Communications Act, 131
Rather, Dan, 41–42
RCA, 125–26
Reader Rabbit, 198
Reading Rainbow, 197, 235
Reagan, Ronald, 19, 157
     1980s deregulation crusade, 19, 46,
        78, 94, 136–41, 227, 228
Real TV, 113
Recording Industry Association of Amer-
     ica (RIAA), 64, 221–22
Red Lion case, 131–33
Redstone, Sumner, 167, 210, 224
Regulation, *see* Censorship; Deregulation;
     Government
Reiner, Rob, 79
Religious groups, 246
Ren and Stimpy, 208
Republican Party, 122, 155, 160–62, 176
Rhino, 31
Rideout, Vicky, 63

Rivera, Henry M., 139
RJ Reynolds/Nabisco, 161
Roberts, Donald, 64, 66, 84
Robertson, Pat, 172
Roosevelt, Franklin D., 120
Ross, Rich, 146
Rothenberg, Marc, 109
Rugrats, 47, 208, 210, 211
Rule, Elton, 218
Rushkoff, Douglas, 47, 85, 86
Ruskin, Gary, 100

Saban, Haim, 101–2, 167, 171–73, 207,
     227
Saban Entertainment, 101, 167, 172
Sabrina, the Teenage Witch, 113
Sanders, Dave, 93
Scannell, Herb, 14, 74, 146, 211–14
Schmidt, Eric, 165, 166
Schoolhouse Rock, 139
Schools, 114
     marketing in, 114–17
     media literacy in, 195–97, 236, 249
     violence, 69–71, 80, 82–84, 87, 89,
        93–95
Scooby-Doo, 47
Scream, 73, 74, 81, 113
Screen Actors Guild, 157
Script Development Initiative, 215–16
Seabrook, John, 113
Seagram's, 160, 161
Sega of America, 93
Self-regulation, 220
September 11 terrorist attacks, 25, 76, 83,
     90, 193, 207, 219, 234, 242, 243,
     250
Sesame Street, 76, 111, 143, 144, 197, 209,
     211, 235, 245
Sesame Workshop, 76, 143, 144, 197, 212
Seventeen, 112
Sex, media, 5, 6, 7, 12, 14, 15–16, 25, 38,
     40, 44–68, 82, 119, 129–30, 135,
     183, 192, 195, 202, 204–7, 229, 248
     Internet, 66–67
     movie rating system, 56–60
     music lyrics, 63–66
     parent's role, 49–51, 55, 67
     taboo-free zone, 47–49
     teaching expectations, 51–53
     teenagers and, 52–68
     TV rating system, 60–63
Sex and the City, 47
Sexually transmitted diseases (STDs), 54
Shalek, Nancy, 100
Shales, Tom, 168, 169
Sharing media with kids, 191–93, 197–98
Silicon Valley, and media politics, 152–56,
     161–67

Simon & Schuster, 31
Simpsons, the, 8
Sinatra, Frank, 157
Singer, Drs. Jerome and Dorothy, 198
Slayer, 84, 85
Smurfs, The, 99
Snow Day, 211
Sony, 30
Sony Pictures Entertainment, 82
Sony PlayStation, 116
South Park, 94
Spears, Britney, 52, 113
Spice, 135
Spice Girls, 7–8, 37, 52, 113
Spielberg, Steven, 70, 157
Spinner.com, 31
SpongeBob SquarePants, 211
Sports, 6, 31, 35, 36, 185, 198
Sports Illustrated, 31
Stanford University, 10, 22, 77, 90, 129, 251
Stanton, Frank, 218
Star Wars, 104
Stern, Howard, 134
Stewart, Potter, 128
Stone, Rob, 113
Sugar and Spice, 82–83
Supreme Court, 128–34, 228
Sweden, 117, 235
Sweeney, Anne, 146
Syndication, 27–28

Taina, 212
Tauzin, Billy, 170
TBS, 31
TechNet, 154, 164, 165, 222
Teenage Mutant Ninja Turtles, 78
Teenagers, 37–38
    marketing, 37–38, 110–17
    pregnancy, 53–54
    sexualized, 52–68
    violence and, 69–71, 80–88, 92
Telecommunications Act (1996), 20, 41, 147, 174, 177, 237, 247
Telephones, 31, 121, 122, 173
    digital, 175
Teletubbies, 96–98, 103
Television, 3, 6, 9, 13, 21, 29, 30, 31, 122, 124, 170, 183, 223, 232
    cable, *see* Cable television
    censorship issues, 128–35, 206, 219
    creation of, 44
    digital, 7, 173–78, 212
    "family hour" policy, 136, 238
    government role, 119–49, 226–40
    limited use, 185, 187–90, 199, 248
    location of, in home, 186–87
    marketing, 96–108, 113, 214–16, 223

news, 6, 8, 39, 41–42, 73, 76, 116, 149
Nickelodeon values and profits, 207–14
of 1950s–1970s, 4, 6, 44, 45, 48, 101, 112, 125–28, 131, 136, 139, 142, 229
1980s deregulation, 6–7, 19, 46, 78, 94, 99, 101, 103, 136–41, 227, 228
parents watching with kids, 191–93, 197–98
permission to watch, 190–91
political ads, 163–64
profit motives, 11–15, 17–21, 26–43, 143, 144, 201–7, 220–21, 250
public fund for, 231–32
ratings system and V chip, 9, 60–63, 226, 239
sexual content, 6–7, 15–16, 44–55, 60–63, 204–5, 207, 248
syndication, 27–28
as "vast wasteland," 123
violence, 6–7, 16–17, 37, 62, 70, 72, 75, 76–83, 94, 101–2, 173, 205–7
Temptation Island, 37, 141, 169, 205
There's Something about Mary, 60
Thomason, Harry, 157
Thompson, Robert, 46
Three's Company, 46
Time, 31, 69
Time Life Music, 31
Time Warner, 24, 33, 34, 104, 160, 205, 206, 207, 227
    AOL merger, 30–31
Tinker, Grant, 216, 218
TNT, 31
Tobacco industry, 79, 93, 161, 206
Tollin, Michael, 56, 57, 74
Toon Disney, 30, 34
Touchstone, 30, 34
Toys, 34–35, 116, 139
    licensed products, 34–35, 86, 96–118, 172–73, 234
    "pester power" and, 105–6
    violence-themed, 78
Training, for media professionals, 222–23, 232, 243
Tribune Company, 123
TriStar Pictures, 50
Tucker, C. DeLores, 206
Turley, Jeffrey, 76
Turner, Ted, 13, 33, 40
"Turn-Off-the-TV Week," 189, 248
Twentieth Century Fox Studios, 167

UCLA Center for Communications Policy, 222–23
Unis, Dr. Alan, 87–88

United Artists Theatre, 59
Universal Studios, 60
UPN, 31
USA Networks, 30

Valenti, Jack, 158, 161
Variety, 38
VCR, 4, 34, 107, 116
VH-1, 31
Viacom, 12, 20, 30, 31, 42, 121, 148, 160,
        167, 204, 208, 210, 212
    -CBS merger, 121, 145, 146, 148, 219
Video games, 5, 7, 12, 17, 107
    parents playing with kids, 191–93
    rating system, 91–93
    violent, 17, 69, 70, 77, 79, 88–94, 205
Videos, 4, 34–35, 107
    music, 38, 86–88, 112–14, 204–5
Vietnam War, 89
Violence, media, 5, 6, 7, 12, 14, 16–17,
        25, 37, 38, 60, 62, 69–95, 101–2,
        119, 135, 136, 148, 173, 183, 189,
        192, 202–7, 227, 229, 243
    blame for, 71–72
    "mean world" syndrome, 72–75
    no consequences of, 77–79
    profits from, 80–82, 94, 205–7
    school violence, 69–71, 80, 82–84,
        87, 89, 93–95
    sold to children, 82–88
    video games, 88–93
Vivendi Universal, 30–32, 86, 161

Wallace, Aurora, 32
Wall Street Journal, 148, 228

Ward, L. Monique, 51, 52
Warner Bros. Animation, 31
Warner Bros. Pictures, 31, 59, 104, 207
Warner Bros. Records, 31
Warner Bros. Television, 31
Washington Post, 168, 177
Wayans, Keenen Ivory, 48
WB Television Network, 11, 31, 61, 146,
        216
Wehling, Bob, 214–16, 223
Welch, Jack, 204
Westinghouse, 19–20, 218
White, Byron, 131
White, Rick, 165, 166
Whitman, Meg, 222, 246
Wildmon, Reverend Donald, 223
Wiley, Richard, 136
Williamson, Kathleen, 115
Winky Dink and You, 101
WNET, 27, 141
World War II, 89, 112, 125
Woodham, Luke, 70
Workshops, for media professionals,
        222–23, 243
World Wrestling Federation (WWF), 17,
        88
Wrestling, TV, 17, 31, 78, 88
Wright, Bob, 204
Writers Guild of America, 136

Yahoo!, 165, 206, 217, 233
Yang, Jerry, 217, 222, 224, 246
You Can't Do That on Television, 210

ZapMe!, 117